Perspectives in
Personal Construct
Theory

Perspectives in Personal Construct Theory

Edited by D. Bannister
Bexley Hospital, Dartford Heath, Bexley, Kent, England

1970

Academic Press LONDON and NEW YORK

ACADEMIC PRESS INC. (LONDON) LTD
Berkeley Square House
Berkeley Square,
London, W1X 6BA

U.S. Edition published by
ACADEMIC PRESS INC.
111 Fifth Avenue,
New York, New York 10003

Library of Congress Catalog Card Number: 78–129782
ISBN: 0–12–077960–9

Printed in Great Britain at the Pitman Press, Bath

List of Contributors

JACK R. ADAMS-WEBBER, *Department of Psychology, Brock University, St. Catharines, Ontario, Canada.*

D. BANNISTER, *Bexley Hospital, Dartford Heath, Bexley, Kent, England.*

FAY FRANSELLA, *Bexley Hospital, Dartford Heath, Bexley, Kent, England .*

DENNIS N. HINKLE, *Miami University, Oxford, Ohio, U.S.A.*

RAY HOLLAND, *Department of Humanities, Chelsea College of Science and Technology, Manresa Road, London, England.*

†GEORGE A. KELLY.

GRAHAME LEMAN, 9 *Tudor Court, Gunnersbury Avenue, London, England.*

J. M. M. MAIR, *Academic Department of Psychiatry, Middlesex Hospital Medical School, London, England.*

W. DONALD OLIVER, *Department of Philosophy, University of Missouri, Columbia, Missouri, U.S.A.*

PHILLIDA SALMON, *Department of Humanities, University of Surrey, Guildford, Surrey, England.*

JOHN SHOTTER, *Department of Psychology, The University of Nottingham, University Park, Nottingham, England.*

† Deceased.

Preface

The quality of psychological theory which George Kelly most esteemed was fertility. By this, he did not mean mean simply hypothesis generating capacity. Any fool with a variable-speed pursuit rotor, three age-groups, two questionnaire measures and a penchant for intellectual permutation can "generate" hypotheses by the score. He meant rather the capacity of a theory to inspire people, to move them to new ventures, to puzzle them into asking new questions.

In this sense the present book is an experiment to test the hypothesis that personal construct theory is fertile. Between the opening and closing papers, which are by the late George Kelly, are ten essays. Ten people were each invited to write an essay around the theme of personal construct theory—the instructions were no more explicit than that. Thus the reader can fairly judge whether the theory has inspired or dulled them, freed their thinking or imprisoned them in dogma.

The book is additionally a test of the cohering properties of personal construct theory. The writers knew nothing of any essay but their own until the work was complete. Thus the reader can judge the degree to which the theory has provided a bonding theme so that under the varied literary styles and personal preoccupations, there are common issues and relatable concerns.

The book may also prove a test of the reader's stance towards modern psychology. If you feel that current psychological undertakings, or a fair proportion of them, hold promise, and assiduous work along proven lines will advance the discipline—then the book may well seem to you to be intellectual shadow-boxing. If you have grave doubts as to whether psychologists know what they are about and cannot scan a current journal in psychology without a sinking heart, then the book may seem to you properly preoccupied with basic issues.

The fate of personal construct theory, since its formal presentation in 1955, has been strange in that is had had neither the kinds of acceptance nor the kinds of rejection that are customary for new ideas in the field. It has not, like "notions" such as cognitive dissonance or n-ach or technique-concepts such as the semantic differential, had any fashionable flowering. It has not, like learning theory, ingested a multitude of issues to seep on, contorted but vastly influential. It has not, like the Allportian psychology of the individual, stood admired and unused. Rather it has had a slow, almost unvarying momentum, such that uses of it and curiosity about it, mount steadily; while as yet there does not seem to be the beginnings of an awareness that personal construct theory is the most massive and carefully elaborated theoretical invention in the psychology of the last fifty years.

This book is designed to illustrate both the rewards and tribulations of attempting to confront personal construct theory.

D. BANNISTER

June 1970

Acknowledgements

The Editor is grateful to Mrs. Gladys Kelly and to Dr. Jean Tippett and Dr. Frances Lemcke for agreeing to the publication of the two essays by the late George Kelly.

The Editor and the publisher also wish to thank the following for their kind permission to reproduce material quoted from other volumes:

M.I.T. Press for a quotation from "Aspects of the Theory of Syntax" by Noam Chomsky; Basil Blackwell, Publisher, for a quotation from "Philosophical Investigations" by L. Wittgenstein; Yale University Press for a quotation from "Essays on Man" by Ernst Cassirer; The University of Chicago Press for a quotation from "The Structure of Scientific Revolution" by T. S. Kuhn; *The Journal of Individual Psychology* **20,** pp. 137–152 (1964), from an article "The Language of Hypothesis: Man's Psychological Instrument"; Eyre and Spottiswoode Ltd. for a quotation from "Behaviour" by D. E. Broadbent; John Wiley and Sons Ltd. for various quotations from "Clinical Psychology and Personality: The Selected Papers of George Kelly"; The Hutchinson Publishing Group Ltd. for a quotation from "Concept of Mind" by G. Ryle and also to Barnes and Noble Inc., for the U.S. rights to reproduce this material; Laurence Pollinger Ltd. and the Estate of the late Mrs. Frieda Lawrence, and to the Viking Press for permission to reproduce a quotation from "Fantasia of the Unconscious" by D. H. Lawrence; the American Psychological Association for a quotation from *American Psychologist*; and W. W. Norton & Co., Inc. for quotations from "The Psychology of Personal Constructs" by George A. Kelly.

Contents

A Brief Introduction To Personal Construct Theory*

George A. Kelly

Who can say what nature is? Is it what now exists about us, including all the tiny hidden things that wait so patiently to be discovered? Or is it the vista of all that is destined to occur, whether tomorrow or in some distant eon of time? Or is nature, infinitely more varied than this, the myriad trains of events that might ensue if we were to be so bold, ingenious, and irreverent as to take a hand in its management?

Personal construct theory neither offers nor demands a firm answer to any of these questions, and in this respect it is unique. Rather than depending upon bedrock assumptions about the inherent nature of the universe, or upon fragments of truth believed to have been accumulated, it is a notion about how man may launch out from a position of admitted ignorance, and how he may aspire from one day to the next to transcend his own dogmatisms. It is, then, a theory of man's personal inquiry—a psychology of the human quest. It does not say what has or will be found, but proposes rather how we might go about looking for it.

Philosophical Position

Like other theories, the psychology of personal constructs is the implementation of a philosophical assumption. In this case the assumption is that whatever nature may be, or howsoever the quest for truth will turn out in the end, the events we face today are subject to as great a variety of constructions as our wits will enable us to contrive. This is not to say that one construction is as good as any other, nor is it to deny that at some infinite point in time human vision will behold reality out to the utmost reaches of existence. But it does remind us that all our present perceptions are open to question and reconsideration, and it does broadly suggest that even the most obvious occurrences of everyday life might appear utterly transformed if we were inventive enough to construe them differently.

* This essay was written in 1966 to introduce a projected book on research in personal construct theory.

1

This philosophical position we have called *constructive alternativism*, and its implications keep cropping up in the psychology of personal constructs. It can be contrasted with the prevalent epistemological assumption of *accumulative fragmentalism,* which is that truth is collected piece by piece. While constructive alternativism does not argue against the collection of information, neither does it measure truth by the size of the collection. Indeed it leads one to regard a large accumulation of facts as an open invitation to some far-reaching reconstruction which will reduce them to a mass of trivialities.

A person who spends a great deal of his time hoarding facts is not likely to be happy at the prospect of seeing them converted into rubbish. He is more likely to want them bound and preserved, a memorial to his personal achievement. A scientist, for example, who thinks this way, and especially a psychologist who does so, depends upon his facts to furnish the ultimate proof of his propositions. With these shining nuggets of truth in his grasp it seems unnecessary for him to take responsibility for the conclusions he claims they thrust upon him. To suggest to him at this point that further human reconstruction can completely alter the appearance of the precious fragments he has accumulated, as well as the direction of their arguments, is to threaten his scientific conclusions, his philosophical position, and even his moral security. No wonder, then, that, in the eyes of such a conservatively minded person, our assumption that all facts are subject—are wholly subject —to alternative constructions looms up as culpably subjective and dangerously subversive to the scientific establishment.

Facts and Conclusions

But wherein does responsibility lie? Can we ever make facts, even facts that turn out as predicted, responsible for conclusions? I think not. Whatever the world may be, man can come to grips with it only by placing his own interpretations upon what he sees. While his ingenuity in devising suitable constructions may be limited, and many misfortunes therefore come to pass, still it is he, not facts, who holds the key to the ultimate future. This, it seems to me, makes him responsible, and suggests that it is quite inappropriate for him ever to claim that his conclusions have been dictated by any nature other than his own.

This, of course, is how I construe it; and in this undertaking I, too, have chosen to bear responsibility for where my constructive alternativism is leading me. So, also, my reader, if he accepts this invitation to join me, will, like any other Adam or Eve who chooses to understand for himself, be held responsible for his choice—though no more so than I should think him responsible for any other choice he might make, including the choice of *not* accepting this invitation.

None of this is a denial that men customarily share each other's insights and prejudices. Our ingenuity in devising alternative constructions is limited by our feeble wits and our timid reliance upon what is familiar. So we usually do things the way we have done them before or the way others appear to do them. Moreover, novel ideas, when openly expressed, can be disruptive to ourselves and disturbing to others. We therefore often avoid them, disguise them, keep them bottled up in our minds where they cannot develop in the social context, or disavow them in what we believe to be loyalty to the common interest. And often, against our better judgment, we accept the dictates of authority instead, thinking thus to escape any personal responsibility for what happens.

But though our devices for interpreting circumstances are still meager, and the human adventure continues to be fraught with dire uncertainties, it does not follow that facts ever dictate our conclusions, except by the rules we impose upon our acts. Events do not tell us what to do, nor do they carry their meanings engraved on their backs for us to discover. For better or worse we ourselves create the only meanings they will ever convey during our lifetime. The facts of life may even be brutal, but they are nonetheless innocent of any evil intent, and we can scarcely accuse them of taking sides in our epistemological disputes. Our ever present task is to devise ways of anticipating their occurrences, and thus to prepare ourselves for assuming a more and more responsible role in the management of the universe.

The Meaning of Events

Constructive alternativism stresses the importance of events. But it looks to man to propose what the character of their import shall be. The meaning of an event—that is to say, the meaning we ascribe to it—is anchored in its antecedents and its consequents. Thus meaning displays itself to us mainly in the dimension of time. This is much more than saying that meanings are rehearsals of outcomes, a proposition implicit in behaviouristic theory, or that the ends justify the means—the ethical statement of the same proposition.

Besides including anticipated outcomes, meaning includes also the means by which events are anticipated. This is to suggest that different meanings are involved when identical events are correctly anticipated by different sets of inferences. It suggests also the implication of quite different meanings when the basic assumptions are different, even when the chains of inference are otherwise more or less similar.

In all of this we look to events to confirm our predictions and to encourage our venturesome constructions. Yet the same events may confirm different constructions, and different, or even incompatible, events may appear to validate the same construction. So, for each of us, meaning assumes the shape of the arguments which lead him to his predictions, and the only outside

check on his personal constructions are the events which confirm or disconfirm his expectations. This is a long way from saying that meaning is revealed
by what happens, or that meaning is something to be discovered in the natural
course of events, or that events shape men and ideas. Thus in constructive
alternativism events are crucial, but only man can devise a meaning for them
to challenge.

When we place a construction of our own upon a situation, and then
pursue its implications to the point of expecting something to happen, we
issue a little invitation to nature to intervene in our personal experience. If
what we expect does happen, or appears to happen, our expectation is confirmed and we are likely to think that we must have had a pretty good slant
on the trend of affairs, else we would have lost our bet. But if we think the
matter over carefully we may begin to have doubts. Perhaps a totally
different interpretation would have led to an equally successful prediction;
and it may, besides, have been more straightforward, or more consistent
with our conscience. Or perhaps our vivid expectations overlaid our perception of what actually happened.

So, on second thought, even when events are reconciled with a construction,
we cannot be sure that they have proved it true. There are always other
constructions, and there is the lurking likelihood that some of them will turn
out to be better. The best we can ever do is project our anticipations with
frank uncertainty and observe the outcomes in terms in which we have a bit
more confidence. But neither anticipation nor outcome is ever a matter of
absolute certainty from the dark in which we mortals crouch. And, hence,
even the most valuable construction we have yet contrived—even our
particular notion of God Himself—is one for which we shall have to continue
to take personal responsibility—at least until someone turns up with a better
one. And I suspect he will! This is what we mean by *constructive alternativism*.
Our view might even be called a philosophical position of *epistemological
responsibility*.

The Conduct of Inquiry

One of the most exciting aspects of constructive alternativism is its bearing
upon the conduct of human inquiry. According to the canons of logic a
statement, if meaningful, is either true or not true. Indeed, the logical posi-
tivists have reversed the logic and argued that the criterion for meaningfulness
is whether or not a statement can be proved true or not true. This means, I
take it, that we should not ask a question until we have answered it. But
constructive alternativism suggests that the canon itself is not fruitful, or at
least that it tends to stultify fruitful endeavour. Besides, I note that most of
the members of the famous Vienna Circle abandoned their extreme position—
bursting with unanswerable questions, no doubt.

Since ultimate truth is such a long way off, it seems as inappropriate to try to capture it by, say, five o'clock on Tuesday as it is to claim we already have it in our grasp. Thus any proposition we contrive must be regarded as a crude formulation of a question which, at best, can serve only as an invitation to further inquiry, and one that can be answered only through personal experience and in terms of the *ad interim* criterion of anticipated events. Indeed, the answer we get is not likely to be exactly an answer to our question at all, but an answer to some other question we have not yet thought to ask.

To this way of thinking the verbs in all significant statements a man makes are implicitly cast in an "invitational mood", rather than in the indicative mood, or in one of the other moods recognized by English grammar. "What", he says, "would happen if . . . ?" We suspect, furthermore, that this is psychologically characteristic of man whenever he is not in a defensive posture, and that it characterizes his unspoken impulses as well as his articulate sentences. "Please", he means to say, "join me in pursuing the implications of this pose I have assumed."

In this light, then, it is not necessary to disprove one proposition before entertaining alternatives to it. In certain situations, as in psychotherapy for example, it may even be disastrous to start with disproof, at least until we know what alternatives will drop into place once the disproof is taken seriously. Constructive alternativism is therefore an invitation to immediate adventure. By not insisting on disproof as a precondition for initiative it saves a lot of wear and tear on nerves and it should release a great deal of scholarly manpower for more productive and less disputatious occupations.

So, under constructive alternativism, even the appearance of some objective certainty may be taken as a flagrant challenge to throw—without waiting for the courage that disillusionment provides—a new light on the very circumstances that make it seem so obvious. Yet constructive alternativism tells us also that the reconstructive enterprise may be forestalled even earlier in the sequence. If one cautiously insists that truth must be compiled and cross-validated in fragments before he ever ventures further in the human quest, he may never reach the point where he can sense the challenge of upending smug certainties. He will be so eager to nail down his bits of truth once and for all that he will never back off and treat himself to a fresh look.

Generally, propositions cannot be effectively refuted unless we accept their terms of reference. But unless the terms are better stated than they usually are, it may be more appropriate to discard an old proposition than to go through the contortions necessary to disprove it. This seems to be mostly what we do with old propositions anyway! In any case, constructive alternativism suggests that we need not become bogged down in tedious refutations and that audacious proposals, including some that are badly put, may well serve as springboards for novel inquiry—even while we still retain a preference for their traditional alternatives.

Generating Psychological Theory

But now, since we are already on the threshold of psychological theorizing, we might as well get on with it, even though there is much more that could be said about the philosophical position of constructive alternativism. So let us talk about personal construct theory itself. We can come back to philosophy later if necessary.

The question of just how a theory is generated is about as complicated as the whole of human psychology. Since theories—so far, at least—are devised by men, it seems unreasonable to claim that they are shaped by any process other than a psychological one. Yet for a long time we have been saying that one moves from old propositions to new ones by the logical procedures of induction or deduction, as if this could happen independently of the personal disposition of man. Indeed, I have come to doubt that the notions of induction and deduction tell us very much about what goes on. In the one case I suppose it means we listen to ourselves making a clutter of assertions only to end up trying to say them all in one mouthful. In the other we let loose with a high-sounding remark and then, like a four-year-old child trying to "read" his own "writing", struggle to figure out what we meant by it.

In formulating the theory I have called *the psychology of personal constructs* I cannot say that I actually launched out deductively from the assumption of constructive alternativism as I have phrased it here, though now I can see how, with the help of a certain amount of idiosyncratic bias along the way, one could start with constructive alternativism and end up with personal construct theory. And I believe I can see how the clutter of events I experienced was important. Now that I think of it, I can remember a lot of relevant things that happened over the years. But not for one moment would I claim that these events converged to shape my theory. They seemed only to keep challenging it—and not always to be very constructive about it either. It may even be that I can remember these incidents now only because, on hindsight, they seem to confirm what my present formulation would forecast. And I am sure that I found myself perplexed and aggravated by many circumstances I have long since forgotten, and that what I came to think as a psychologist was what, over the years, I had jury-rigged as a man to cope with what was going on.

So let us not be hasty. Perhaps constructive alternativism was my basic assumption all along. I may only have delayed putting it into words. I recall that I have often felt that personal construct theory was as much an account of what had long been running through my noggin as it was the outcome of my laboured thinking after I told myself to go ahead and dare to write a theory.

All of this is to suggest that the psychological postures, mine included, that we accent with words, or dignify in philosophical terms, may be quite personal and may considerably antedate our verbal statements about them. There is even reason to dread bringing such nascent constructions to light lest they betray us as foolish or even crazy. And I must say, at some risk to myself I suppose, that to propose a statement of such sweeping proportions as constructive alternativism is to flirt with grandiosity—a symptom more often associated with psychosis than with genius. But just as good cannot be accomplished without risking evil, so enlightenment cannot be sought wholeheartedly without approaching the brink of what may turn out to be insanity. There is no such thing as adventure with safety guaranteed in advance, not even when sitting alone with a typewriter. Not that I have ever lost any sleep over the matter!

Scientific Behaviour as a Paradigm of Human Behaviour

Legend has it that many theories originated with simple observations, often occurring under the most commonplace of circumstances. Archimedes is supposed to have been dallying in his bath when he made the observation that led to the notion of specific gravity. And there is the story about Newton napping under the apple tree. Then there is Bernoulli. I have long had my suspicions about what Bernoulli was doing.

Not to be outdone in fictionalizing itself, personal construct theory also can lay claim to an initial anecdote. In this case it is an observation of an amusing human, and even better than that, a psychologists' foible—which happily lowers it, I think, to the level of a caricature. So let us say that personal construct theory is a bit of humour that examined its own implications. And what, may I ask, could be more candidly psychological than that?

Psychologists are likely to be very much in earnest about making their discipline into a science. (Unfortunately, not many are as concerned as they might be about making science into something.) And they are never more deadly serious about staking a claim to scientific respectability than they are when they are writing elementary textbooks. It struck me rather suddenly one day that all the elementary texts I had read contained at least two theories of personality—one covert, lucid, and facile, and the others labelled, abstruse, and laboured.

"Psychology is a science", each author would say as soon as he had finished his initial exhortation to his young readers to stop relying upon common sense, "and a scientist is one who observes, construes relationships, articulates theories, generates hypotheses, ventures predictions, experiments under controlled conditions, and takes candid account of outcomes." This is to say that if the student is to understand a psychologist's commitment to life, here is the way to make sense out of it. Not bad! It gives us a pretty clear picture of what it is like to be a psychologist. Altogether it is a most penetrating and perceptive theory of personality, albeit one reserved for the scientifically elite.

Later on in the book, after the writer has explained that the eye really sees things upside down, that dogs' mouths water when they hear the dinner bell, and that the child's confrontation with the school system at age sixteen turns out about the same way it did when he was six (proving that it is *the child's* intelligence that does not change) he takes up the matter of personality theories, making it clear that he is really talking about organisms and being careful not to anthropomorphize his explanations—even his explanations of man. And how do organisms, such as human organisms (still being careful to avoid the use of such a compromising term as *persons*), behave? Why, they are *conditioned* (meaning that learning is something they must have had done to them—probably when they weren't looking), they are propelled by drives (anyone can see that otherwise they would just sit and do nothing at all), deluded by their motives (why else would they disagree with us?), and stalked by the ghosts of their childhood fantasies (note how they read the comic strips in the newspaper).

But what would happen if one were to envision all human endeavour in those same terms the psychologists have found so illuminating in explaining themselves to their students? And, indeed, might it not be that in doing so one would see the course of individual life, as well as human progress over the centuries, in clearer perspective? Scientists are men, and, while it does not follow that men are scientists, it is quite appropriate to ask if it is not their human character that makes scientists what they are. This leads us to the question of how that human character can better be construed so as to account for scientists, and whether our construction can still explain as well the accomplishments that fall far short of what we, at this transient moment in our history, think good science is.

This is not a question of whether or not men do, in fact, live by the canons of science? That, except to an accumulative fragmentalist, is not even an appropriate question. We are not in search of such a neat conclusion, but of a strategic advantage in a long term quest for understanding. No theory can offer us more than that. The issue, then, is what this constructive alternative of seeing man as an incipient scientist will contribute at the present state in the search for a psychological understanding of him. Who knows—a by-product of this venture may be new light on scientific endeavour itself. In fact, I think I can see such a by-product emerging as personal construct theory suggests ways in which psychological processes we have hitherto spurned may enliven the scientific enterprise.

Basic Postulate

A person's processes are psychologically channelized by the ways in which he anticipates events. This is what we have proposed as a fundamental postulate for the psychology of personal constructs. The assumptions of constructive alternativism are embedded in this statement, although it may not be apparent until later in our exposition of the theme just how it is that they are.

We start with a *person.* Organisms, lower animals, and societies can wait. We are talking about someone we know, or would like to know—such as you, or myself. More particularly, we are talking about that person as an event—the processes that express his personality. And, since we enter the system we are about to elaborate at the point of a process—or life—rather than at the point of a body or a material substance, we should not have to invoke any special notions, such as dynamics, drives, motivation, or force to explain why our object does not remain inert. As far as the theory is concerned, it never was inert. As we pursue the theoretical line emerging from this postulate I think it becomes clear also why we do not need such notions to account for the direction of movement—any more than we need them to explain the movement itself.

This is to be a psychological theory. Mostly this is a way of announcing in the basic postulate that we make no commitment to the terms of other disciplines, such as physiology or chemistry. Our philosophical position permits us to see those other disciplines as based on man-made constructions, rather than as disclosures of raw realities, and hence there is no need for the psychologist to accept them as final, or to limit his proposals to statements consistent with them.

In addition, I think the theory sounds more or less like the other theories that are known as psychological. This gives me an inclusive, as well as an exclusive reason for calling it a psychological theory, although this is more or less a matter of taste rather than of definition. Certainly I have no intention of trying to define psychology; there are just too many things called psychological that I do not care to take responsibility for.

Some have suggested that personal construct theory not be called a psychological theory at all, but a metatheory. That is all right with me. It suggests that it is a theory about theories, and that is pretty much what I have in mind. But I hope that it is clear that it is not limited to being a metatheory of formal theories, or even of articulate ones.

There is also the question of whether or not it is a cognitive theory. Some have said that it was; others have classed it as existential. Quite an accomplishment; not many theories have been accused of being both cognitive and existential! But this, too, is all right with me. As a matter of fact, I am delighted. There are categorical systems in which I think the greater amount of ambiguity I stir up, the better. Cognition, for example, strikes me as a particularly misleading category, and, since it is one designed to distinguish itself from affect and conation, those terms, too, might well be discarded as inappropriately restrictive.

Personal construct theory has also been categorized by responsible scholars as an emotional theory, a learning theory, a psychoanalytic theory (Freudian, Adlerian, and Jungian—all three), a typically American theory, a Marxist theory, a humanistic theory, a logical positivistic theory, a Zen Buddhistic theory, a Thomistic theory, a behaviouristic theory, an Apollonian theory, a pragmatistic theory, a reflective theory, and no theory at all. It has also been classified as nonsense, which indeed, by its own admission, it will likely some day turn out to be. In each case there were some convincing arguments offered for the categorization, but I have forgotten what most of them were. I fear that no one of these categorizations will be of much help to the reader in understanding personal construct theory, but perhaps having a whole lap full of them all at once will suggest what might be done with them.

The fourth term in the postulate—*channelized*—was chosen as one less likely than others to imply dynamics. This is because there is no wish to suggest that we are dealing with anything not already in motion. What is to be explained is the direction of the processes, not the transformation of states into processes. We see states only as an *ad interim* device to get time to stand still long enough for us to see what is going on. In other words, we have assumed that a process can be profitably regarded as more basic than an inert substance. We have had to do this notwithstanding the commitments of the centuries to quite another kind of language system. There are some disadvantages that come with this notion of what is basic, but we are willing to accept them for the time being in order to explore the Heraclitean implications more fully than psychologists have ever done before.

In specifying *ways of anticipating events* as the directive referent for human processes we cut ourselves free of the stimulus-response version of nineteenth century scientific determinism. I am aware that this is a drastic step indeed, and I suspect that others who claim to have taken similar steps have not always seriously taken stock of the difficulties to be encountered. For one thing, the very syntax of the language we must employ to voice our protest is built on a world view that regards objects as agents and outcomes as the products of those agents.

In our present undertaking the psychological initiative always remains a property of the person—never the property of anything else. What is more, neither past nor future events are themselves ever regarded as basic determinants of the course of human action—not even the events of childhood. But one's way of anticipating them, whether in the short range or in the long view—this is the basic theme in the human process of living. Moreover, it is that events are anticipated, not merely that man gravitates toward more and more comfortable organic states. Confirmation and disconfirmation of one's predictions are accorded greater psychological significance than rewards, punishments, or the drive reduction that reinforcements produce.

There are, of course, some predictions we would like to see disconfirmed, as well as some we hope will indeed materialize. We should not make the mistake of translating personal construct theory back into stimulus-response theory and saying to ourselves that confirmation is the same as a positive reinforcement, and that disconfirmation nullifies the meaning of an experience. Disconfirmation, even in those cases where it is disconcerting, provides grounds for reconstruction—or of repentance, in the proper sense of that term—and it may be used to improve the accuracy and significance of further anticipations. Thus we envision the nature of life in its outreach for the future, and not in its perpetuation of its prior conditions or in its incessant reverberation of past events.

Personal construct theory is elaborated by a string of eleven corollaries which may be loosely inferred from its basic postulate. Beyond these are certain notions of more limited applicability which fall in line with personal construct thinking—notions about such matters as anxiety, guilt, hostility, decision making, creativity, the strategy of psychological research, and other typical concerns of professional psychologists. These latter notions need not be considered part of the formal structure of the theory, although our theoretical efforts may not come to life in the mind of the reader until he has seen their applicability to the daily problems he faces.

Construction Corollary

A person anticipates events by construing their replications. Since events never repeat themselves, else they would lose their identity, one can look forward to them only by devising some construction which permits him to perceive two of them in a similar manner. His construction must also permit him to be selective about which two are to be perceived similarly. Thus the same construction that serves to infer their similarity must serve also to differentiate them from others. Under a system that provides only for the identification of similarities the world dissolves into homogeneity; under one that provides only for differentiation it is shattered into hopelessly unrelated fragments.

Perhaps it is true that events, as most of us would like to believe, really do repeat aspects of previous occurrences. But unless one thinks he is precocious enough to have hit upon what those aspects will ultimately turn out to be, or holy enough to have had them revealed to him, he must modestly concede that the appearance of replication is a reflection of his own fallible construction of what is going on. Thus the recurrent themes that make life seem so full of meaning are the original symphonic compositions of a man bent on finding the present in his past, and the future in his present.

Individuality Corollary

Persons differ from each other in their constructions of events. Having assumed that construction is a personal affair, it seems unlikely that any two persons would ever happen to concoct identical systems. I would go further now than when I originally proposed this corollary and suggest that even particular constructions are never identical events. And I would extend it the other way too, and say that I doubt that two persons ever put their construction systems together in terms of the same logical relationships. For myself, I find this a most encouraging line of speculation, for it seems to open the door to more advanced systems of thinking and inference yet to be devised by man. Certainly it suggests that scientific research can rely more heavily on individual imagination than it usually dares.

Organization Corollary

Each person characteristically evolves, for his convenience in anticipating events, a construction system embracing ordinal relationships between constructs. If a person is to live actively within his construction system it must provide him with some clear avenues of inference and movement. There must be ways for him to resolve the more crucial contradictions and conflicts that inevitably arise. This is not to say that all inconsistencies must be resolved at once. Some private paradoxes can be allowed to stand indefinitely, and, in the face of them, one can remain indecisive or can vacillate between alternative expectations of what the future holds in store for him.

So it seems that each person arranges his constructions so that he can move from one to another in some orderly fashion, either by assigning priorities to those which are to take precedence when doubts or contradictions arise, or by arranging implicative relationships, as in boolean algebra, so that he may infer that one construction follows from another. Thus one's commitments may take priority over his opportunities, his political affiliations may turn him from compassion to power, and his moral imperatives may render him insensitive to the brute that tugs at his sleeve. These are the typical prices men pay to escape inner chaos.

Dichotomy Corollary

A person's construction system is composed of a finite number of dichotomous constructs. Experience has shown me that this is the point where many of my readers first encounter difficulty in agreeing with me. What I am saying is that a construct is a "black and white" affair, never a matter of shadings, or of "grays". On the face of it, this sounds bad, for it seems to imply categorical or absolutistic thinking rather than any acceptance of relativism or conditionalism. Yet I would insist that there is nothing categorical about a construct.

When we look closely the initial point of difficulty in following personal construct theory usually turns out to lie in certain unrecognized assumptions made earlier while reading the exposition, or even carried over from previous habits of thought. Let us see if we can get the matter straightened out before any irreparable damage is done.

Neither our constructs nor our construing systems come to us from nature, except, of course, from our own nature. It must be noted that this philosophical position of constructive alternativism has much more powerful epistemological implications than one might at first suppose. We cannot say that constructs are essences distilled by the mind out of available reality. They are imposed *upon* events, not abstracted *from* them. There is only one place they come from; that is from the person who is to use them. He devises them. Moreover, they do not stand for anything or represent anything, as a symbol, for example, is supposed to do.

So what are they? They are reference axes, upon which one may project events in an effort to make some sense out of what is going on. In this sense they are like cartesian coordinates, the *x, y* and *z* axes of analytic geometry. Events correspond to the points plotted within cartesian space. We can locate the points and express relations between points by specifying *x, y* and *z* distances. The cartesian axes *do not represent* the points projected upon them, but serve as guidelines for locating those points. That, also, is what constructs do for events, including ones that have not yet occurred. They help us locate them, understand them, and anticipate them.

But we must not take the cartesian analogy too literally. Descartes' axes were lines or scales, each containing in order an infinite number of imaginary points. Certainly his *x* or *y*-axis embodied well enough the notion of shadings or a succession of grays. Yet a construct is not quite such an axis.

A construct is the basic contrast between two groups. When it is imposed it serves both to distinguish between its elements and to group them. Thus the construct refers to the nature of the distinction one attempts to make between events, not to the array in which his events appear to stand when he gets through applying the distinction between each of them and all the others.

Suppose one is dealing with the construct of good versus bad. Such a construct is not a representation of all things that are good, and an implicit exclusion of all that are bad. Nor is it a representation of all that are bad. It is not even a representation of all things that can be called either good or bad. The construct, of itself, is the kind of contrast one perceives and not in any way a representation of objects. As far as the construct is concerned there is no good-better-best scale, or any bad-worse-worst array.

But, while constructs do not represent or symbolize events, they do enable us to cope with events, which is a statement of quite a different order. They also enable us to put events into arrays or scales, if we wish. Suppose, for example, we apply our construct to elements, say persons, or to their acts. Consider three persons. One may make a good-bad distinction between them which will say that two of them are good in relation to the third, and the third is bad in relation to the two good ones. Then he may, in turn, apply his construct between the two good ones and say one of them is good with respect to the other formerly "good" one and the one already labelled "bad".

This, of course, makes one of the persons, or acts, good in terms of one cleavage that has been made and bad in relation to the other. But this relativism applies only to the objects; the construct of good versus bad is itself absolute. It may not be accurate, and it may not be stable from time to time, but, as a construct, it has to be absolute. Still, by its successive application to events one may create a scale with a great number of points differentiated along its length. Now a person who likes grays can have them—as many as he likes.

But let us make no mistake: A scale, in comparison to a construct, is a pretty concrete affair. Yet one can scarcely have himself a scale unless he has a construct working for him. Only if he has some basis for discrimination and association can he get on with the job of marking off a scale.

Now note something else. We have really had to fall back on our philosophical position of constructive alternativism in order to come up with this kind of an abstraction. If we had not first disabused ourselves of the idea that events are the source of our construct, we would have had a hard time coming around to the point where we could envision the underlying basis of discrimination and association we call the construct.

The Geometry of Psychological Space

While we are at it, let us keep on going with this kind of abstract thinking and envision an equally abstract construction system made up of many constructs. If we can hold on we shall be well on our way to understanding personal construct theory's underlying mathematics or metaphysics. But we dare not fall back on our cartesian analogy, once we have reached this point in the argument, lest we find ourselves envisioning systems of lines intersecting at common points. That may be all right for dimensioning physical space—though I am not so sure—but certainly it will not do for structuring psychological space.

To catch a glimpse of psychological space we may imagine a system of planes, each with two sides or aspects, slicing through a galaxy of events. One does not measure distances on these planes, he notes only, at any one instant of application, which side of each plane faces which events when the set is suspended in the galaxy. The set, or construct system, can, of course, be moved around in the galaxy in the manner I have described when a single construct is used to devise a scale. If the set is moved into all possible positions it generates a paracartesian hyperspace with its relatively concrete scalar axes. But that is a rather large undertaking, and one likely to fall through because man is inventive enough to keep thinking of new constructs he would like to add to the system. Another way of saying this is to suggest that even the simplest personal construct system can hardly get around to putting all events in order, and, unless the man is pretty unimaginative, he will have to keep starting over each time he thinks of a new way to discriminate or associate.

One thing more has to be said. In order to make the point, I have had to talk about constructs in such an explicit manner that I have probably given the impression that a construct is as highly articulate and cognitive as my discussion has had to be. If I had been able to say what I have said in metaphor or hyperbole I might have left the impression that a construct had something to do with feeling or with formless urges too fluid to be pinned down by labels. But personal construct theory is no more a cognitive theory than it is an affective or a conative one. There are grounds for distinction that operate in one's life that seem to elude verbal expression. We see them in infants, as well as in our own spontaneous aversions and infatuations. These discriminative bases are no less constructs than those the reader may have been imagining during the reading of the preceding paragraphs. Certainly it is important not to consider a construct as another term for a concept, else a major sector of the arena in which constructs function will be obscured from view.

Choice Corollary

A person chooses for himself that alternative in a dichotomized construct through which he anticipates the greater possibility for the elaboration of his system. It seems to me to follow that if a person makes so much use of his constructs, and is so dependent upon them, he will make choices which promise to develop their usefulness. Developing the usefulness of a construction system involves, as far as I can see, two things: defining it and extending it. One defines his system, by extension at least, by making it clear how its construct components are applied to objects or are linked with each other. He amplifies his system by using it to reach out for new fields of application. In the one case he consolidates his position and in the other he extends it.

Note that the choice is between alternatives expressed in the construct, not, as one might expect, between objects divided by means of the construct. There is a subtle point here. Personal construct theory is a psychological theory and therefore has to do with the behaviour of man, not with the intrinsic nature of objects. A construct governs what the man does, not what the object does. In a strict sense, therefore, man makes decisions which initially affect himself, and which affect other objects only subsequently— and then only if he manages to take some effective action. Making a choice, then, has to do with involving oneself, and cannot be defined in terms of the external object chosen. Besides, one does not always get the object he chooses to gain. But his anticipation does have to do with his own processes, as I tried to say in formulating the basic postulate.

So when a man makes a choice what he does is align himself in terms of his constructs. He does not necessarily succeed, poor fellow, in doing anything to the objects he seeks to approach or avoid. Trying to define human behaviour in terms of the externalities sought or affected, rather than the seeking process, gets the psychologist pretty far off the track. It makes more of a physicist of him than a psychologist, and a rather poor one, at that. So what we must say is that a person, in deciding whether to believe or do something, uses his construct system to proportion his field, and then moves himself strategically and tactically within its presumed domain.

Men change things by changing themselves first, and they accomplish their objectives, if at all, only by paying the price of altering themselves— as some have found to their sorrow and others to their salvation. The choices that men make are choices of their own acts, and the alternatives are distinguished by their own constructs. The results of the choices, however, may range all the way from nothing to catastrophe, on the one hand, or to consummation, on the other.

Range Corollary

A construct is convenient for the anticipation of a finite range of events only. A personal construct system can hardly be said to have universal utility. Not everything that happens in the world can be projected upon all the dichotomies that make up a person's outlook. Indeed I doubt that anyone has ever devised a construct that could cover the entire range of events of which he was aware. There are patches of clouds in every man's sky. This is to say that the geometry of the mind is never a complete system. The lines of reference here and there become lost in irrelevancies and make it practically impossible to write formulas that are universally applicable.

The classical notion of a *concept* is that it embraces all elements having a common property, and excludes all others. But this kind of notion will not do for *constructs*. A construct is a distinction which has the effect of distributing objects tentatively into two associations. If one says that a man is tall he does more than exclude all objects that are not tall. He denies that the man is short. He asserts that there are other objects that are both not tall and are short. And he excludes only those objects which are outside his range of concern.

Logicians, accustomed to thinking about concepts and not yet altogether clear about what I mean by constructs, might take issue with me at this point. They might say that all one has disclaimed is the possibility that the man is not tall. But we must remind ourselves that here we are talking about the psychology of man's actions and intents, and we can be sure that if the person who makes the remark has nothing more on his mind than what formal logic suggests, he will keep his mouth shut. Psychologically, the only point in commenting on the man's being tall is to deny some alternative that needed denying. What is excluded, therefore, includes some pretty important considerations, as well as some irrelevancies.

If we are to understand a person's statement we had better take into account just what it was he felt he must negate, as well as what he used as the subject or the predicate of his sentence. This, again, is a way of saying that the construct is a basis of making a distinction and, by the same act, creating an association, as one does when saying that a man is tall and implying thereby that he is like some other objects in that respect. Especially, one must keep in mind that a construct is not a class of objects, or an abstraction of a class, but a dichotomous reference axis.

A construct has its *focus of convenience*—a set of objects with which it works especially well. Over a somewhat larger range it may work only reasonably well; that is its *range of convenience*. But beyond that it fades into uselessness and we can say the outer array of objects simply lies beyond that range of convenience.

It would be nice, mathematically, if every event in a man's world could be projected onto every construct he had. Then we might hope to check out the whole system and all its internal relationships. It would be even nicer if every event could be projected upon every construct of every man. Then we could check one man's outlook precisely against another's—hoping that neither would change his mind before the wallpaper came out of the computer. But I don't think this is very likely to happen, at least not during the natural life of personal construct theory.

Experience Corollary

A person's construction system varies as he successively construes the replications of events. Here again our analytic geometry model does not quite fit the mathematics of psychological space. Rather than remaining altogether fixed, as the axes of analytic geometry do when points are plotted within them, the tendency is for personal constructs to shift when events are projected upon them. The distinctions they implement are likely to be altered in three ways: (1) The construct may be applied at a different point in the galaxy, (2) it may become a somewhat different kind of distinction, and (3) its relations to other constructs may be altered.

In the first of these shifts it is a matter of a change in the location of the construct's application, and hence not exactly an intrinsic change in the construct itself. In the second case, however, it is the abstraction itself which is altered, although the change may not be radical enough for the psychologist to say a new construct has been substituted. Finally, in the third case, the angular relations with other constructs are necessarily affected by the transition, unless, by some chance, the construct system were rotated as a whole. But that is not a very likely contingency.

The first kind of shift might be observed when a person moves to an urban community. Some of the actions he once regarded as aloof and unneighbourly he may come to accept as relatively friendly in the new social context. But he may also rotate the axis of his construct as he gains familiarity with city life, and, as a result, come to see "aloofness" as a neighbourly respect for his privacy, something he had never had very clearly in mind before. This would be an example of the second kind of shift. The third kind of shift comes when he alters his notion of respect as a result of the experience, perhaps coming to sense it not so much a matter of subservience or adulation but more a matter of empathy and consideration. As a matter of fact, we might regard the whole transition as leading him in the direction of greater maturity.

Keeping in mind that events do not actually repeat themselves and that the replication we talk about is a replication of ascribed aspects only, it begins to be clear that the succession we call experience is based on the constructions we place on what goes on. If those constructions are never altered, all that happens during a man's years is a sequence of parallel events having no psychological impact on his life. But if he invests himself—the most intimate event of all—in the enterprise, the outcome, to the extent that it differs from his expectation or enlarges upon it, dislodges the man's construction of himself. In recognizing the inconsistency between his anticipation and the outcome, he concedes a discrepancy between what he was and what he is. A succession of such investments and dislodgments constitutes the human experience.

A subtle point comes to light at this juncture. Confirmation may lead to reconstruing quite as much as disconfirmation—perhaps even more. A confirmation gives one an anchorage in some area of his life, leaving him free to set afoot adventuresome explorations nearby, as, for example, in the case of a child whose security at home emboldens him to be the first to explore what lies in the neighbour's yard.

The unit of experience is, therefore, a cycle embracing five phases: anticipation, investment, encounter, confirmation or disconfirmation, and constructive revision. This is followed, of course, by new anticipations, as the first phase of a subsequent experiential cycle gets underway. Certainly in personal construct theory's line of reasoning experience is not composed of encounters alone.

Stated simply, the amount of a man's experience is not measured by the number of events with which he collides, but by the investments he has made in his anticipations and the revisions of his constructions that have followed upon his facing up to consequences. A man whose only wager in life is upon reaching heaven by immunizing himself against the miseries of his neighbours, or upon following a bloody party-line straight to utopia, is prepared to gain little experience until he arrives—either there, or somewhere else clearly recognized as not the place he was looking for. Then, if he is not too distracted by finding that his architectural specifications have been blatantly disregarded, or that the wrong kind of people have started moving in, I suppose he may begin to think of some other investments he might better have been making in the meantime. Of course, a little hell along the way, if taken more to heart than most heaven-bound people seem to take it, may have given him a better idea of what to expect, before it was too late to get a bit of worthwhile experience and make something out of himself.

Modulation Corollary

The variation in a person's construction system is limited by the permeability of the constructs within whose ranges of convenience the variants lie. While the Experience Corollary suggests that a man can revise his constructions on the basis of events and his invested anticipations of them there are limitations that must be taken into account. He must have a construct system which is sufficiently open to novel events to let him know when he has encountered them, else the experience cycle will fail to function in its terminal phases. He must have a system which also will admit the revised construct that emerges at the end of the cycle. If the revised construct is left to stand as an isolated axis of reference it will be difficult for him to chart any coordinated course of action that takes account of it; he therefore can do little with respect to it except vacillate.

Perhaps it is clear from these remarks that what is meant by permeability is not a construct's plasticity, or its amenability to change within itself, but its capacity to be used as a referent for novel events and to accept new subordinate constructions within its range of convenience. A notion of God, for example, which includes an unabridged dictionary of all things holy is likely to be impermeable. Anything new that turns up—such as an unbiblical event or idea—is likely to be excluded from the construct's realm of concern. Unless the novelty can fit elsewhere into some more permeable part of the construct system, it is likely to be ignored.

Fragmentation Corollary

A person may successively employ a variety of construction subsystems which are inferentially incompatible with each other. We must be careful not to interpret the Modulation Corollary to mean that a construct system has to be logically intact. Perhaps in any proximate transition in the human process there is an inferential relationship between antecedent and consequent at some constructive level in the person's system. But persons move from *a* to *b*, and on to *c* without always taking into account the fact that their overview of *c* cannot be inferred from their overview of *a*. A man may move from an act of love to an act of jealousy, and from there to an act of hate, even though hate is not something that would be inferred from love, even in his peculiar system. This is the kind of psychological fact to which the Fragmentation Corollary calls particular attention.

Perhaps I should add that I do not see this kind of "irrationality" as necessarily a bad thing. For man logic and inference can be as much an obstacle to his ontological ventures as a guide to them. Often it is the un-inferred fragment of a man's construction system that makes him great, whereas if he were an integrated whole—taking into account all that the whole would have to embrace—the poor fellow would be no better than his "natural self".

Commonality Corollary

*To the extent that one person employs a construction of experience which is similar to that employed by another, his processes are psychologically similar to those of the other person.** On the face of it, this corollary appears to assert pretty much what personal construct theory seems to stand for: The notion that behaviour is governed by constructs. But there is more to it than what such a simplified statement might be taken to imply.

If we do as most behaviouristically influenced psychologists do, and use behaviour as a synonym for all human process, we then might, I suppose, substitute the term "behaviours" for "processes" in stating this corollary. But what thoughtful behaviourists have in mind when they make behaviour the focus of their concern is the logical positivist position that anything that cannot be identified as behaviour is untestable and therefore a scientific distraction. If we were to take this stand—as I would prefer not—we would be concerned only with that phase of the experiential cycle I have called "personal investment". Personal construct theory would lead us, I think, to be

---

* To my mild dismay I have only now realized that the word "psychological" was misplaced in my original phrasing of this corollary. Instead of modifying "processes", as I originally had it, the term should modify "similar", as constructive alternativism would suggest. Sorry about that!

concerned with the whole experiential cycle and the process which it represents, rather than with the behavioural phase only.

There is something more. I have used the expression, "construction of experience", rather than "construction of events". I wanted it to be clear that the construction would have to cover the experience itself, as well as the external events with which experience was ostensibly concerned. At the end of an experiential cycle one not only has a revised construction of the events he originally sought to anticipate, but he has also a construction of the process by which he reached his new conclusions about them. In launching his next venture, whatever its concern might be, he will have reason to take account of the effectiveness of the experiential procedures he employed in his last.

To be sure, in writing this corollary it would have been literally correct to say simply, "construction of events", a phrase that appears so frequently in this exposition. This would have included "experience", since an experience, once it has been enacted, is itself an event. But experience is such an important event in charting what comes next, it seemed important to single it out for special mention. Besides, since experience, as I have defined it, already embraces the events with which the experiencing person has involved himself, the term is sufficiently inclusive, as well as exclusive, to pinpoint what needs to be said. What I especially want to make clear is that the extent of the psychological similarity between the processes of two persons depends upon the similarity of their constructions of their personal experiences, as well as upon the similarity in their conclusions about external events.

But let us also be especially clear about something this corollary does not say, and what that means for the psychology of man in motion. It does not say that the two persons must have experienced "the same" events and it does not say their two experiential cycles have to be "the same". And, to go further, it does not even say they must have experienced "similar" events or that the two experiential cycles must actually have been similar in some way. What has to be similar, in order for their processes to be similar in the same degree, is their construction of experience. And that includes similarity of the construction of events that emerges in the terminal phase of the experiential cycle.

The reason for this being so important is that the outcome of an experience is not merely a tendency to repeat or to avoid it thereafter, as reinforcement theory presumes, but that the conclusions reached through experience are likely to be in the form of new questions which set the stage for new ventures. One does not fully understand human behaviour, or human processes, except as he understands also the flashes of ingenuity that intersperse human monotonies. While novel undertakings can be construed in ways which show replications, as the Construction Corollary suggests, it is not behaviour or process itself which is concretely re-enacted. But in construing replications, rather than in claiming he has seen concrete repetitions, one may project a view of man engaged in ventures, rather than always repeating concretely what has been reinforced.

This corollary makes it possible to say that two persons who have confronted quite different events, and who might have gone through experiential cycles which actually seem to us to be quite different, might nevertheless end up with similar constructions of their experiences, and, because of that, thereafter pursue psychologically similar processes of further inquiry. Thus personal construct theory further releases psychology from assumptions about the identity of events and man's dependence upon them. It leaves us free to envision man coping with "familiar" events in new ways and co-operating with other men to produce novelties which make their world a different place to live in. Neither behaviourism nor phenomenology, as I see them, provides a psychological basis for this kind of forward movement in man.

Sociality Corollary

To the extent that one person construes the construction processes of another, he may play a role in a social process involving the other person. The implications of this corollary are probably the most far reaching of any I have yet attempted to propound. It establishes grounds for understanding *role* as a psychological term, and for envisioning thereupon a truly psychological basis for society. As far as I can see, the term has only extrapsychological meaning elsewhere. This view offers, moreover, an approach to certain puzzling aspects of psychopathy, and it permits one to understand guilt in far more intimate terms than are possible within more conventional "personality" theories, or within current theological doctrines. It leads us also to a position from which we can distinguish personality theories from others.

Perceptive psychologists are keenly aware that there must be some important relationship between what they call "role", "guilt", and "psychopathic personality" on the one hand, and the viability of society on the other. Yet there is little in the stimulus-response kind of theorizing that throws psychological light on what the relationship may be. There is scarcely more to be found in the so-called dynamic theories, although the literature associated with them richly documents a vaguely disquieting awareness of what may be transpiring in the community of man.

Let me start by trying to differentiate two levels at which I may try to understand another person—say, my reader. It is not hard for me to imagine him—*you*, I mean—at this moment a figure bending over a book. It—the figure—is skimming the paragraphs with the right fore-finger in a position to turn to the pages that follow. The eye movements zig zag down the page and quickly the next leaf is flipped, or perhaps a whole section—a chapter or more—is lifted with the left thumb and drawn horizontally aside.

What I am envisioning is a moving object, and whether or not I am correctly describing the movements that are taking place can be reasonably well confirmed—or disconfirmed—by an observer who has been watching you for the past few moments, or if he saw a motion picture film of what has been taking place. This is to say I have couched my picture of you in the terms of "objective" psychology. I have offered a hypothesized description of a "behaving organism".

Ordinarily, if I wanted to play the game by the rules of objectivity, I would not stoop to ask you outright whether or not my description of your actions was correct; the noises you might make in reply could be taken in so many different ways I can be sure of being "a scientist" only if I stick to what can be confirmed. Being a "scientist" may be so important to me that I dare not risk sullying myself with your delusions. I shall therefore play my part and retain my membership in Sigma Xi by referring to your reply as a "vocal response" of a "behaving organism". *Hello there, Behaving Organism*!

But now let me say it quite another way. There you are, my reader, wondering, I fear, what on earth I am trying so hard to say, and smiling to yourself as the thought crosses your mind that it all might be put in a familiar phrase or two—as indeed it may. You are hunched uncomfortably over the book, impatiently scanning the paragraphs for a cogent expression or a poignant sentence that may make the experience worth the time you are stealing from more urgent duties. The right forefinger is restlessly poised to lift the page and go on to discover if perhaps anything more sensible follows.

Let me confess that I feel at this moment like urging you not to try so hard. While it has taken me hours to write some of these paragraphs—the four preceding ones, for example—and I would like to think the outcome has been worth some of your time too, they were not meant to be hammered into your consciousness. They are intended, instead, to set off trains of thought. And, in following them, I earnestly hope we shall find ourselves walking along the same paths.

There now, isn't that the way it really is? It isn't? Then, tell me, what *are* you doing? And while we are at it, tell me also how my efforts strike you— I mean, what do you think I am trying to do, not merely whether I am making sense or not. Only please do not tell me that all I am really doing is pounding a typewriter in an effort to keep my wife awake; I have other psychoanalytically oriented friends who are only too happy to offer me that kind of "interpretation".

Although these two descriptions of my view of the reader both represent a wide departure from accepted literary style, I hope they will make clear the contrast between construing the construction processes of another person and construing his behaviour merely. In the first instance, I construed only your behaviour. There is nothing wrong with that, as far as it goes. In the second case I went further and placed a construction upon the way in which I imagined you might be thinking. The chances are that I was more or less mistaken in both instances, particularly in the second. But the point I want to make lies in the difference in my mode of construing you. In both formulations I was indeed concerned with your behaviour, but only in the second did I strive for some notion of the construction which might be giving your behaviour its form, or your future behaviour its form. If immediate accuracy is what I must preserve at all costs, then I had better stick to the first level of construction. But if I am to anticipate you, I must take some chances and try to sense what you are up to.

One does not have to be a psychologist to treat another person as an automaton, though training in "experimental psychology" may help. Conversely, treating him that way does not make one into a scientist—though some of my colleagues may wish to dispute this. It is easy enough to treat persons we have never met as behaving organisms only, and many of us think that is the sophisticated way to go about secondary human relations. We may even treat our neighbours that way, especially if there are more of them than we care to know. I have even observed parents who go so far as to treat their children so, and they sometimes come to me for psychological advice on how to do it. I sometimes suspect it is because they have more children than they care to know. To be very frank about it, my construction of you, while writing some of these passages, has often lapsed into no more than that. And, if you are like me in this respect, there must have been moments when you regarded me as a disembodied typewriter, or as an Irish name on the title page of a book, or as a kind of animated sentence ejector.

Points About Roles to be Emphasized

I know from past experience in attempting to explain this notion of role that two things need especially to be made clear, particularly if I am trying to explain it to a thoroughly trained fellow psychologist. First, my construing of your construction processes need not be accurate in order for me to play a role in a social process that involves you. I have seen a person play a role, and do it most effectively—even in a manner quite acceptable to his colleagues—when he grossly misperceived their outlooks, and they knew it. But because he did what he did on the basis of what he thought they understood, not merely on the basis of their overt acts, he was able to play a collaborative role in a social process whose experiential cycle led them all somewhere. Experiential cycles which are based on automaton-like constructions do not, I think, generate social processes, though they may lead to revisions of the manipulative devices by which men try to control each other's actions.

The second point that experience has led me to stress is that my construction of your outlook does not make me a compliant companion, nor does it keep us from working at cross purposes. I may even use my construction of your view as a basis for trying to undo your efforts. But there is something interesting about this; there is still a good chance of a social process emerging out of our conflict, and we will both end up a good way from where we started—in my case, because the experiential cycle will reflect back upon my construction of your outlook, not of your behaviour only, and, in your case, because you would find that something beyond your overt behaviour was being taken into account, and you might revise your investments accordingly.

There is a third point that sometimes needs mentioning. What I have proposed is a psychological definition of role, and therefore it does not lean upon sociological assumptions about the nature of society or economic assumptions about the coordination of human labour. Being psychological, it attempts to derive its terms from the experience of the individual, though, once the derivations have been made, there are no necessary restrictions on pursuing implications on out into the world of the sociologist, or even into that of the mathematician.

What comes out, then, is a definition that permits us to say that roles are not necessarily reciprocal; you may indeed enact a role based on your construction of my outlook, but my failure to construe you as anything more than a "behaving organism" may prevent me from enacting a role in relation to you. The social process that results from such an exchange stems from you but not from me. It involves you because your behaviour tests out a version of my outlook, and the experiential cycle in which you invest yourself leads you to a reinterpretation of our social relationship. It does not involve me because the only hypotheses to which I have made an experiential commitment are hypotheses about your overt behaviour.

Role and Experience

If I fail to invest in a role, and relate myself to you only mechanistically, then the only thing that disconfirmation can teach me is that the organism I presumed you to be is not wired up to produce the behaviours I thought it would—just as my typewriter does not always behave in the way I expect it to. When my typewriter behaves unpredictably I look to see if there isn't a screw loose, or if something hasn't gotten into the works. Sometimes I find I have struck the wrong key; I'll strike a different one next time.

And if I insist on construing you as I do my typewriter, I shall probably take my predictive failures as an indication only that I should look to see if there isn't "a screw loose somewhere" in you. Or perhaps I shall wonder if

I haven't "struck the wrong key", or if something hasn't "gotten into your works", like a "motive" or a "need", for example. I may even conclude that you are a brand of "typewriter" that has been badly put together. Certainly if this is the way I go about concluding my experiential cycle, I can scarcely claim that I have engaged myself in a social process. Mine might be the kind of experience that gets the commonwealth's work done, but it would not be the sort that builds viable societies.

When one construes another person's outlook, and proceeds to build an experiential cycle of his own upon that construction, he involves himself, willy nilly, in an interesting way. He can test his construction only by activating in himself the version of the other person's outlook it offers. This subtly places a demand upon him, one he cannot lightly reject if his own experience is to be completed. He must put himself tentatively in the other person's shoes. Only by enacting that role can be sense the impact of what happens as a result of taking the point of view he thinks his friend must have.

This means making a behavioural investment of his own, following the hypothesized lines, and experiencing the consequences. The enactment by which he pursues this experiential venture comes close to what is popularly regarded as role-taking. While not all enactments constitute roles in the personal construct sense, and not all role enactments culminate in completed experiential cycles, these brief comments may serve to suggest why the term *role* has been given such a salient part in the development of this theory.

Guilt

It is in the context of the Sociality Corollary that one can begin to develop a truly psychological definition of *guilt*. This is not to say that such a definition has to be at odds with ecclesiastical or legal definitions, though it may indeed suggest quite different courses of human action where misdemeanor is involved. We shall be speaking, of course, about the experience of guilt and what it is like, psychologically.

Most psychological theories, both "mechanistic" ones and "dynamic" ones, regard the experience of guilt as a derivative of punishment. One feels guilty because he thinks he has made himself eligible for punishment. But suppose one does not see punishment as the appropriate treatment of wrong-doing, only as revenge by injured persons serving simply to make clear that they have been hurt. Or suppose one does not see wrong-doing as something for which he has been systematically punished. Can he still feel guilty? I think he can. I think Jesus thought so too, though very few ecclesiastics appear to agree with either of us on this point. Even the term "repentance", which I think might better be taken to mean rethinking or reconstruing, as its etymology suggests, has come to stand for undertaking something irrelevantly unpleasant or punitive in compensation for disobedience, rather than doing something which will throw light on past mistakes.

As far as I can see, both from what I have observed and what I have figured out for myself, a person who chronically resorts to this kind of penitence to bring his guilt feelings back into comfortable equilibrium, or to write off his wrong-doing, ends up as a well-balanced sanctimonious psychopath. His only possible virtue is obedience and the society he perpetuates has no purpose except to uphold its own laws. I suspect, furthermore, that this is the net effect of any stimulus-response-reinforcement kind of theory, whether in psychology, religion or politics. And I have been moved to say, on occasion, that a psychopath is a stimulus-response psychologist who takes it seriously— a remark I find does not endear me to all my colleagues.

From the standpoint of personal construct theory, guilt is the sense of having lost one's core role structure. A core structure is any one that is maintained as a basic referent of life itself. Without it a person has no guidelines for staying alive. To the extent that one's core structure embodies his role also, as we have defined role, he is vulnerable to the experience of guilt. He has only to perceive himself dislodged from such a role to suffer the inner torment most of us know so well.

To feel guilty is to sense that one has lost his grasp on the outlook of his fellow man, or has unwittingly played his part in a manner irrelevant to that outlook by following invalid guidelines. If the role is based on one's construction of God's outlook, or The Party's, he has only to fail to play it or to find that in playing it he has grossly misinterpreted its principal dimensions, to experience a religious sense of guilt. With this goes a feeling of alienation from God, or man, or from both. It is not a pleasant experience, and if the perception of excommunication is extensive or the core role deeply disrupted, it may be impossible for life to continue. Indeed, among primitive people, life may be extinguished within a few days, and, among more civilized ones, it may be abandoned by suicide.

A person who has never developed a role, or who has never allowed his life to depend on it, need not experience guilt. Guilt follows only from the loss of such a central part in the affairs of man. Persons who have always lacked a sense of role, such as psychopaths are said to be, may become confused or even anxious, as they contemplate the disconfirming outcomes of their experiences, but what they display is usually clinically distinguishable from guilt. But, then, neither do such persons play any substantial part in the developments by which societies emerge. Guilt is thus a concomitant risk in any creative social process by which man may seek to transcend blind obedience. The author of the Book of Genesis seems to have perceived this a good deal more clearly than his readers have.

Hostility

At this point let us turn back to the Experience Corollary and examine its contribution to our understanding of another puzzling matter—hostility. The experience cycle described in that section included a terminal phase embodying an assessment of the construction in terms of which the initial anticipation had been cast and the behavioural commitment had been made. If outcomes emerging successively from ventures based on the same construction continue to leave a trail of disconfirmations behind, it becomes increasingly clear, even to the most dim-witted adventurer, that something is wrong with his reference axes.

Of course, all he has to do when this happens is to start revising his constructs. But, if he procrastinates too long or if his core constructs are involved, this may prove to be a major undertaking. Constructs which are in the process of revision are likely to be pretty shaky, and if he has a great deal of importance resting on one of them, with no others nearby to take up the load, he may find himself on the verge of confusion, or even guilt.

Ordinarily one can loosen his constructs by falling back on more permeable constructions, as suggested by the Modulation Corollary. But if his superordinate constructs are impermeable he will find himself unable to range any new constructions under them. He will then be confronted with a far more extensive revision of his system than he would if he had more open-ended constructions to fall back upon. The upshot of all this may be that he will find himself precariously poised between the minor chaos that his recent disconfirmations have disclosed, and the major chaos that might engulf him if he attempted to make the needed repairs in his reference axes. In this predicament he may look for some way to avoid both.

One way to avoid the immediate chaos is to tinker with the validational evidence which has recently been giving trouble. There are several ways of doing this. One is to stop short of completing one's experiments. Graduate students are quick to catch on to this one. Another is to loosen up one's construction of outcomes, though this is likely to invite charges of being unrealistic. Still another is to claim rewards as valid substitutes for confirmations, the way doting parents and reinforcement theorists do. One does this by exploiting his dependency on people who are over eager to be helpful.

But there is still another way. That is to force the circumstances to confirm one's prediction of them. A parent who finds that his child does not love him as much as he expected may extort tokens of affection from the helpless youngster. A nation whose political philosophy has broken down in practice may precipitate a war to draft support for its outlook. A meek and trembly spinster, confronted at last by the fact that it is her impregnable posture that renders her unmarriageable, may "prove" the validity of her stand by enticing one of the male brutes to victimize her. A child, unwilling to concede his parents' better judgment because of its far-reaching implications for himself, may seize upon the first opportunity to engage in spiteful obedience by following their advice legalistically in a situation to which it obviously does not apply.

Each of these illustrates an instance of hostility. What personal construct theory has to offer in this matter differs radically from what conventional psychological theory implies. As with other topics with which it deals, personal construct theory attempts to define psychological constructs in terms of the personal experience of the individual to which they are to be applied. Thus, in defining hostility, we do not say that it is essentially an impulse to destroy—even though that may be its consequence—for that sounds more like a complaint of the victim than a prime effort of the hostile person. Instead, hostility is defined as the continued effort to extort validational evidence in favour of a type of social prediction which has already proved itself a failure.

Further Implications of Personal Construct Theory

Since this presentation is intended to be a brief introduction to personal construct theory, rather than a condensation of it, much has had to be omitted. The important decision cycles and creativity cycles which the theory envisions remain unmentioned until this moment, as does a radically different view of dependency. There are strictly psychological definitions of threat, impulsivity, anxiety, transference, preemption, constellatoriness, and propositionality. There is a linguistic system called the language of hypothesis, an ontology exemplified in orchestrated approaches to psychotherapy, and a methodology of psychological research. The notions of motivation, needs, and psychodynamics vanish under the light of the Basic Postulate which accepts man as alive to begin with, and the principle of the elaborative choice which takes care of the directionality of man's moves without invoking special motivational agents to account for each of them.

The concept of learning evaporates. The boundary between cognition and affect is obliterated, rendering both terms meaningless. Fixed role therapy illustrates one of a variety of psychotherapeutic approaches which, at first glance, appear to violate most accepted canons of mental treatment by recognizing man as his own scientist. A new view of schizophrenia emerges, as well as fresh interpretations of "the unconscious", depression, and aggression.

But this is enough to mention now. All it has been possible to accomplish in these pages is to state the basic propositions from which hypotheses may be drawn, to illustrate a few of the lines of inference that may be pursued, and to encourage the more impatient readers to seek out the theory's most exciting implications for themselves.

Actual Structure and Potential Chaos: Relational Aspects of Progressive Variations Within a Personal Construct System

J. R. Adams-Webber

Introduction

George Kelly (1955) derived the formal principles of his system from the fundamental postulate that, "A person's processes are psychologically channelized by the ways in which he anticipates events". His basic unit of analysis, the *personal construct*, is defined as a "templet" or representational schema which a person "creates and then attempts to fit over the realities of which the world is composed". It is assumed that each individual employs his personal constructs both to forecast events and to assess the accuracy of his previous forecasts after the events have occurred, thereby testing his constructs in terms of their predictive efficiency. In short, "A person anticipates events by construing their replications" (*Construction Corollary*). As events subject a person's anticipations to a validational process, confirming some of them and disconfirming others, his constructs undergo progressive changes as a function of the fact that he successively revises them in the light of this "feedback". Thus, "A person's construction system varies as he successively construes the replication of events" (*Experience Corollary*). In general, an individual attempts to elaborate his conceptual framework in such a way that it remains functionally integral with respect to the anticipation of events as he gradually increases its deployability and scope. It is assumed that he always chooses to enhance his anticipations, that is, "the person moves out toward making more and more of the world predictable".

Kelly posited that, "Each construct is convenient for the anticipation of a finite range of events only" (*Range Corollary*). Every construct has a specific "range of convenience" which comprises "all those things to which the user would find its application useful". Moreover, each construct has a particular "focus of convenience" which is defined as that sector of its range of convenience wherein it is maximally useful. Neither a construct's range of

31

convenience nor its focus of convenience is identical to its "context" which is composed of all those elements to which it ordinarily is applied. The latter usually is more constricted than the range of convenience, but more extensive than the focus of convenience. For example, the range of convenience of a person's construct of "masculine-feminine" might encompass French nouns, types of master key, electrical points as well as biological and social sex differences between persons. The usual context of this construct might consist of the speech, manners, dress, activities and appearance of his personal acquaintances, whereas its focus of convenience might be limited to his own unique relationship with his wife. This set of definitional propositions clearly implies the possibility of some degree of specialization of each construct in terms of the domain of elements within which it provides efficient predictive coverage. It is precisely this possibility of functional differentiation among constructs which gives rise to what Kelly termed the "Minimax Problem", which he formulated as follows:

> "One way to be aware of greater variety is to conjure up more constructs. But the number of constructs does not increase in direct ratio to the number of events to be distinguished. So what we have is a minimax problem; how to discriminate meaningfully the greatest variety of events with the least number of constructs. Since constructs are not only hard to come by, but are difficult to keep in mind once you get them, it becomes psychologically strategic to devise a system which will do the most with the least . . . Moreover, the minimax solution must vary within certain human limits from person to person" (Kelly, 1965, p. 5).

This basic issue underlies two seemingly distinct and unrelated lines of investigation within the framework of Kellian theory. The first of these is concerned with the process of functional differentiation among personal constructs as an aspect of individual cognitive development. The second deals with the progressive disintegration of cognitive structures in the genesis of clinical thought disorder. The purpose of the following discussion will be to show how both these strands of inquiry, by logical extension, converge upon the same fundamental principles governing progressive variation within a personal construct system.

The Structural Model

Kelly argued that "Each person characteristically evolves, for his own convenience in anticipating events, a construction system embracing ordinal relationships between constructs" (*Organization Corollary*). He asserts:

> "Construction is systematic in that it falls into a pattern having features of regularity. Since construing is a kind of refinement process involving abstraction and generalization, it is a way of looking at events as having a kind of identity with each other and as not being wholly unique. These features of identity and

regularity are given shape through construction which itself has been shaped up as a system" (Kelly, 1955, p. 72).

RELATIONSHIPS BETWEEN CONSTRUCTS

No construct stands alone within the system because a necessary condition for organized thought and action is some degree of "overlap" between constructs in terms of their respective ranges of convenience. In order for any event to be anticipated or interpreted it must occupy the intersect of the extensions of at least two constructs. Furthermore, the more constructs which can be brought to bear upon a given event, the more clear and distinct its meaning within the context of the system. Kelly pointed out that:

"An event seen only in terms of its placement on one dimension is scarcely more than a mere datum. And about all you can do with a datum is just let it sit on its own continuum. But as the event finds its place in terms of many dimensions of consideration it develops psychological character and uniqueness" (Kelly, 1965, p. 4).

In other words, predictive inference depends on specific relationships between constructs which lend articulate structure to an individual's personal construct system.

We can conceptualize these relationships between constructs in terms of Boolean set theory, upon which the traditional logic of propositions is based. Given that a construct is the kind of thing which defines a set of elements in terms of one of their perceived common aspects, we can determine the relationship between the set defined by a given construct and the set defined by any other construct within a specific domain of elements. In comparing the extensions of any two constructs we can encounter any one of five possible cases:

(1) construct A defines a subset of the set defined by construct B;
(2) construct B defines a subset of the set defined by construct A;
(3) there is a relation of one-to-one correspondence between the two sets;
(4) there is at least one member of the intersect of the two sets, but neither is a subset or equivalent set of the other;
(5) the two sets are mutually exclusive.

Each of these relationships can be plotted on a simple Venn diagram. Recently, Deese (1969) has suggested that the reason why Venn diagrams are so useful to us in the solution of abstract logical problems is because they reveal the "parallel between the more general psychological process and the logical one". He contends that:

". . . relationships in thought are fundamentally perceptual in derivation. Thus, it is possible that the relationship A implies B is not a fundamental operation, though the relationship A is inside of B, or B includes A, is" (Deese, 1969, p. 519).

At the level of operational definition Bannister reasons that:

"If a subject nominates 40 people known personally to him and categorises each in turn as *moral* or *not-moral* and then re-sorts them as *honest* or *not-honest* and if we find that the 20 designated as *moral* are also designated as *honest* and the 20 designated as *not-moral* are designated as *not-honest*, then we can infer a high positive relationship (which can be measured in terms of its binomial probability) between the constructs *moral-not-moral* and *honest-not-honest* for that subject" (Bannister, 1965, p. 977).

Thus, the nature of construct relationships in general can be represented in terms of various degrees of overlap between groupings which themselves reflect underlying judgments of similarity and contrast between elements along the relevant dimensions. However, Kelly warned:

"It is important for us to keep in mind that it is not the accumulation of the elements in the context that constitutes the construct, nor is it the differential grouping of the elements. Rather the construct is the basis on which the elements are understood. It is a matter of how the person construes the elements, in order to deal with them, not where they happen to appear when he decides to set them down" (Kelly, 1955, p. 109).

The advantage of representing construct relationships in terms of set theory is that they can be "translated" into logical propositions of the form "if p, then q" according to the principle that all members of a subset of a given set are also members of that set. This rationale underlies many of the uses of Kelly's "repertory grid technique", summarized by Bannister and Mair (1968).

CONSTRUCTS AS PREDICTIONS

In general, it is assumed that each construct by virtue of its specific relationships with other constructs within the explicit framework of an individual's system "implies" a set of predictions about each of the range of elements to which it is applied. That is to say, whenever a person anticipates a particular event, essentially he construes it in terms of its expected similarities and contrasts with other events within the context of a specific set of interrelated constructs. For example, if a person's constructs *kind, unselfish,* and *considerate* are interrelated, he will tend to anticipate unselfish and considerate behaviour on the part of an individual whom he construes as kind.

SYSTEM AND SUBSYSTEM

It is also necessary to take into consideration the nature of functional relationships between differently organized subsystems of constructs within a construct system as an operational whole. It is the first premise of Kelly's "Constructive Alternativism" that events do not inherently belong to any particular set of constructs, but rather the same events can be viewed in the light of alternative construction systems or subsystems, although not necessarily with the same degree of predictive efficiency. In addition, Kelly's

Fragmentation Corollary asserts that "A person may successively employ a variety of construction subsystems which are inferentially incompatible with each other". It follows that a person's successive constructions of the same set of events are not necessarily derivable from one another. Kelly also assumed that, in general, systematization can be enhanced by restricting the range of convenience of a particular system or subsystem. He reasoned that by limiting the domain of a given set of related constructs they can be developed into a highly integrated structure without undue concern about the inconsistencies which certain "peripheral events" might reveal. It seems to follow that when a person's construct system includes several subsystems of constructs, he may employ some of those subsystems to accommodate events which are outside the ranges of convenience of other subsystems.

Each subsystem can be viewed as providing one of a set of alternative cognitive strategies or lines of inference which an individual may pursue in successively formulating predictions about a sequence of events. Moreover, this functional differentiation among subsystems may increase the efficiency of the overall system. As Ashby (1968) suggests, the division of the operations of a cybernetic problem solving system in terms of a set of subprocesses, "each of which can be carried out without reference to the other subprocesses has the effect, when it can be done, of lowering by great orders of magnitude the demands for information processing". It can be argued that the differentiation of a construct system into relatively independent operational subsystems, by permitting the discriminative allocation of elements among relatively specialized sets of constructs, and thus, parallel processing of information input, increases the deployability of the system as a whole. In short, the more differentiated the structure of an individual's construct system, the greater the variety of events which can be meaningfully discriminated within its framework at any one time.

STRUCTURAL EXTREMES

On the other hand, an individual's system might become so fragmented in structure that, although he would have available a highly complex repertory of constructs, there may be insufficient overlap among the ranges of convenience of his various dimensions to enable him to relate one aspect of a set of events to another. As a result a given construction would have few, if any, predictive implications within the framework of his system. Thus, Kelly's "minimax problem" seems to involve two ideal limiting cases. One extreme would be a system so unidimensional in structure that all a person's constructions of events would converge upon the contrasting poles of a single construct which fixes the realm membership of its elements across all other dimensions in the system. In general, the more unidimensional the structure of an individual's system, the fewer the alternatives which are available to him in interpreting events since, the more closely related all constructs constituting the system, the more his successive constructions will fit the logical constraints of a single set of construct relationships. The other possible extreme would be the total absence of relationship between constructs precluding the possibility of ordered thought. For example, Bannister (1960, 1962, 1963, 1965) proposes the hypothesis that the genesis of clinical thought disorder involves the progressive "serial invalidation" of an individual's predictive inferences in the course of which one group of related constructs after another "loosens" in structure and eventually collapses. Ultimately, the entire construct system—"reduced steeply by the loss of possible combinations"—ceases to function effectively.

A Developmental Perspective

Kelly (1955, p. 79) maintained that, "if we are to see a person's psychological processes operating within a system which he constructs, we need also to account for the evolution of the system itself in a similarly lawful manner". In contrast to the progressive disintegration of cognitive structure in the genesis of thought disorder hypothesized by Bannister, it will be argued here that the normal course of development of a personal construct system involves the progressive differentiation of the system into relatively independent, internally organized, subsystems and increasing functional integration of subsystems within the overall system as an operational whole. This assumption contains explicit parallels with the developmental models of both Piaget (1950) and Werner (1957). Piaget submits that psychological structure evolves through the progressive differentiation and reintegration of operational schemata at increasingly higher levels of logical abstraction. Similarly, Werner's "orthogenetic principle" entails the general hypothesis that cognitive development proceeds from states of relative globality and undifferentiated structure to states of increasing differentiation and hierarchical integration of concepts. The basic problem, as it has been defined by Piaget (1969, p. 164), is "that of development or evolution, in the sense of the gradual production of organized forms with qualitative transformations taking place in the course of the various stages of their development".

COMPLEXITY VERSUS CHAOS

It was Bieri who first introduced into Kellian theory the idea of analysing the developmental level of an individual's construct system in terms of the relative degree of functional differentiation between constructs. Focusing upon the problem of the influence of individual differences in cognitive structure upon social judgment, Bieri proposed that,

> "Cognitive complexity may be defined as the tendency to construe social behaviour in a multidimensional way, such that a more cognitively complex individual has

available a more versatile system for perceiving the behaviour of others than does a less cognitively complex person" (Bieri, 1966, p. 14).

Research based on Bieri's paradigm has revealed that the more uni-dimensional the structure of an individual's "interpersonal construct system", the less he distinguishes between persons in forming impressions in social situations and the more he assumes that others are similar to himself (Bieri, 1955; Leventhal, 1957; Adams-Webber, 1970). Relationships between differentiation of cognitive structure and other facets of social judgment are reviewed by Bieri *et al.* (1966).

Bieri seems to regard the relative number of constructs in a cognitive system alone as an index of its structural complexity. A more elaborate definition of "cognitive complexity" is that put forward by Crockett (1965), which is grounded in the developmental theories of Werner (1957). Crockett argues that the structural complexity of an individual's "cognitive system with respect to other people" can be viewed as a function of both its degree of differentiation, operationally defined in terms of the number of constructs; and its level of hierarchic integration, operationally defined in terms of the pattern of logical relationships between constructs and the extent to which subsystems are interrelated by superordinate constructs. Whereas Bieri has focused exclusively upon the problem of differentiation, Crockett's model deals also with the equally important issues of logical integration and flexibility of organization in the developmental analysis of a construct system.

Bannister's (1960, 1962) investigations have demonstrated clearly that severely thought disordered schizophrenics exhibit a high degree of differentiation between their constructs; however, their social judgments seem more random than "cognitively complex" in organization in that they are highly unstable and inconsistent over time. Kelly stated the problem thus:

> "Schizoid persons have a complex repertory, but their constructs lack sufficient ranges of convenience to enable the person to relate one of them to another. Thus, the system fails to function as a whole" (Kelly, 1961).

Their systems can be viewed as lacking integration as a function of the fact that each construct has such a narrow range of convenience that other constructs cannot be organized under it. As a result, there are few, if any, linkages between constructs, which is a necessary condition of ordered inference. Their constructs tend to relate directly only to concrete objects or persons and not to each other. Thus, the experiences of these persons must be hopelessly kaleidoscopic and discontinuous. It seems to follow that it cannot be differentiation alone which determines the level of functioning of a construct system, but rather the progressive differentiation *and* reintegration of substructures at increasingly higher levels of abstraction.

Schroder and co-workers have given the following exceptionally clear formulation of this point:

"The number of dimensions taken alone, then, has no necessary relationship to the level of information processing; but *given complex combinatory rules*, the potential for generating new attributes of information is higher, and the degree to which one stimulus can be discriminated from another is increased, as the number of perceived dimensions increases" (italics mine) (Schroder *et al.*, 1967, p. 14).

WORKABLE ALTERNATIVES

It was noted above that Kelly's *Fragmentation Corollary* asserts that "a person may successively employ a variety of construction subsystems which are inferentially incompatible with each other", and consequently, not all a person's successive constructions of the same events are necessarily derivable from one another. Let us consider what would follow if this were not the case. The whole of an individual's construct system would have to be integrated in terms of a single set of hierarchical relationships. Such a system would be the ideal prototype of Bieri's notion of cognitive simplicity. All a person's constructs would be concretely pyramided so that at any given level the rules of organization would be absolute. Regardless of the number of dimensions constituting the structure, events would be construed in accordance with one fixed pattern of possibilities. Ultimately, all a person's anticipations would converge through an "if-then-but-not" form of reasoning upon the contrasting poles of the most superordinate dimension in the system. Since the rules of integration would be inflexible, there would be no way to deal with sequences of events which did not fit the current logical constraints of the system. These "ambiguous" occurrences would remain outside the range of convenience of the system as a whole.

If, on the other hand, an individual's construct system were differentiated into several relatively independent subsystems, which the *Fragmentation Corollary* explicitly permits, he will be able to employ the cognitive strategy of using some subsystems of constructs to accommodate events which are outside the ranges of convenience of other subsystems. This implies a fairly high degree of functional specialization of separate subsystems, but it does not necessarily preclude any degree of overlap between them in terms of their respective domains. It might be said that each subsystem has its own focus of convenience, that is, the domain within which it functions with maximum predictive efficiency. Thus, specialization of function among subsystems can be viewed in relative rather than absolute terms. It is assumed that an individual may find some subsystems *more useful* than others in construing a particular range of events.

Thus, Kelly's *Fragmentation Corollary* entails not only the possibility of differentiation of structure, but also flexibility of organization. Combining and successively using two or more alternative subsystems in processing information would increase the capacity of the system to integrate a sequence of events into a variety of patterns or "themes". For example, a person who can employ more than one set of related constructs in interpreting the same social situation is in a better position to see it in terms of two or more different points of view. He could perhaps use one subsystem to organize his own outlook and an alternative one to subsume another's different constructions of the same events.

CONSTRUING THE CONSTRUCTION PROCESSES OF OTHERS

Specifically it has been found that the more unidimensional the structure of an individual's "interpersonal construct system", the less accurate are his attempts to identify the personal constructs of a new acquaintance following a brief social interaction with him (Adams-Webber, 1969). Kelly's (1955) *Sociality Corollary* asserts that "To the extent that one person construes the construction processes of another he may play a role in a social process involving the other". The hypothesis can be inferred that the more uni-dimensional the structure of an individual's construct system, the less success-ful will be his attempts to construe the personal axes of reference of other persons as a basis of effective communication and understanding, that is, "sociality". Cameron (1947, p. 167) submits that the less a person is able to construe the perspectives of others, "the less opportunity he will have of finding out how different from himself other ordinary people can be . . . [and] the more likely is he to extend assimilative projection further than actual conditions warrant". The fact that it has been found that relatively "cogni-tively simple" subjects predict more inaccurate similarities (assimilative projection) between others and themselves than relatively "cognitively complex" subjects (Bieri, 1955) directly supports this argument.

NOVELTY AND AMBIGUITY

It can be hypothesized further that new structure evolves within a personal construct system to accommodate elements which are ambiguous within the context of existing structure. Of particular relevance to this hypothesis is Piaget's (1950) concept of "need-to-function" arising from the temporary instability of schematic organization following an attempt to assimilate a "novel" element into a psychological system prior to a fully adequate accommodation of specific structures to the intrinsic demands of that element. It is the "novelty" or ambiguity of the element in the context of current structure which stimulates a circular reaction of "reciprocal assimilation and accommodation" effecting progressive modifications in the organization of the system until it is reintegrated, and thus, returns to a state of dynamic equilibrium. From Piaget's point of view the ideal focus of this developmental sequence is a hypothetical "stage" of functional differentiation between schemata and their logical integration at sufficiently high levels of abstraction such that the introduction of novelty does not create any disequilibrium or "need-to-function". Consequently, a newly assimilated element will no longer alter mental structures which refer to it, nor the relation of mental structures to each other, because thought is "reversible" and a compensatory thought is available which will restore the equilibrium. Specifically, Piaget (1950) asserts that the principle "implies an equilibrium such that the structure of operational wholes is conserved while they assimilate new elements". It is important to bear in mind that this is an ideal definition of psychological adaptation and not a series of concrete observations. As Schroder *et al.* (1967) suggest, at the most complex levels of organization "abstractness (that is, lack of fixity) becomes a formal rule of the system." Biggs also makes the point that:

> "The emphasis of Piaget (e.g. 1950) upon the growth, with age, of increasingly abstract structures is another way of saying that the growing child becomes adept at handling more and more environmental information with increasing economy of means" (Kelly's "minimax" principle) (Biggs, 1969, p. 289).

The Wider Bounds of Construct Validity

A set of developmental principles which are strikingly parallel to those of Piaget can be derived within the explicit framework of Kelly's theory. It is assumed that changes within a construct system occur only in response to validation or invalidation of a person's predictive inferences. Kelly defined validation as compatibility (subjectively construed) between an individual's expectations and the outcome as he observes it. Invalidation is defined as perceived incompatibility between prediction and outcome. In general, events invite a person to place new constructions on them whenever something unexpected happens, that is, when he encounters a person or object whose behaviour does not "fit" the patterns of construct relationships which define the structure of his system. As Bannister and Mair (1968, p. 212) suggest, "Such an unpredictable figure might be seen as *kind* and *hypocritical* and *stupid* and *successful* by a subject who lived in a world where he expected kind people to be sincere and stupid people to fail". Since the notion of system implies a grouping of elements in which incompatibilities and in-consistencies have been minimized, such a novel figure would become a source of cognitive strain or disequilibrium within the system. A novel element can be said to create a "need-to-function", in Piaget's sense of the term, to the extent that it emerges as the focus of inconsistent constructions in terms of specific relationships between constructs within the system. It was assumed above that when a particular element does not fit the pattern of construct relationships within one subsystem, a person will attempt to assimilate it more consistently to the structure of an alternative subsystem. It should be noted that this hypothesis is consistent with Heider's (1946) "principle of equifinality" which asserts that cognitive organization takes the course of least resistance to a logically balanced situation. It was argued also that the more differentiated the structure of an individual's system into functionally specialized subsystems, the more likely that he will be able to "fit" a given element into one of them. If, on the other hand, a novel element is ambiguous within the context of all existing structure in its present state of development, it will be necessary to evolve new substructure in order to accommodate it adequately. This will involve a further differentiation of the system and a reintegration of both new and existing substructures at higher levels of abstraction. In other words, developmental change involves a progressive evolution of the system as an operational whole rather than grafting onto the system of new structures from the outside.

Kelly emphasized this point when he asserted that,

". . . progressive variation must, itself, take place within a system . . . one's personal constructs can only be changed within subsystems of constructs and subsystems only within more comprehensive systems" (Kelly, 1955, p. 79).

Whatever systematic changes take place, the person must be able to construe them, and thus *anticipate* them, within the context of his current conceptual framework.

PARAMETERS OF CHANGE

Kelly's *Modulation Corollary* stipulates that, "The variation in a person's construction system is limited by the permeability of the constructs within whose range of convenience the variants lie". A construct is permeable if it is so constituted that "new experience and new events can be discriminately added to those which it already embraces", that is, it will admit to its range of convenience new elements which are not yet included within its context. Kelly (1955, p. 81) contended that, "it is under the regency of such constructs that the more subordinate aspects of one's construction system can be systematically varied without making his whole psychological house fall down". Conversely, when superordinate structure reaches the point of relative impermeability it cannot be used to meet new situations or readjust to old ones, because new substructures cannot be organized under it. Thus, the *Modulation Corollary* clearly implies that, the more permeable the superordinate constructs within a system, the greater the amount of systematic change which can occur within the substructures which they subsume. Although Kelly's *Fragmentation Corollary* explicitly permits the differentiation of an individual's construct system into relatively independent subsystems, the extent of this fragmentation is directly limited by the degree of permeability of the superordinate constructs within whose ranges of convenience it occurs. Kelly specifically stipulated that:

> "The *Fragmentation Corollary* follows as an explicit statement of the kind of inconsistency which the *Modulation Corollary* implicitly tolerates. The *Modulation Corollary* tolerates inconsistency between subsystems. More specifically, it tolerates the successive use of subsystems which do not themselves add up" (Kelly, 1955, p. 87).

When an individual's superordinate constructs, that is, the constructs at the highest levels of abstraction within his system, are relatively permeable, they can provide a thread of consistency throughout his system as a whole by virtue of the fact that they permit him to abstract features of similarity and difference across separate substructures. In short, subsystems which are functionally differentiated at lower levels of abstraction can be reintegrated at higher levels when they are scanned for recurring regularities and "abstractly cross-referenced" within the context of superordinate constructs. However, it is only within the context of the most permeable aspects of the superordinate structures that overall consistency can be maintained. Further developmental change is possible only when no damage to the functional integrity of the system as a whole will result from extending its range of convenience to subsume new substructures. In order to systematically incorporate new components of structure it is essential that an individual be able to continually readjust his superordinate constructs so as to minimize incompatibilities and inconsistencies at the highest levels of abstraction.

THOUGHT DISORDER

Clinical thought disorder as defined by Bannister in terms of "loosening" of structure might often result from the failure of superordinate structures to subsume adequately changes in the rest of the system. When superordinate constructs are too impermeable, variations in the system cannot be anticipated and may prove disruptive when they are forced upon one by events. Kelly observed:

> "Frequently on a clinical basis, we can see the so-called 'decompensation' taking place in a client in the space of a few days or weeks. We are able to see how the brittleness and impermeability of his construction system failed to support the alterations which he was finding it necessary to make" (Kelly, 1955, p. 81).

Specifically, many thought disordered persons may be floundering in the wreckage of what was once a highly unidimensional construct system organized under a set of relatively impermeable superordinate constructs. Given highly impermeable superordinate constructs there can take place little in the way of progressive differentiation of substructures and their reintegration at higher levels of abstraction. Therefore, most of the constructs within the system will be directly linked and a person's successive constructions of events will converge upon a single tightly organized pattern of expectancies. The range of convenience of the entire system will be relatively narrow. The person will not be able to resolve inconsistencies in his experience by assimilating elements which emerge as foci of incompatible predictions within the context of one set of related constructs to the range of convenience of an alternative, relatively independent, substructure; or to evolve new substructures within which they could be accommodated more adequately. The impermeability of superordinate structures will preserve the unidimensionality of the entire system and preclude the emergence of new subsystems. Moreover, the more closely related all constructs within the system, the greater will be the impact of any invalidating feedback. Each successive predictive failure, because of the inflexibility of present structure, will present a prospect of impending chaos. Because of his great dependence on a single pattern of construct relationships, he cannot risk adjustments at any level within the substructure in the face of invalidating feedback for fear that this may place him in an even more ambiguous position with respect to the anticipation of events.

The person may then withdraw more and more into a narrow, constricted, but still predictable world. All events outside the impoverished range of convenience of his unidimensional system will be "meaningless" in that palpable features of regularity can not be abstracted from them. Thus, he may lose most of the predictive capacity which he previously acquired. Since constructs are most susceptible to invalidation when they are used to predict immediate happenings, he may largely give up trying to make sense of everyday events.

However, fragmentation when it does occur in the face of increasing ambiguity and predictive failure, may be sudden and lead rapidly to further variation, thereby precipitating a major shake up in the brittle organization of his system. As this rigid structure begins to collapse under the impact of repeated invalidation, his superordinate constructs will begin to lose definition as a function of the fact that their specific relationships with other constructs at various levels will become increasingly vague and unstable. Thus, he may have to abandon them and seek frantically for new ways of making sense out of life. "Eventually he may be thrown back on a more primitive and less effectual system, albeit a more permeable one", that is, a system with relatively few levels of abstraction, and thus, within which most constructs are related not to other constructs but directly to concrete events.

Kelly offers the following brief summary of this decompensation process:

"There is no clearer example of the limitation of one's ability to adjust to the vicissitudes of life, due to the impermeability of his superordinate constructs, than the case of a compulsion-neurosis client who is undergoing a marked de-compensation process. The construct system of such a client is characteristically impermeable; he needs a separate pigeonhole for each new experience and he calculates his anticipations of events with minute pseudomathematical schemes. The variety of construction subsystems which are inferentially incompatible with each other may, in the train of rapidly moving events, become so vast that he is hard put to find ready made superordinate constructs which are sufficiently permeable or open ended to maintain overall consistency. He starts making new ones. While he has very little successful experience with concept formation at the permeable level, these are the kinds of constructs which he tries to develop. They may turn out to be generalized suspicions of the motives of other people. They may have to do with reevaluation of life and death. They may lead him to anticipate reality in bizarre ways" (Kelly, 1955, p. 89).

Kelly assumed that validational "feedback" affects a system at various levels which follow a gradient: constructs which are more closely related to the constructs upon which the original prediction was based will be more affected by predictive failure. Thus, the more closely related all an individual's constructs, the greater will be the impact throughout the system of a single invalidational experience. Bannister (1963, 1965a) reasons that in the face of repeated predictive failure—"serial invalidation"—an individual "loosens" the definition of his constructs in terms of their logical relationships with other constructs in order to minimize the effects of invalidation. Although this loosening is undertaken to conserve the system, progressive loosening of construct relationships, by definition, must lead ultimately to the collapse of all logical structure. However, a question which still requires an answer is why an individual who eventually becomes clinically thought disordered in this manner was so unfortunate in the first place to experience repeated predictive failures in his successive attempts to anticipate events. It is proposed here that it is the impermeability of the superordinate aspects of an individual's system which continually arrest the developmental changes which are a necessary condition for psychological adaptation in the face of environmental variation. The more impermeable one's superordinate structures, the less one's daily commerce with events in terms of anticipation and feedback will result in the progressive evolution of one's construct system which is essential to extending its range of convenience to meet new circumstances, and thereby, maintaining its functional integrity with respect to the anticipation of events in a continually changing environment.

Variable Stability

In summary, it seems clear within the context of the basic assumptions of Kellian theory that psychological development entails the progressive differentiation of the structure of an individual's construct system into subsystems which are relatively specialized with respect to their foci of convenience, under the terms of the *Fragmentation Corollary* and a corresponding reintegration of these operational components at increasingly higher levels of abstraction. Viewed in terms of its own internal organization the information processing activity of a given subsystem is a direct expression of the specific relationships between constructs which define its structure. On the other hand, its *function* within the construct system as an operational whole must be regarded, in Piaget's (1969, p. 165) words, "as the part (i.e. the sector of activity or functioning sector) played by a sub-structure in relation to the functioning of the total structure and, by extension, the action of the total functioning on the functioning of the sub-structures".

Moreover, systematic developmental change can only occur within the range of convenience of permeable superordinate structures, under the terms of the *Modulation Corollary*. Whenever superordinate aspects of the system are not sufficiently well defined or are too impermeable to subsume structural variation and still maintain overall consistency, fragmentation under the pressure of events will be chaotic and may lead to partial or total disintegration of the system. However, to the extent that variations are modulated by permeable superordinate constructs, the progressive differentiation and reintegration of structure will permit the continuous extension of the range of convenience of the total system in terms of the variety of events which can be discriminated meaningfully within its framework. Thus, permeability is a necessary condition of cognitive development because only in the context of relatively permeable superordinate constructs can new experience lead to progressive orderly change in existing structure (which has evolved in the course of earlier experience) so that its range of convenience can be extended to accommodate novel elements without prejudice to overall continuity in the functioning of the system as an operational whole.

References

Adams-Webber, J. R. (1969). Cognitive complexity and sociality. *Brit. J. soc. clin. Psychol.* **8**, 211–216.

Adams-Webber, J. R. (1970). An analysis of the discriminant validity of several repertory grid indices. *Brit. J. Psychol.*, **61**, 83–90.

Ashby, R. W. (1968). The contribution of information theory to pathological mechanisms in psychiatry. *Brit. J. Psychiat.* **114**, 1485–1498.

Bannister, D. (1960). Conceptual structure in thought-disordered schizophrenics. *J. ment. Sci.* **106**, 1230–1249.

Bannister, D. (1962). The nature and measurement of schizophrenic thought disorder. *J. ment. Sci.* **108**, 825–842.

Bannister, D. (1963). The genesis of schizophrenic thought disorder: a serial invalidation hypothesis. *Brit. J. Psychiat.* **109**, 680–686.

Bannister, D. (1965a). The genesis of schizophrenic thought disorder: re-test of the serial invalidation hypothesis. *Brit. J. Psychiat.* **111**, 377–382.

Bannister, D. (1965b). The rationale and clinical relevance of repertory grid technique. *Brit. J. Psychiat.* **111**, 977–982.

Bannister, D. and Mair, J. M. M. (1968). "The Evaluation of Personal Constructs", Academic Press, London and New York.

Bieri, J. (1955). Cognitive complexity-simplicity and predictive behavior. *J. abnorm. soc. Psychol.* **51,** 263–268.

Bieri, J. (1966). Cognitive complexity and personality development. *In* "Experience Structure and Adaptability", (Harvey, O. J. ed.), Springer, New York.

Bieri, J., Atkins, A. L., Briar, S., Leaman, R. L., Miller, H. and Tripodi, T. (1966). "Clinical and Social Judgement", John Wiley & Sons, New York and Chichester.

Biggs, J. B. (1969). Coding and cognitive behavior. *Brit. J. Psychol.* **60,** 287–305.

Cameron, N. (1947). "The Psychology of the Behavior Disorders", Houghton Mifflin, Boston.

Crockett, W. H. (1965). Cognitive complexity and impression formation. *In* "Progress in Experimental Personality Research", (Maher, B. A. ed.), Vol. 2., Academic Press, New York and London.

Deese, J. (1969). Behavior and fact. *Am. Psychol.* **24,** 515–522.

Heider, F. (1946). Attitudes and cognitive organization. *J. Psychol.* **21,** 107–112.

Kelly, G. A. (1955). "The Psychology of Personal Constructs", Vols. 1–2, Norton, New York.

Kelly, G. A. (1961). The abstraction of human processes, *Proc. 14th Congr. appl. Psychol.* (Copenhagen).

Kelly, G. A. (1965). The strategy of psychological research. *Bull. Brit. psychol. Soc.* **18,** 1–15.

Leventhal, H. (1957). Cognitive processes and interpersonal predictions. *J. abnorm. soc. Psychol.* **55,** 176–180.

Piaget, J. (1950). "The Psychology of Intelligence", Routledge and Kegan Paul, London.

Piaget, J. (1969). The problem of common mechanisms in the human sciences. *The Human Context* **1,** 163–185.

Schroder, H. M., Driver, M. J. and Streufert, S. (1967). "Human Information Processing", Holt, Rinehart and Winston, New York.

Werner, H. (1957). "Comparative Psychology of Mental Development", International Universities Press, New York.

Science Through the Looking Glass

D. Bannister

"If we view the scientist as a man we must regard his science with the same incredulity we apply to human behaviour in general. This is to say that most of us would then have to claim that one's science is a symptom of his psychodynamics, or perhaps a product of his operant conditioning, though modulated, to be sure, by the psychodynamics—or the conditioning of—those with whom he is dynamically identified, or to whom he is conditioned. Thus, if we were to persist in accounting for scientists in terms of current psychological theories about men, I think we would soon be led to the conclusion that science is more a human predicament than a vital undertaking. On the other hand, if we apply the science paradigm to man, we someday are going to catch ourselves saying, in the midst of a heated family discussion, that our child's temper tantrum is best understood as a form of scientific inquiry."

G. A. Kelly

A pervasive assumption of psychologists seems to be that, since we have arrived on the scene to find a number of highly developed sciences in existence, we must needs adopt a scientific approach as it is currently defined and create thereby an acceptable science of psychology. The science club exists, it is argued, therefore we must set about qualifying ourselves for membership. Or, conversely, it is assumed that we cannot meet the club requirements and should therefore resign ourselves to being non-scientists engaged in the non-science of psychology. Both these postures imply that the nature of "science" is largely ordained and that it is within or without this settled framework, that psychology must develop.

Thus, most basic textbooks in psychology begin with some sort of *me and Copernicus* passage in which the canons of science are set out as demanding careful observation, controlled experimentation, falsifiability of hypotheses and so forth; science is congratulated and psychologists are congratulated on their readiness to live up to it's known and traditional standards. Wundt's laboratory is cited as our birthplace because is was *a laboratory.*

What does not seem to be commonly envisaged is that rather than traditional science moulding psychology: psychology might be the new venture which will remould science. When Gods have been thought to frown upon new undertakings, men have been known to alter their theology rather than abandon their undertakings.

Three linked arguments concerning the peculiar and particular nature of psychology as an endeavour, imply that "science" must be enlarged if it is to encompass the study of the person.

Firstly, psychologists, as part of what they have to say in their role as psychologists, must subsume science, so that psychology is to be looked upon as simultaneously a science and also a meta-discipline which overviews science. This, because science is a human undertaking, a category of human behaviour and thereby a legitimate topic for psychology. This statement is meant to imply a good deal more than an occasional sociopsychological article on the lives of great scientists: it implies that all aspects of science, including the meaningfulness of traditional scientific models and approaches in psychology, must inevitably come up for review and analysis.

Secondly, we must recognize the problems attendant upon having the subject matter of a science propounding scientifically upon itself. Psychologists generally seem to recognize their reflexive predicament only insofar as they struggle to mitigate what they imagine might be its disastrous consequences. Thus, in order to lock the persons they are studying into the paradigm of "an object of study" they frequently deceive their subjects as to the nature of the experimental situation and their experimental purpose—this in order to claim kinship with the chemist who has never had to deceive an acid in his life. Aware that the subject might assert similar rights, the psychologist rushes to embed a lie scale in his questionnaire to reduce this knowing counter to a measurable "response". Rosenthal investigating experimenter bias effect or Orne assessing the social characteristics of the experimental situation, have moved from a purely defensive stance to an attempt to look on reflexivity as a topic for investigation. Yet it can be argued that the common human experience of "psychologists" and "subjects" is not a hindrance to the advance of psychology, nor one more "topic" for it, it is the very basis on which psychology can elaborate. For sure, we will not find the problem catered for in the traditional rules of the science club: the rules will have to be rewritten.

Thirdly, moral issues are raised by the very process of developing a science of psychology and not, as seems the case with the natural sciences, only in relation to the consequences of application. If you say, as a physicist, that your purpose as a scientist is the prediction and control of physical phenomena, you have not thereby posed—in most people's view—a moral issue. If you say, as a psychologist, that your purpose as a scientist is the prediction and control of human behaviour, then you have thereby posed a moral issue. Psychology, practised as a public endeavour, is a politically significant act. Since men can influence men (the basic assumption of experimental psychology) then psychologists may—by virtue of the self fulfilling prophecy—make rather than discover their laws. Thus, for psychologists, the question of values must be a daily concern and not only in relation to simple issues of cruelty in experimentation. Such a perpetual concern, woven into the fabric of the science, might yield us a significant outcome—a race of moral scientists: scientists who are by training and inclination unwilling to sell themselves to merchants who want to market trash more quickly or to tyrants who yearn for more detailed methods of control. Thus, the moral forebodings of psychologists might signify before they construct a psychological "nuclear weapon" rather than manifest themselves, in fear, after the event.

A Duelling Ground for Psychologies

If we accept as legitimate the idea that psychological theories should number among their tasks an explanation of the nature of science as a human undertaking, then we can set up a common ground of tourney between differing psychological approaches.

As between the various psychological theories, notions overblown and presented as theories and assorted eclectic stances in psychology, the so called crucial experiment is more than something of a myth. Each theoretical framework in psychology tends uniquely to define its purpose and to categorize and phrase human behaviour completely in its own terms, so that a common area in which theories may compete is well nigh impossible to find. Thus, psychoanalytic theory and learning theory may duel sporadically with each other at some quasi-boundary such as therapy (entrammelled in non-relatable notions of "cure") or some Gestalt and retinal idea of perception, may be forced into an uneasy juxtaposition for comparison purposes, but a clearcut issue on which varying psychological faiths can flex their muscles, is hard to come by.

But such a one may be this very issue of the psychological nature of a science. We may reasonably give forth a kind of general challenge to psychologists to speak up and explain the nature of sciences in terms of their favoured psychological language and principles.

Clearly, in such a contest, personal construct theorists have loaded the dice in their favour by taking "man the scientist" as the model man of their psychological theory. However, of itself, such a notion cannot explain science. It can only assure us that construct theory will see science as no Godlike, unique or freakish undertaking, but will depict it as an extension of ordinary human questing, as a formalization of sloppy human curiosity, as a Sunday best version of man in an everyday mood.

So that, if sense should fail us, we shall at least be left with formal structure, each section of this essay will propose a defining requirement of a science in terms of construct theory; comment on the degree to which modal modern psychology meets such a requirement, and evaluate the degree to which personal construct theory (looked on then as *a science* rather than as a definer of science) meets such a requirement.

A Science is a Subsystem

In construct theory terms a subsystem is a group of constructs which have a great many defined internal lines of implication and relatively few and less defined relationships with constructs outside the subsystem—it is a large and elaborate *cluster* of constructs. In terms in more general use then, it is a conceptual framework, a language system, a discipline, a universe of discourse, a defined field of study.

Obviously, this characteristic alone cannot define a science since music, theology, chess, banking, grammar, flower arrangement, politics, and billiards can equally be seen as subsystems with separate codes, distinct languages, usages and terms which work well within each encapsulating system but which only a poet or a man in search of a new idea, would try to cross-refer. Be it noted then, that combining, cross-referring, punning and analogical reasoning are useful in the early circumspective and creative phases of thinking about problems, but for a scientist, such thinking has to be tightened and brought back into the pure language of the subsystem if it is to extend theory and inspire significant experimentation.

However, although it is not a sole defining criterion, the subsystem quality of sciences seems manifest and the impressive degree of definition which sciences such as chemistry, astronomy and physics attain, seems to reflect their status as subsystems.

It would seem that what sciences or other subsystem modes gain by their separate nature, is freedom of action. A person using an integrated and separate construct cluster can elaborate it aggressively without the constraint of having to account to other subsystems for the intellectual ventures which he undertakes. The astronomer havering between steady state and big bang theories does not have to feel responsible for the biologist who is polishing up evolutionary theory, any more than the composer dabbling in diatonic scales has to footnote implications for strong centre theory in chess. Thus, individual sciences and scientists have the kind of freedom which we grant ourselves in our personal life when we keep a degree of separation in our construing of our working life, our loving life, our political life. Granted, if the individual makes the separation ultimate and invariable, he will have to face the perhaps lethal problem of where has gone the "I" who is living these various lives, and similarly scientific subsystems seem to retain lines of implication into common meta-systems such as logic, mathematics and philosophy in order to retain a consensus about intellectual sanity.

Psychology fares badly if we regard being an integrated subsystem as the hallmark of a science. On the one hand it is fragmented into unrelatable subsystems in pursuit of the mini-psychologies of memory, emotion, cognition, perception and so forth and on the other hand it has cluttered its boundaries by desperate attempts to cross-refer to inappropriate language systems such as physiology and biology.

Apart from reductionism—the strange urge to establish an authoritarian hierarchy among subsystems—which has been used as intellectual justification for this confusion, there would seem to be two tendencies which have inspired psychologists to their particular version of the Tower of Babel.

Firstly, psychologists seem unwilling to specify the subject matter of their discipline beyond the vague notion that it is "man". But a concept as generalized as "man" has too many "properties" to provide a usable model. We must determine for ourselves what we wish to see man as, we must look upon man *as if* he were something or other. Thus, biology is a systematic and successful attempt to construe man *as an animal* and physiology is equally successful in construing man *as an organic system*. Because psychologists are unwilling to commit themselves to a clear model, they have constructed a crazy patchwork consisting partly of these two models which are already adequately dealt with and which have been elaborated in ways that are not particularly useful to psychologists, while lunging sporadically towards other temporary visions of what man might be thought to be—a "social unit", "a digital computer", "a hydraulic drive system" and so forth.

Secondly, many psychologists seem to harbour an atavistic fear of the bleakness of a unitary language. True, psychology as a science should not gainsay human experience, but it should not attempt to reflect the variety of terms in which we customarily express our experience. It is as if a physicist had suddenly panicked at losing everyday terms like cumbersome, fluffy, painted, steep, grubby, and so forth from the converse of theoretical physics, and sought to reintroduce them into his universe of discourse. Thus on the one hand psychology suffers from the micro-theorists who erect pure but tiny language systems with ranges of convenience so minute that they do not merit the name of subsystems. On the other hand, we have psychologists busily jargonizing an endless array of lay concepts and stuffing them into the semantic ragbag which is modern psychology. Be it clear that the prime complaint being made is not that this or that language system has not been accepted as mandatory for psychology, but that psychologists do not appear to be very much aware of the need to strive towards a unified language system—in construct theory terms a construct subsystem.

There are three main aspects to the solution which construct theory offers to the subsystem requirement for a science of psychology. Firstly, it proposes a specific subject matter for psychology, a particular model around which to integrate the discipline. It proposes that psychology be the study of man *as a person.*

Obviously the defining of a "person" (as distinct from "an organism") is part of the ongoing task of any construct theory oriented psychology, but a provisional definition would (*by* definition) have to locate the source of the defining characteristics in the person's concept of himself. It might thereby include specifications such as that a person entertains notions (1) of his own uniqueness; (2) of the integrity of his experience; (3) of his continuity over time; (4) of other persons by analogy with himself; (5) of the causal nature of his acts; (6) of himself as self-inventing. The adoption of such a central model (or of any central model) for the subject matter of psychology, slices out great sections of the ramifications which we now enjoy and with which we are encumbered. Thus, comparative psychology could be bequeathed to the zoologists because, while it might carry implications for the study of man *as an animal*, it blatantly carries no implications for the study of man *as a person*.

Secondly, construct theory would seek to solve the subsystem problem by proposing itself to *be* psychology rather than a theory or topic *within* psychology. Note that this is not a political proposal for what students should be taught, but is a directional requirement for all serious theories in psychology. If Freudian theorists or learning theorists are content to regard their theory as *ultimately* a topic *within* psychology, then clearly they are intending no solution to the subsystem problem, but are accepting the idea that there can be no science of psychology, only assorted psychologies. This view does not dispute that theories ought to be progressively replaced as they are found wanting (and the ultimate discarding of personal construct theory is specifically contracted for in the idea of constructive alternativism), rather it asserts that the standard continually referred to in the building of any particular theory is that it be elaboratable into the science of psychology as such.

A final problem in connection with the subsystem requirements of psychology as a science—to which construct theory proffers a solution—is the problem of reflexivity. Being a psychologist, conducting experiments, formulating theories and so forth, is a human activity, it is "behaviour" and it therefore follows that in trying to account for human behaviour, any psychological theory should account for psychologizing, it should account for the processes which led to its own construction. This is an exceptional demand in that it seems to apply only in psychology. While a physiologist's account, say of the functions of the liver, must potentially explain the functioning of his own liver, he is not involved in the trickier problem of explaining the processes whereby he comes to be explaining processes. It seems that, with the exception of construct theory, all theories in psychology are non-reflexive. Skinner does not (actually or potentially) analyse the schedule of reinforcements which shapes men into advocates of Skinnerian psychology; Freudians do not itemize what fixation in what developmental stage results in man the psychoanalytic theorist and gives psychoanalytic theories their particular flavour. Thus it follows that, when psychologists are theorizing, hypothesizing, experimenting (and writing in the journals), they are using a second language system quite distinct from the one which they are using to describe the processes of their subjects. The subsystem rule is breached right from the beginning of the psychological discussion. Construct theory in viewing a person as a scientist and accepting that he has hypotheses (anticipations), theories (construct systems) and experiments (behaviours), integrally accounts for its own construction. It enables the personal construct psychologist to use the same constructs about say tight and loose construing, permeability, construct validation and invalidation and so forth about himself and his colleagues and the very process of carrying out research, that he uses about his "subjects".

Reverting to the status of modern psychology with regard to the subsystem requirement, the unsatisfactory current position is perhaps most vividly experienced by laying side by side a standard scientific text book of any discipline and a psychological textbook. If we glance casually from one to the other, the most striking difference is the unity of language in any standard scientific textbook—different topics and areas and problems may be discussed but the same units of interpretation recur time and time again, carrying common and standard implications into various "parts" of the science. In the psychological textbook we see at least as many languages as there are chapter headings, and within each chapter we see mini-languages conjured into being and abandoned again whenever the immediate explanatory occasion demands.

A Science as an Issue Choosing Venture

As predicated by personal construct theory, a science is a deliberate articulation of the choice corollary of that theory. The choice corollary states that "a person chooses for himself that alternative in a dichotomised construct through which he anticipates the greater possibility for the elaboration of his system". There are a number of ways of rephrasing this, but one is to take it as meaning that a person *predicts that which makes most sense*. Or going back a little further into the process we can say that a person chooses to ask those questions which, if an answer of some kind is forthcoming, will open up the greatest reaches to his understanding; he tries to understand that which, if he succeeds in understanding it, will contribute most, either to the clarity of, or to the extension of, his system for understanding.

Taken into the context of science, this suggests that scientists, even when they are focusing on details, try to focus on the details of those *issues* which are central and which have the most far reaching implications for their discipline.

This requirement is obviously intimately connected with the previously discussed idea that a science is a subsystem. Given an integrated conceptual framework, it is possible to decide what issue would most effectively lead to the extension of that framework if tackled: given a multiplicity of disintegrated frameworks, it becomes impossible to *locate* a crucial issue.

Our varying psychologies (it is reasserted that there is no such thing as modern psychology, only modern psychologies) have sought to locate crucial issues, each within their own conceptual framework. To this extent, they have met this primary requirement of a science (though inevitably the many central issues have not proved cross-referrable). But many visions in modern psychology can be judged myopic, in that a blurring of issues has been accepted in the name of simple empirical prediction. Psychologists often seem to behave as if prediction, at any price, were the essence of a science. It seems to be believed that since a scientist is a person who makes testable predictions, then a scientist is a person who does *nothing but* make testable predictions, regardless of whether the fulfillment or negation of these predictions will contribute, in any crucial way, to the conceptual framework of psychology.

This has led to numberless experimental studies which are devoted to one or another type of short term payoff and which are asking questions of such a nature that it does not matter one iota what the experimental answer turns out to be. Competence, plus a deep lack of interest in psychology can (and does) produce endless studies variance analysing the effects of number relationships and electrically induced stress on rote memory for digits; factor analysing the pattern of responses to standard American questionnaires completed by middle class Sudanese or testing differences between firstborn and lastborn in musical pitch discrimination. The justification for the asking of such experimental questions seems to be that they can be answered—not that the answer will generate more significant questions.

When it is claimed that it does not matter what the experimental answer turns out to be, so far as many psychological experiments are concerned, it is not thereby claimed that the experimental answer will be without practical value for manipulative purposes. However, such an applied criterion of the purpose of prediction and question asking, is essentially what discriminates a technology from a science. A technology does not need to concern itself with the question of the *elaboration* of its own conceptual framework, it can substitute for this requirement of a science any immediate socioeconomic return.

A reflection of this attitude appears in the emphasis placed in teaching research on techniques and methods rather than on issues. Thus, students are taught every detail of experimental method, the fine points of statistical analysis and the most exquisite convolutions of research design but not, necessarily, to chose a problem that matters in that its solution will ultimately contribute to the elaboration of a science of psychology. The question of choice of issue, choice of problem, is little discussed in teaching discourses on research.

Just as the philosophy of reductionism has often been used as justification for garbling the language of psychology, so the principle of parsimony is given as grounds for asking questions of little point. Preferring the simpler of two hypotheses is a sensible practice if you intend the then hypothesis to be the last you will ever make. If you are trying to build links to some larger issue, then the hypothesis with more links back into its parent theory, and forward into a potential extension of that theory, may well be a better bet.

As a comment on the way in which experimental procedures can be designed to avoid rather than pose issues, consider the work of Spence as analysed by Kessel (*American Psychologist*, 1969). He first quotes Spence and goes on to comment.

"Consider Spence's acknowledgment that recent research . . . has revealed that higher mental processes (inhibitory and facilitory sets, etc.) play a much more prominent role in human conditioning than has sometimes been realized.

However, having further noted 'our lack of knowledge concerning these factors', Spence states:

Obviously the additional uncontrolled variables minimize the role of these *basic theoretical factors* ($_sH_R$, D, etc.), tending to hide their effects. Under such circumstances it is necessary to have reasonably large samples so that the effects of these *confounding variables* (higher processes) are more likely to be equalized in the comparison groups" italics added).

After later experiments "designed to control this cognitive factor", Spence was able to conclude that:

"extinction of conditioned eyelid responses in humans proceeds at a relatively slow rate, as in animals. The basic behaviourist tenet that humans and animals 'learn' in essentially the same manner is thus experimentally supported, potentially refuting facts having been eliminated by appropriate 'control of confounding variables'."

Construct theory's candidate for a central issue in psychology can be argued to be *change*. Kelly's definition of man as *a form of motion* makes it central and the fundamental postulate and virtually all of the eleven elaborative corollaries of the theory, specifically refer to *process*.

A Science as a Hierarchical System

A science, in construct theory terms, is a systematic articulation of the organization corollary. This corollary states that "each person characteristically evolves for his convenience and anticipating events, a construction system embracing ordinal relationships between constructs".

Consider the following hierarchy of constructs as derived from an individual by the Hinkellian procedure of laddering.

happier	*vs*	Unhappier
closer personal relationships	*vs*	poorer personal relationships
more accepted by people	*vs*	not so well accepted by people
makes a good first impression on people	*vs*	makes a poor first impression
well dressed	*vs*	badly dressed

The person was asked whether he would prefer to see himself as *well dressed* or *badly dressed* and replied that he would like to see himself as *well dressed*. He was asked "why" and he replied that it was in order to make a *good first impression on people* (presumably the contrast pole here is making a *poor first impression on people*). When asked "why" he said that once you have made a good first impression on people then you are *more accepted by them* and in response to "why" he said that in that way you could go on to form *better personal relationships with them*. When asked "why" he wanted to form better personal relationships he said that in that way he would be *happier*. When asked why he wanted to be *happier* he gave no direct answer but argued that it wasn't in aid of anything—it was what life was about. Thus he appeared to have reached his personal ceiling for this particular hierarchy—the over-arching principle which, for the time being, was at the top of this particular ladder and which had no verbally accessible "why" to it.

Each of the constructs as we go up the list can be viewed as superordinate to the constructs below it and conversely the one's below are termed subordinate in relation to the constructs above. Perhaps if we had started with *well dressed-badly dressed* and asked questions like "*what constitutes* a well dressed person" or something of the sort, we might have got further subordinates down the ladder (e.g. *wears well cut clothes*). In formal terms the subordinate-superordinate relationship is defined by reference to the fact that the superordinate construct includes its subordinate constructs as elements within its context. In formal logic a similar issue is dealt with by the idea of class inclusion and the idea of "level of abstraction" is similarly used inside and outside construct theory. References to the "importance" of certain ideas or distinctions between "detail" and "generality" or the idea of something being "an operational definition" of a more "general hypothesis" all seem to be terms concerned with the same issue.

This pyramidal structure of construct systems seems to serve a variety of purposes in science and in living. For example, if we accept that the more superordinate constructs will have more implications and a wider range of convenience than their subordinate constructs, then "climbing up our system" may be a way of finding strategies for cross-referring more subordinate constructions which cannot be directly related to each other "across" the system. Thus the old adage that you can't add *horses* and *cows* is nonsense as soon as you climb up the subsystem and subsume them both as *farm animals* and you can blithely add in *hermit crabs* if you are prepared to climb up as far as *forms of organic life*.

Equally you may use the hierarchy as a conflict resolving process by taking decisions in terms of the most superordinate, relevant construct. For example, for some of us *courteous-discourteous* may be a subordinate construct to *kind-unkind* and if this is so, we may in exceptional circumstances decide to be *discourteous* if we feel that in the long run this is the *kindest* way to be (say in curtailing a mutually disastrous relationship). However, if that is the way we organize our constructs, then it would not make sense for us to be *cruel* in order to be *courteous*. Going down the pyramid if we assume that for us *spitting in the spitoon-spitting on the carpet* is a subordinate construction (one possible operational definition if you like) of the construct *courteous-discourteous* then again, in exceptional circumstances, (say in a culture which has reversed our particular rituals) we may find it makes sense to *spit on the carpet* in order to be *courteous*.

(As a pure digression we may note that one equivalent of "the Unconscious" in construct theory may be these higher order, superordinate implications which are not readily verbalized, yet may be points of reference for whole areas of construing.)

One of the hallmarks of science seems to be the care with which the superordinate-subordinate status of constructs is defined and the attention paid to this problem. Thus, in biology, notions of family, genus and species or in physics the notions of nucleus, atom, molecule, substance and so forth are carefully elaborated in superordinate-subordinate terms.

In current psychology, on the contrary, there is a tendency to produce one abstraction at almost any level, supply it with one or two operational definitions, with no explication of the lines of subordinate-superordinate relationship, and start it up in business. Thus, for example, the very chapter headings in psychological textbooks such as "Affect", "Cognition", "Personality", and so forth, represent sliding levels of abstraction; sliding because they were never positioned into any hierarchical network. Lines of research, theories and general textbook expositions are arbitrarily centred on concepts such as "arousal", "attention", "anxiety", "meaning", "motivation", "social groups", "response styles", "field dependence", and so forth, entirely without regard to the hierarchical relationship between such constructs and others extant in the field. Equally, in test construction or more general research, psychologists of factor analytic bent, are fond of labelling newly discovered factors "succorance", "neuroticism", "hostility", "authoritarianism" and so forth, again without reference to the level of abstraction at which such terms are to be read or the implicatory steps that are supposed to intervene between them and the most concretistic constructs at subordinate levels.

Construct theory clearly represents an attempt to position its own constructs within a hierarchy and because, reflexively, the construct theorist applies the theory to his own processes, he is continually reminded of the need to elaborate constructs in hierarchical terms. Granted, obscurities as to relative "heights" within the system exist in the theory. For example, the apparent parity in level of abstraction between constructs such as constriction-dilation, tightness-loosening and other constructs of transition such as anxiety, hostility, guilt and so forth, presents a problem for users of the theory.

However, in relation to current psychology we may note that a partial failure of attempt is being compared with an often bland indiscipline, in that psychologists seem to be unconcerned with the issue of hierarchy as part of their general lack of concern with the coherence of subsystem language.

A Science as a Creativity Cycle

In personal construct theory terms, a science is a systematic articulation of the circumspection-preemption-control cycle.

Kelly argued that construct systems are elaborated and new interpretations of a person's world are developed by first circumspecting, i.e., construing loosely and imaginatively, feeling and dreaming, so that at this stage the nature of the problem is not defined but all kinds of possibilities are explored. Eventually, the person is enabled to move into the preemption phase in which he chooses the terms in which he will try and solve "the problem", i.e., he will decide what kind of problem he is faced with, what are the issues, what are the alternative choices. Finally, he can move into the control phase in which he selects the actual path he will go down, selects the pole of the construct in terms of which he will operate, specifies the alternative he will select. As the experiment (behaviour) which the control phase of the cycle generates, brings in its mixture of affirming, negating and downright irrelevant data, the person will eventually be forced back into new circumspection and the cycle begins again.

Such a cycle can be viewed as characterized initially by loose and ultimately by tight construing. Kelly defines a tight construct (or more accurately a construct used "tightly") as a construct which leads to unvarying predictions whereas a loose construct is one which can lead to varying predictions, but which, nevertheless, can be identified as a continuing interpretation. Another way of describing the difference, would be to consider the relationships between constructs as being inferences with varying degrees of probability. Thus, when we are construing tightly, we are essentially arguing to ourselves that A inevitably implies B which inevitably implies C which totally implies D. When we are construing loosely we are saying to ourselves that A might imply B (or a variant of B) but just possibly X or Y. Interestingly enough, our conversation seems to be studded with marginal notes which indicate to the listener whether he is to read us in a loose or a tight mode. Thus phrases like "sort of", "more or less" and "at a guess" seem to indicate loose construing, while "the fact that" and "bloody" seem to indicate tight construing. Neither tightness nor looseness are "healthy" or "correct", since they are phases in a continuous movement whereby we can invent and move forward. They help us to vary our stance in the light of changing validational fortunes. By risking a little chaos we can avoid obsessionality, by reaching for our brass tacks we can avoid schizophrenia.

This kind of process, within which new ideas, new experimental ventures are generated, is essential in the life movement of an individual person and equally essential in a science, if it is to continually evolve and elaborate. Over a long time line, it seems to relate to what Kuhn was describing as paradigm change and revolution in his "The Structure of Scientific Revolutions".

It is one of the most marked and disastrous characteristics of current psychology that there has been a cleavage into loose and tight *types of psychology*. This is to say that many psychologists seem to fail to move repeatedly through the cycle but rather take up a permanent intellectual residence at one or other end of the cycle.

Thus, we have almost totally loose circumspective psychologies such as Freudian or Existential psychology. This is the kind of speculative, vague psychologizing which leads to papers of the *Unconscious aggression and overt sexual fantasies as quasi-religious substrata for international conflicts* type. At the other end of the spectrum we have the tight world of the pure learning theorist dealing in the highly defined and fragmentary and providing us with the *Short term memory for T mazes under electrically induced stress conditions in the decorticate wood louse* type of paper. Thus, psychologists tend to take up residence and spend their lives with either the vaguely significant or the specifically irrelevant rather than accept that it is a continuous movement between loose and tight construing that enables the arguments which constitute a science to elaborate. This kind of frozen positioning seems to underlie much of the tough minded *versus* tender minded argument in science and is obviously referred to by phrases concerning the problem of vitality of material *versus* precision of method.

In equating science with operational precision and failing to involve their personal imaginations, psychologists have meekly accepted the widespread popular distinction between Arts and Science. The extent and nature of the distinction is indicated in the following experiment. Subjects were given twenty pairs of opposites and asked to underline the adjective in each pair they thought related to Science as contrasted with Art. Almost unanimously they chose for Science the pole italicized in the following list.

emotion—*thought*
new—old
day—night
soft—*hard*
passion—*reason*
plain—coloured
religious—*atheist*
male—female
duty—pleasure
curved—*straight*
actuality—dream
Cavalier—*Roundhead*
sane—mad
public—personal
chaos—*order*
excited—*calm*
plain—beautiful
free—*disciplined*
realist—idealist
lax—*careful*

This pervasive dichotomy seems frustrating in that it does not necessarily deny Art tools, techniques and concrete realizations, while it seems to deny Science personal involvement and adventure. Certainly it implies much more than the contrasting emphasis on commonality and individuality of construing which construct theory suggests as the basis for the Science-Arts polarity.

Personal construct theory includes an attempt to write a tight-loose clause into the theoretical contract. The philosophy of constructive alternativism, Kelly's idea of the invitational mood and propositional (*as if*) construing, all stress the idea of imagination as a primary basis for science, while the formal propositions of the theory and the elaboration of grid method and fixed role therapy, offer the continuous possibility of tightening. Already difficulties seem to be arising because personal construct theorists—perhaps as a function of their scientific birthplaces—tend to opt permanently for tight or loose stances within the theory and thus become either grid methodologists or speculative theorists, rather than accept that it is the distance the person can move between tight and loose that is the measure of his personal and scientific potential.

Therefore

To view Science through the goggles of personal construct theory, is to see it as kin to many human activities which do not have a capital letter to distinguish them, to date it long before the beginning of the Renaissance, to note that being invented by men it has its own repetitive and uninspiring rituals. Thus, while acknowledging the imagination which it represents, we can find it less awesome. Of course, finding things less awesome has its advantages—the young male who ceases to be awed by the young female, finds thereby that he can do something with her.

What might psychologists do with, to, for, by or from "science"? They might, perhaps, raise their eyes from the rules written down by scientist-psychologists who are always congratulating themselves on being scientist-psychologists and note the vision of an arch non-scientist sketched thus.

> "Only let me say that to my mind that there is a great field of science which is, as yet, quite closed to us. I refer to the science which proceeds in terms of life and is established on data of living experience and of sure intuition. Call it subjective science if you like. Our objective science of modern knowledge concerns itself only with phenomena, and with phenomena as regarded only in their cause and effect relationship. I have nothing to say against our science. It is perfect as far as it goes. But to regard it as exhausting the whole scope of human possibility in knowledge seems to me just puerile. Our science is a science of the dead world. Even biology never considers life, but only mechanistic functioning and apparatus of life" (D. H. Lawrence "Fantasia of the Unconscious", 1963).

And thus we might set about enlarging science. Perhaps from the starting point that when the natural scientist says of a changing object "what does this change signify", he is not asking the same question as when we ask of a changing person "what does this change signify *for him*"—for this latter is truly a psychological question.

References

Lawrence, D. H. (1963). "Fantasia of the Unconscious, W. H. Heinemann, London.

... And Then There Was One

Fay Fransella

It has always seemed to me that one of the sad things about a scientific approach to the study and understanding of human behaviour is the way in which it curtails the richness of speculation. With the advent of the hypothesis and methods of measurement, magnificently creative ideas are denuded down to their bare bones. It is only these that lend themselves to quantification. Hard data are most assuredly dull data in the vast majority of cases.

One of the most fertile fields for imaginative thinking is that of psychotherapy. Whatever opinion one may hold of Freudian theory, few would deny the originality of his ideas. Perhaps one of the reasons why these ideas have not been emasculated is that, by and large, they are not susceptible to experimental investigation. If we are not "scientific" we can continue to indulge in the intellectual excitement of allowing our minds to wander through those magnificent realms of fantasy before closing in on an idea so as to look more closely at what we have created. But very likely it will be beyond our wit to bring it under experimental control. With an increasing emphasis on objectivity goes a tendency to restrict these flights of fancy in the hope that any ideas emerging will the more likely be amenable to measurement.

George Kelly's theory (1955) or, as some prefer to say, metatheory of personal constructs is unusual in psychology. It is a theory that gives us scope to use our imagination, while at the same time providing a technique for quantifying some of the resulting ideas. The theory can, in its turn, be used to describe and account for the creative ideas of the thinker. It would be untrue to state that the technique allows *complete* freedom of movement, it certainly imposes many restrictions. But there seems reason for hoping that these restrictions reflect more the inadequacy of the user than the limitations of the tool.

The focus of convenience of Personal Construct Theory is the psychotherapeutic situation. As with Freud, it was within this setting that Kelly formulated his theory. It was here that he construed how people go about the business of conceptually organising their world and anticipating events each on the basis of his own personal construct system. It was here that he construed how people could be trapped by these very constructions and the invalidating evidence they sometimes evoke. It was within this context that he developed those parts of his theory which describe dimensions of diagnosis and transition and the process of reconstruction.

Kelly, along with many others, was of the opinion that psychologists do not have to use the "medical model" when describing psychological change. He points out that one has to communicate and so must use familiar terms, but his view of "therapy" is best expressed in his own words:

> "Our view of the ultimate concern of clinical psychology as a discipline, and our notion of *therapy*, is that of a psychological process which changes one's outlook on some aspect of life. It involves construing, or, more particularly, reconstruing. That which is reconstrued is usually one's own life or the role he envisions for himself through his understanding of others' outlooks. Not only does he reconstruct life in an ordinary biographical sense, but he also reconstructs his own life processes, even those which are commonly called vegetative. The reconstruing is what some psychologists would call "learning"; but again we are inclined to avoid a term because of its customary implications—in this case, because of its stimulus-response implications.
>
> Since we see processes psychologically channelized by one's construction system, we can view them as being changed, either by rerouting through the same system of dichotomous constructs, or by reconstruction of the system of channels. In the clinic one is more apt to be concerned with the latter kind of readjustment . . . (this) is a much more ambitious undertaking and involves many technical difficulties, both in communication and in timing. Yet we see it as the ultimate objective of the clinical-psychology enterprise, and have used it as the basis for the theme of this book—*the psychological reconstruction of life*. We even considered using the term *reconstruction* instead of *therapy*. If it had not been such a mouth-filling word we might have gone ahead with the idea. Perhaps later we may! (Kelly, 1955, vol. I, pp. 186–187)."

When thinking and working within the framework of Personal Construct Theory it seems meaningless to continue using the term "therapy" as if there were no alternative. On the other hand, "reconstruction" *is* a mouth-filling word and does not lend itself easily to modification. It is too inelegant to speak of a person who attempts to bring about a process of reconstruction as a "reconstructionist". So I shall use the terms "reconstruction" and "therapy" as if they were synonyms, choosing whichever seems the more appropriate in a given setting.

As this essay is concerned with a study of one psychotherapy group, the discussion of the Personal Construct Theory approach to psychotherapy must be followed by an account of the theoretical view of some social phenomena.

Interactions Between People

One of the very important aspects of the theory of personal constructs is that dealing with interactions between people. This is formally set out in the Sociality Corollary which states that "to the extent that one person construes the construction processes of another, he may play a role in a social process involving the other person". This procedure of placing oneself in the shoes of another so as to be better able to understand and predict his present and subsequent behaviour, can be applied to therapeutic as well as to social situations. Wherever there is interaction there must be at least some understanding of the other person. So central are these ideas in Personal Construct Theory that Kelly remarks how, in the early days of the theory's development, his students called it "role theory".

Viewing another as a construer and thus playing a role in relation to him, means that our role constructions are validated in terms of the expectancies of those with whom we have established this role. Thus, the expectancies of a group may act as validators of each individual's personal constructs. As with all constructs, validation is achieved by checking predictions. People living in the same environment may well develop many similar expectancies and so behave similarly. It is in this way that constructs of *individual* members are seen as being constantly validated by the expectancies of the group.

Kelly describes three ways in which these group expectancies operate as validators of personal constructs. The first is when we accept the opinions of others on matters on which we cannot personally obtain validational evidence, such as that the world is a sphere. The second is exemplified by the colleague who suddenly behaves in a totally unpredictable way and so is viewed askance. He may, however, find this a more interesting way in which to behave and so start to construe himself as a person who "keeps people guessing". The expectancies and reactions of his colleagues have caused him to reconstrue himself, but he has made no attempt to understand them, he has only observed their behaviour. But in a third instance, this same man may decide that his colleagues now *construe* him differently and see him as an unpredictable person; if he went on behaving in a similar way he would be playing a role in relation to them.

Role Relationships in Psychotherapy

Some therapists try to impose their own theoretical constructs on the patient and to a greater or lesser extent ignore the patient's own construction of events. Among the worst offenders in this respect are those found in the ranks of the behaviour therapists. While the systematic desensitizer fondly believes that the patient is climbing obediently up his hierarchy, say, the agoraphobic to the great outdoors, the agoraphobic is constantly construing the construction processes of the therapist. It is becoming more and more clear that the therapist who is construed as "believing" in the procedure and the patient will have a better record of "improvements" than the therapist who is seen as being disinterested or sceptical. But more than this, there is mounting evidence that changes in construing, and thus in anticipation, directly affect behaviour. For instance, Marcia *et al.* (1969) found it possible to desensitize people to snakes and spiders solely by systematically altering their expectancies. Although there is increasing awareness among behaviour therapists of the importance of cognitive factors in conditioning procedures, there is still a reluctance to place much importance on the role played by the therapist.

In a psychological reconstruction programme, the therapist aspires to understand the client by subsuming his construct system and thus plays a role in relation to him. But the construct theory therapist may take this one stage further and deliberately *role play*. For instance, he may deem it important that the client enlarge the range of convenience of "authority figures". Having established himself in the role of such a figure, he may vary the behaviour he adopts in the presence of the client. The client in his turn tries out new behaviours in relation to the therapist's role. In time he will be encouraged to try out some of these new behaviours with the relevant figures in his environment.

Responses to Invalidating Evidence

Supposing the group suddenly starts producing invalidating evidence for a person's role expectancies? In Personal Construct Theory terms several things can happen. The individual can accept the evidence philosophically, cut his losses and try another construct to see whether its predictive capacity is better. Or he can argue that there was something unusual about that particular experiment, there was some aspect of the situation that he had failed to take into account, so he repeats the experiment. Or he can attempt to *alter* the events so that they conform to his predictions and thus behave in a hostile way. He can become anxious and so "loosen" his construct system in the relevant places to incorporate the new evidence. Or he may feel threatened by the unpredicted responses and perhaps "tighten" his system in an attempt to define more clearly exactly what it was he was predicting.

The last four of these possible responses to invalidating evidence need further discussion as these constructs will be used when the psychological changes occurring in the group psychotherapy research are evaluated.

Hostility is defined as "the continued effort to extort validational evidence in favour of a type of social prediction which has already proved itself a failure". Hostility can itself be a reaction to anxiety or threat. Supposing a colleague whom you construe as a fool suddenly invalidates this construction by talking in a most intelligent way. For some reason it is important for you to continue to construe him as a fool, so you deliberately start a topic of conversation on which you *know* he has some "foolish" ideas. You are extorting validational evidence in favour of a prediction that has proved to be a failure. You do this because the implications of his being a "non-fool" are threatening for some reason or cause anxiety. There is too much invested in the prediction to allow it to fail. Scapegoating in groups might be seen in this light.

Anxiety is defined as "recognition that the events with which one is confronted lie outside the range of convenience of one's construct system". Providing the person has an alternative construction to place on events there is no great problem. But anxiety may occur when invalidation of a construct leaves the individual with no alternative to take its place.

Threat is "the awareness of imminent comprehensive change in one's core structures". A therapist himself is a great potential source of threat. He can, for example, expect a person to behave in a way that is reminiscent of how that person behaved in the past, but which he has now abandoned. In other words, the therapist may be seen as expecting the client to regress. Or he may expect the client to behave in a manner that is substantially different from the way in which he behaves at present. The group reconstruction situation is potentially more liable to produce anxiety or be more threatening than the individual situation. In the former there are two sources of threat instead of one, there are the group members as well as the therapist. It is important to bear in mind that the presence of a feeling of threat often militates against the formation of new constructs; the person either falls back on older constructions or may "tighten" his construing.

One of the most important constructs about constructs is the dimension of "loose *vs* tight". A loose construct is one leading to varying predictions while retaining its identity. A tight construct is one which leads to unvarying predictions. Loosened construing is seen in its extreme form in the abnormal thinking of thought disordered schizophrenics and in the normal process of dreaming. But everyone can indulge in loose construing in waking life. Sometimes for fun as in day-dreaming and fantasy building, sometimes for real as in the desperate search for a theory to account for some experimental findings. In loose construing the elements play snakes and ladders along the construct dimensions. Bannister (1965) has shown experimentally how persistent invalidation can produce a loosening of relevant parts of a person's construct system.

The importance of loose construing for our present purpose is that it is the lynch pin of creative thinking. In a therapy situation, the Creativity Cycle is repeated again and again. I should perhaps qualify this by saying any therapy situation that is successful in producing some degree of reconstruction in the client. The Creativity Cycle is "one which starts with loosened construction and terminates with tightened and validated constructions". In psychotherapy loosening can be deliberately encouraged by the use of relaxation, word association, recounting dreams or by uncritical acceptance by the therapist. Or, as has been mentioned, it can occur as a reaction, particularly to anxiety and to invalidation of constructs.

Group Psychotherapy: Theories and Research

The relative recency of the development of group psychotherapy has resulted in a multiplicity of theories and speculations. Group psychotherapists or those interested in the subject are prolific writers. In a review of the 1967 literature, MacLennan and Levy (1968) record that almost three hundred papers were published on the subject during the year. Amongst the writers there seems to be general agreement as to the almost total lack of systematic theory and research in this area. A closer look reveals that the writers are bemoaning the fact that original and interesting ideas abound but no attempts are made to test them—in fact, too much imagination and too little "science".

Probably because of the difficulty of conducting experiments and research on the group process itself, most studies have concerned themselves with looking at the group from without. What sort of group composition is the most efficient? Are groups comprising patients with a variety of complaints better than homogeneous groups? Who talks to whom and what is the proportion of verbs, adjectives and nouns in their speech? Is a group better for having a leader or for being leaderless?

A common criticism is that many therapists have taken ideas developed in the sphere of individual psychotherapy and grafted them on to therapy using group methods. Many have stated that no one theory has yet been expounded whose range of convenience will encompass both individual *and* group reconstruing. Personal Construct Theory can do precisely this. There are many examples of its application with the individual case and the research about to be discussed gives a few of the ways in which the theory and measuring technique can be used in the group setting.

A Group of Ten People

This group, which met once a week for one year, was made up of eight adult out-patients, who had asked for help with a variety of psychological complaints, and two psychiatrists. One was psychoanalytically-orientated and led the group the other acted as an observer who played no active part at all in the group procedures. Everyone in the group knew that they were to meet for one year only and that this time limit would be enforced.

Repertory grid technique

A form of repertory grid was the only method used for quantifying change in thought structure and patterning and was administered in standard form to each of the group members and to both psychiatrists on five occasions. The first testing took place within two days of the initial group meeting and at three-monthly intervals thereafter.

Repertory grid technique started life as the Role Construct Repertory Test (or Rep Test) and several variants are now in existence. Full details of these and related research are given in Bannister and Mair's book entitled "The Evaluation of Personal Constructs" (1968).

This technique is an integral part of Kelly's work. It is the method he devised for assessing the relationship between a person's constructs. It can be used without any reference to the theory and, indeed, has been on many occasions. But I consider that a vast amount of the richness of information is lost when such a decision is made. Many psychologists to-day feel happier without a theory breathing down their necks, but they buy comfort at the expense of clarity. This present study, in fact, started life as a piece of "grid" work. It was designed to quantify psychological changes postulated to occur in certain supplied constructs over time and to test a few specific hypotheses. I hope to demonstrate that, with the use of the theory, some very fundamental group phenomena may have been described.

The particular modification of the grid employed was that of rank ordering the *elements* in terms of the *constructs*. In this particular instance, the eight people in the group served as the elements. The name of each patient group member was written on a card, each person having his own name replaced by the word SELF. These cards were then laid out before the person to be tested and he was presented with the first construct, in the present study this was THE LEADER OF THE GROUP. He was then asked to rank the people from those to whom the construct most applied to the one who was least like a leader of the group. As there were twenty such constructs for the (patient) group members, each ended up with a matrix of 8 × 20 rankings. The identical constructs and elements were readministered on each of the assessment occasions, which resulted in forty matrices of rankings by the end of the research. Both the active psychiatrist and the observer completed five grids each as well. The only differences being that they were supplied with seventeen constructs instead of twenty and they did not rank themselves as one of the elements.

What lead up to the choice of constructs is detailed in the journal paper (Fransella and Joyston-Bechal, 1970) and is not of particular relevance here. When selection was to test specific hypotheses this will become apparent in the discussion of results. To give a clearer impression of the bases of changes in structure and patterning that occurred, the constructs for patients and psychiatrists are listed below:

PATIENTS' CONSTRUCTS

Leader of the group
Like me in character
Typical of the group as a whole
The person one could have most confidence in
Typical of the group as I would like it to be
The most talkative person
The person who says the most useful things in discussions
The person who has problems that are most like mine
Like I'd like to be in character
The person who annoys me most
Like the observer in character
The most helpful to others
The most dominating person
The one who makes me anxious or worried
A disrupting influence on the group
The most influenced by the group discussions
The one who is different from the rest of the group
The person who depends on other people most
The one I like the least
Like the therapist in character

THE THERAPISTS' CONSTRUCTS

Leader of the group
Typical of the group as a whole
The person I have most confidence in
Typical of the group as I would like it to be
The most talkative person
The person who says the most useful things in discussions
The person who is most unwell
The person the group find most annoying
The one I like the least
A disrupting influence on the group
The one who is different from the rest of the group
The person who is most likely to improve
The scapegoat
The one who makes me anxious or uneasy
The person who most resists change

Like me in character
The person who has improved most (not included in the first grid).

The grid matrices, fifty in all, were analysed in a variety of ways. These included principal component and grid comparison analyses (Slater, 1965, 1968)* and scores derived direct from the rankings.

OUTCOME

Apart from the grids, the other principal measures used were those of "outcome". It seems necessary to put this in parenthesis because sometimes it is difficult to comprehend what people mean by the term. When a person is receiving treatment for some disorder that has been construed as monosymptomatic, measurement is comparatively simple. It is possible, for instance, to see that a person is able to go outdoors with less anxiety than before treatment. But when it comes to something more complex and diffuse in nature and one is faced with assessing improvement after a course of psychotherapy, it is surely naïve at the very least to think one can meaningfully identify this with a few crude measures and assume that these are applicable to all people. This is real wisdom after the event since, in this study, just such a crude attempt at measurement was made.

Crude though it was, it was also excessively time-consuming. It involved two independent assessors, one a clinical psychologist and the other a consultant psychiatrist. The psychologist interviewed each patient and someone who knew the patient both at the start and at the end of treatment (thirty-two interviews in all). She made comprehensive notes during these interviews and then rated the patient on five 5-point scales relating to social adjustment. These scales have each point clearly defined and cover the patient's judged adjustment to work and leisure, to family and non-family and towards sex. The psychologist's notes were then given to the consultant psychiatrist who rated the patients on the basis of the notes alone. The overall interjudge reliability between these two raters was 0·829.

One last point before coming to the results. This concerns the fascinating optimism of many psychotherapists. The psychiatrist's clinical ratings of patient change, based on his notes of the group meetings, and therefore acknowledged to be totally subjective, ran from "no change" to "greatly improved". Parloff (1967) in his paper *A View from the Incomplete Bridge: Group Process and Outcome* says that "while therapists are willing to express varying degrees of modesty, or even subscribe to the more fashionable existentialist concepts of futility, few would take seriously the possibility

* The analyses were carried out by a Medical Research Council service organized by Dr. P. Slater.

that what they do may, in fact, be psychonoxious. . . . The operant conditioner suggests that this too may be an illusion". The operant conditioner is not alone in expressing this disquiet. Truax and Wargo (1966) say, in their paper *Psychotherapeutic encounters that change behaviour: for better or for worse*, "If the technique of change is powerful, it must have the potential to be powerfully therapeutic or, if misused, powerfully anti-therapeutic". The results to this study will be seen to lend some support to these fears.

RESULTS

Process change

(i) Intensity

Construct theorists would argue that there should have been some evidence of movement along the "loose-tight" dimension if any change in construing were to take place.

To find out if any change of this sort had occurred in terms of the "group" grid, it was first of all necessary to get some indication of whether loosening and tightening were occurring throughout the individual's total construct system or whether it might be confined to the group-related constructs and elements. The degree of intensity, that is the relative tightness-looseness of constructs, has been operationally defined by Bannister (1960) as the strength of the correlations between sets of element rankings. The higher the correlation the "tighter" the construct relationship, the more the correlation approaches zero the "looser" the construct relationship. He has shown that the thinking found in thought-disordered schizophrenics is characteristically "loose". A standardized test (Bannister and Fransella, 1967) based on these earlier findings discriminates between the thinking of thought-disordered schizophrenics and various other groups including normal subjects when construing people. This test thus provides normative data for non-psychiatric and psychoneurotic subjects. It was therefore administered to all ten people (eight group members and two psychiatrists) when the group first met and again nine months later.

The mean Intensity score (strength of correlations) for the whole group was 1222·7 on the first occasion and 1552·7 nine months later. Although there was quite a considerable increase here, it was not statistically significant. The means and standard deviations of the group under investigation and the standardization samples, can be seen in Table I. For what is to come it is important to bear in mind that the second testing on this test was coincidental in time with the fourth testing on the "group" grids.

From these test results it was concluded that there was no significant change on these measures in at least some aspects of the group members' construing systems at naught and nine months. Any changes that were found

TABLE I. *Means and standard deviations of the group members' Intensity and Consistency scores on the grid test of schizophrenic thought disorder on two occasions*

	Psychotherapy Group				Standardization Groups			
	0 months		9 months		Neurotics		Normals	
	Mean	S.D.	Mean	S.D.	Mean	S.D.	Mean	S.D.
Intensity	1222	255	1552	427	1383	517	1253	339
Consistency	0·86	0·33	0·87	0·25	0·74	0·45	0·80	0·34

to occur on the "group" grids were, therefore, regarded as being confined to group construing.

On any rank order grid each construct has a correlation with every other construct. If these correlations are squared and multiplied by a hundred, they can be used as scores. These so-called relationship scores can then be added together to yield an Intensity score for each construct. These construct Intensity scores on the five test occasions were subjected to an analysis of variance for each of the ten people. For the two psychiatrists and six of the eight patients, there were significant differences between Occasions and between Constructs. These changes in Intensity on different Occasions can be seen most clearly in Fig. 1, the mean intensity scores for the patient group on each test occasion are plotted along with those for each of the psychiatrists.

From this measure it did begin to look as if the patients and psychiatrists were construing in unison. For those who had significant differences of Intensity between Occasions (six patients and two psychiatrists), a critical ratio was calculated between Occasions 2 and 4. These were significant for all but two of these eight people. Of the deviators, one had a *decrease* in Intensity between Occasions 2 and 4 followed by a significant *increase* between 3 and 4, while the other kept her decrease until Occasion 5.

It will be remembered that there was no significant difference in Intensity on the Bannister-Fransella test between testing at naught months and nine months and whatever difference there was, was in the "tight" rather than the "loose" direction. It could be said that differences in Intensity between the second and fourth Occasions in the "group" grid were being tested, whereas it was between the first and the fourth on the test and that therefore this was not a valid comparison. However, since the Test involves the construing of photographs of strangers, it is extremely unlikely that there is any "getting to know you" process which would operate over three months but not over nine months. In the "group" grids, however, the elements were not strangers but members of the group. At the first testing these group members sometimes had difficulty in remembering who the people were represented by names on the cards. At the second testing they had had three months to get to know them and this was therefore considered a better comparison to make with the fourth Occasion.

What happened on this fourth Occasion to make for such a variation in intensity of correlations for eight of the ten people? Surely here was something resembling a group process. Six out of the ten people had a process of thinking that varied in a similar way to a significant degree. Of the four in the minority, two did not conform to this pattern at all in that with them this process

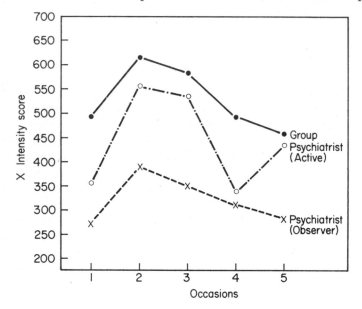

Fig. 1. Mean intensity scores for all constructs of the group and the two psychiatrists (scores prorated) on 5 test occasions.

showed no significant variation between test occasions. The other two did show significant changes but one had this process taking place *before* the others and the other lagged behind, experiencing the decrease in Intensity *after* the others.

One of the features of this part of the analysis that was not predicted in any way at all, was that the non-participant psychiatrist was "in on the act". The degree of relationship (intensity) between his constructs followed directly that of the participating psychiatrist and four of the group members. It has often been reported that "observer" is a misnomer. He cannot remain aloof and "objective", unwillingly he gets involved. Bernardez (1969) has put it this way: "As in the case of the psychoanalytic patient during free association, the observer's reign on his cognitive processes is relaxed, and in a state of free-floating attention he tends to become more attuned to preconscious or unconscious communication."

This link between "loosening" and the group process has been noted by Rogers (1958). In a paper reporting an attempt to measure process in psychotherapy (Walker *et al.*, 1960), the authors report that Rogers ". . . proposed that clients who feel received in therapy tend to move away from a general fixity of functioning and rigidity of structure toward greater openness, fluidity, and changingness, along a continuum from stasis to process." In a recent study of management groups, Argyris (1969) described two patterns of group which he designated A and B. The former is characterized by minimal expression of feelings, is generally task-orientated and indulges in only "tight" construing. The latter type of group expresses its feelings, takes risks, indulges in "loose" construing, and the group itself is seen as the opportunity for individuals to receive invalidating evidence about the self and a chance to reconstrue. Argyris notes that some groups, especially successful T-groups, go from pattern A to pattern B during the course of their meetings. Construct theory and repertory grid technique do seem to present the possibility of quantifying and describing in greater detail these group process phenomena that are being discussed.

(ii) Consistency

Evidence from the Bannister-Fransella test suggested that the reduction in intensity of correlations found at the fourth test occasion was not due to patients and psychiatrists approaching a state of confusion or thought disorder. This conclusion was based on the fact that, not only did the intensity of correlations fail to reduce at all on the test, but also the construct *patterning* remained stable. The test requires the subject to rank order eight photographs on each of six constructs and then to repeat this procedure immediately. A measure of consistency of construct patterning can be obtained. In Table I it can be seen that the mean Consistency for the psychotherapy group was 0·86 at the start of the meetings and 0·87 nine months later.

A check was made to see whether changes in consistency of construing had occurred in the "group" grids along with the variations in Intensity. If there were, then this would look like some kind of group-specific thought disorder. If there were not, then some other explanation of the changes in Intensity would have to be sought.

Bannister has described a method of obtaining what he called a "consistency score" and which is that found in the Thought Disorder Test. The idea behind this score is that a person who is construed as "good" on the first test run-through may be construed as "bad" the second time. However, this person element may likewise have been shifted on all those constructs significantly correlated with "good". This would result in considerable similarity in construct *patterning* between the two matrices of rankings. All constructs have correlations with all other constructs and the *meaning* of any one construct may be said to lie in the relationships it has with these other constructs. Thus, to obtain a measure of construct pattern consistency, the inter-correlations for each construct are ranked. For instance; all the correlations Construct I has with all other constructs are ranked from highest positive, through zero to highest negative for the first test occasion and similarly for the comparison Occasion. A Spearman rho rank order correlation is then run between these two sets of rankings. If all these correlations for all constructs are averaged, a mean Pattern Consistency score can be derived for each person. In the present analysis, it was this degree of similarity of construct patterning that was compared for each individual on each test occasion. It was argued that if the loosening that had occurred at Occasion 4 had not been accompanied by a breakdown in construct patterning, then there should be reasonable stability on this measure between Occasions 2–3 and 3–4.

However, to complicate the issue there are at least two ways in which a low stability can be produced on the rank order form of repertory grid. One can shift the elements around systematically in terms of the constructs and so produce the high construct Pattern Consistency score just described. But this consistency is *across* constructs. If we look at consistency *within* the construct, then shifting elements, no matter how systematically, will result in a low test-retest correlation. Thus, systematic movement of elements results in high Pattern Consistency and low test-retest Consistency, while haphazard movement of elements will result in both Consistencies being low.

Table II shows up the differences that can be produced by these two forms of Consistency score. The test-retest scores are measures of element shift and the construct pattern scores are measures of the degree to which these element shifts are systematic.

Very clearly there is a vast difference between these two measures. The interpretation of these figures is that this person has shuffled the *people* about on the various construct dimensions, but the essential *meaning* of each construct has been retained.

To take the Element Consistency score one step further, just as an overall mean construct Pattern Consistency score can be derived, so it is possible to obtain a measure of total element shift between any two grids having the same elements and constructs (Slater, 1968). For example, if element 6 is ranked fourth on the first grid and eighth on the second grid, then on a grid of element differences it would be given a score of 4. A matrix of all such element difference scores is analysed into its principal components and an overall Index of General Consistency derived.

To give the best idea of the degree to which patients and psychiatrists

TABLE II. *Comparison of two Consistency scores between test occasions 4 and 5 for sixteen constructs*

Construct	Element Consistency (test-retest)	Construct Pattern Consistency
	N = 8	N = 15
1	−0·52	0·96
2	−0·43	0·83
3	0·29	0·63
4	−0·31	0·79
5	−0·24	0·86
6	−0·69	0·94
7	−0·36	0·39
8	0·81	0·48
9	0·55	0·61
10	0·02	0·82
11	0·29	0·78
12	−0·71	0·91
13	−0·57	0·60
14	−0·52	0·70
15	−0·24	0·80
16	−0·07	0·91

reconstrued as opposed to merely shuffling the people elements around along the construct dimensions, the overall mean scores on both measures for each comparison made will be given.

Occasions 1 *to* 2   Not much consistency was expected here, as on the first test occasion the group had only met together once, whereas by Occasion 2, three months later, they presumably knew each other quite well.

	1	2	3	4	5	6	7	8	Psychiatrists	
									9	10
Element Consistency	0·04	0·26	0·23	−0·06	0·32	0·29	0·39	0·37	0·42	0·53
Construct Pattern Consistency	0·12	0·25	0·22	0·28	0·51	0·21	0·11	0·23	0·55	0·52

It would seem fair to say that the eight group members who had consistency indices below 0·4 changed their minds a fair amount about the other members of the group and themselves in relation to the group between Occasions 1 and 2. Neither was there a great deal of stability of construct patterning. The statistical significance of these mean correlations based as they are on individual correlations, would be well below 0·4, but significant correlations accounting for less than 16% of the variance have little psychological meaning in this context. However, the participating psychiatrist (9) and to a greater extent the observer (10) had formed a clearer picture of the members of the group after just one meeting and a preliminary interview. Not only this, but as will be seen in a moment, they did not substantially change this view until the very last test occasion, at the very end of the group meetings.

Occasions 2 *to* 3   Between testings at three and six months, more stability could be expected and was to some extent found. Both types of consistency appear higher, although this applies considerably more to elements than construct patterning. Apart from Person 4, the psychiatrists are more consistent in their judgments as would be predicted; it is not supposed that *they* reconstrue as a result of group meetings—at least, not to any appreciable extent when treating within a psychoanalytic framework. The two types of Consistency score are as follows:

	1	2	3	4	5	6	7	8	Psychiatrists 9	10
Element Consistency	0·46	0·31	0·44	0·62	0·43	0·38	0·41	0·41	0·51	0·58
Construct Pattern Consistency	0·39	0·31	0·21	0·50	0·29	0·41	0·36	0·55	0·74	0·62

Occasions 3 *to* 4   If the loosened construing that was evident in the Intensity scores for Occasion 4 were related to *general* confusion, then both Consistency measures between Occasions 3 and 4 would be expected to be low. From those listed below, it can be seen that confusion can be ruled out as the dominant cause of loosening. There is more stability now than at any other time.

	1	2	3	4	5	6	7	8	Psychiatrists 9	10
Element Consistency	0·48	0·54	0·41	0·75	0·63	0·64	0·37	0·56	0·61	0·54
Construct Pattern Consistency	0·47	0·42	0·36	0·73	0·42	0·52	0·37	0·51	0·76	0·62

The loosening shown on Occasion 4 was independent of any major change in the construing of the patients by both patients as a group and psychiatrists, as it was for the person who loosened significantly on Occasion 3, before the majority did, and for the person who significantly *tightened* his construing system. In previous work, these two variables of the construing process have been found to be significantly correlated for groups of patients but not for non-psychiatric samples. Here however, we have a suggestion that when one is attempting to measure change in thought process and content over time,. these two aspects of thought can to some extent at least, vary independently.

Occasions 4 *to* 5   No predictions were made here. Since loosening was not substantially related to changes in construing, there was no reason to suppose that a period of relative stability on the looseness-tightness dimension would lead to any change either. Yet the following Consistency measures do show that there had been some considerable change in how the group members construed each other, although the consistency of construct *patterning* was no less than it had been between Occasions 3 to 4.

	1	2	3	4	5	6	7	8	Psychiatrists 9	10
Element Consistency	0·00	0·07	0·12	0·01	0·44	0·20	−0·03	0·02	−0·09	−0·14
Construct Pattern Consistency	0·31	0·53	0·32	0·59	0·42	0·45	0·63	0·54	0·80	0·64

It was thought possible that the changes between Occasions 4 and 5 represented a reversion to how they had viewed each other at Occasion I. However, element consistencies for Occasions 5 to 1 do not support this:

	1	2	3	4	5	6	7	8	Psychiatrists 9	10
Element Consistency	0·01	0·11	0·07	0·12	0·13	0·14	0·05	0·10	0·09	−0·01

Whatever changes had occurred over the twelve months in how the group members viewed each other and were viewed by the psychiatrists, they had not reverted to their "first impressions".

An overall analysis of variance of these Element Consistency scores was carried out and, as was to be expected, the difference between the Occasions was highly significant ($p < ·001$) but the difference between subjects was not. So, not only did the majority of patients and the psychiatrists fluctuate significantly in terms of the intensity with which the constructs were interrelated, but they also fluctuated in terms of the degree of stability with which they construed each other from one test occasion to the next.

Content change

(i) Concordance of person perception

One of the things that can happen in groups that cannot occur in the individual situation, is agreement of opinion in the group about each member. It is possible to ask to what extent a person sees himself as others see him. Just as the grid methodology enables one to look at the group construing process, so it enables him to attempt to answer this question. The "concordance of person perception" scores were derived direct from the original grid rankings in the following way. Each of the eight group members ranked each other on, for instance, the construct LIKELY TO BE THE LEADER and produced the set of rankings of elements A to H as given below:

Group Members	A	B	C	D	E	F	G	H
1	1	2	3	8*	4	6	5	7
2	1	6	8*	3	4	2	7	5
3	1	8	7	3	4*	2	6	5
4	1	6	7	5	3	2	8	4*
5	1*	6	5	7	4	3	8	2
6	1	8	6	4	3	5	7*	2
7	2	7	1	5	6	3*	8	4
8	1	8*	6	5	3	2	7	4

The asterisks indicate each individual's ranked view of himself as leader of the group in relation to the other seven members. For example, Person I ranked the elements so as to place himself last, Person 5 placed himself first. Each column was added and then divided by 7 (the self placement being excluded), so as to obtain the mean placement for that element. Thus, Element A had a mean placement of 1·1. Element A is the same as Person 5 and his self-placement (1·0) was deducted from the mean of 1·1 giving him a score of 0·1 on the construct LIKELY TO BE LEADER. This procedure was carried out for every individual on every construct for each of the five test occasions. By totting the discrepancy between the individual's view of himself and the mean of how the others ranked him, a total score for "concordance of person perception" was obtained for that individual—the higher the score, the less he *admitted* seeing himself as others saw him. Without doubt, this measure is greatly influenced by the extent to which the individual is prepared to attribute "good" and "bad" qualities to himself. However, it probably does identify the person who is way out in what he is prepared to say about himself and what the other group members are prepared to say about him.

An analysis of variance of these scores showed there to be a significant difference between People, Occasions and Constructs ($p < 0.001$ in all cases), there were no significant interactions. Thus, people were increasingly aware of, or able to admit to, seeing themselves in the way others saw them up to and including the third test occasion. They then were increasingly *less* accurate, by the fifth test occasion they seemed to have got more totally out of tune than at any other time. As with Intensity and Consistency, it seems that around the fourth test occasion, the ninth month of the meetings, there was a change in trend.

With regard to the individuals, their total scores were ranked in order of "perceptiveness" as follows:

	People							
	1	2	3	4	5	6	7	8
Ranked Position	8	3	1	6	4	5	7	2

A picture starts to emerge at this point. It was People 3 and 8 who were the only ones to have no significant difference in Intensity of correlations between Occasions. Person 3 had no Pattern Consistency scores above 0·36 for any inter-occasion comparison. It is possible to speculate that more reconstruing took place with Person 3 as opposed to the general tendency to shuffle the people elements around on the construct dimensions. This patient will be discussed again later in relation to outcome.

There was a significant difference in the accuracy of interpretation of other's views between the constructs. People were most accurate in seeing themselves as others saw them when it came to being LIKE THE THERAPIST, and least accurate, for whatever reason, in perceiving the extent to which they were LIKED THE LEAST. They were also bad at admitting to perceiving when others thought they were TALKATIVE, but good when it came to being seen as DOMINATING. It is not possible to talk in any detail about these construct differences since they were all supplied to the group and hence may well have different connotations for different people.

(ii) Concordance of therapist and "group" construing

One aspect of the participating therapist's grid to be looked at was the extent to which his construing of the patients and construct patterning was similar to that of the group members. The therapist and patient grids had eleven constructs in common and the overall Element Consistency and Construct Pattern Consistency between each patient and participating psychiatrist are shown in Table III.

There is considerably more similarity in the construct patterning than in the way patients and psychiatrists construed the group members. But the fifth Occasion once again shows a marked disparity between patients and psychiatrists in both construing and how the elements are construed. On this fifth Occasion, the correlations approach zero and are sometimes negative.

(iii) Changes in therapist's construing

What sort of people did the therapist think were likely to improve and did he change his views over time? Table IV shows the significant correlations between the construct LIKELY TO IMPROVE and the other constructs.

TABLE III. *Construct Pattern Consistency (CPC) and Element Consistency (EC) between patient and psychiatrist grids on test occasions 1, 2, 4 and 5*

People	1		2		4		5	
	CPC	EC	CPC	EC	CPC	EC	CPC	EC
1	0·21	0·21	0·38	0·26	0·37	0·31	−0·11	−0·11
2	0·64	0·57	0·55	0·32	0·46	0·31	−0·05	−0·04
3	0·40	0·31	0·42	0·30	0·56	0·37	0·08	0·06
4	0·56	0·44	0·63	0·54	0·56	0·13	0·13	0·13
5	0·44	0·33	0·67	0·46	0·42	0·36	−0·24	−0·22
6	0·56	0·47	0·32	0·27	0·64	0·53	−0·12	−0·13
7	0·55	0·48	0·74	0·63	0·52	0·41	0·02	0·03
8	0·65	0·59	0·68	0·56	0·58	0·43	−0·18	−0·16

There are two things deserving of comment here. The most interesting one is the almost complete loss of structure on Occasion 4. It seems as though the psychiatrist became confused as to who was likely to continue improving by the time the group meetings had been going on for nine months. All he seemed to be certain about was that they did not RESIST CHANGE. A look at the Element Consistency for this construct (no. 12 in Table II) shows that it

TABLE IV. *Significant correlations between the construct LIKELY TO IMPROVE with all other constructs for the participating psychiatrist*

Constructs correlated with LIKELY TO IMPROVE ($r_s > 0·63$)	Occasions				
	1	2	3	4	5
LEADER	0·92	0·79	0·86	—	0·81
TYPICAL OF THE GROUP	—	0·90	0·88	—	0·95
HAVE CONFIDENCE IN	—	0·74	—	—	—
TYPICAL OF THE GROUP AS I WOULD LIKE IT TO BE	—	0·98	1·00	—	0·98
TALKATIVE	0·76	0·88	0·93	—	0·81
SAY USEFUL THINGS	0·74	0·95	0·93	—	0·83
UNWELL	—	0·79	—	—	—
GROUP FIND ANNOYING	—	—	—	—	—
I LIKE THE LEAST	—	—	—	—	—
A DISRUPTING INFLUENCE	—	—	—	—	—
DIFFERENT FROM THE REST	0·92	−0·88	−0·95	—	−0·95
THE SCAPEGOAT	−0·71	—	−0·76	—	−0·76
RESISTS CHANGE	−0·88	−0·93	−0·84	−0·79	−0·83
LIKE ME IN CHARACTER	—	0·90	0·86	—	0·76
MAKE ME ANXIOUS	—	0·69	0·79	—	0·71

is significantly negative (-0.71) from the fourth to the fifth testing. However, he may have changed his view drastically as to who is likely to improve, but there has been no change in the qualities on which his view of improvement is based, as shown by the construct pattern consistency of 0·91. That this radical reconstruing of the elements occurred *after* the loss of Intensity on Occasion 4 is evidenced by the fact that the Element Consistency between Occasions 3 and 4 was still positive (0·65), and the Pattern Consistency 0·76.

That this reduction in Intensity did not occur throughout the constructs used in this grid, is shown by the correlations of all constructs with the self construct in Table V. This is also a good illustration of just how stable some

TABLE V. *Significant correlations between the construct LIKE ME IN CHARACTER with all other constructs for the participating psychiatrist*

Constructs correlated with LIKE ME IN CHARACTER ($r_s > 0.63$)	Occasions				
	1	2	3	4	5
LEADER	0·74	0·93	1·00	0·86	0·93
TYPICAL OF THE GROUP	—	0·81	0·95	—	0·76
HAVE CONFIDENCE IN	—	—	0·64	—	—
TYPICAL OF THE GROUP AS I					
WOULD LIKE IT TO BE	—	0·83	0·86	0·95	0·83
TALKATIVE	—	0·88	0·93	0·95	0·93
SAY USEFUL THINGS	—	0·98	0·93	0·90	0·98
UNWELL	—	—	—	—	—
GROUP FIND ANNOYING	—	—	—	—	—
I LIKE THE LEAST	—	—	—	—	—
A DISRUPTING INFLUENCE	—	0·67	—	—	—
DIFFERENT FROM THE REST	—	−0·74	−0·95	−0·74	−0·71
LIKELY TO IMPROVE	—	0·90	0·86	—	0·76
THE SCAPEGOAT	−0·83	−0·81	−0·76	—	—
RESISTS CHANGE	—	—	−1·00	−0·88	−0·64
MAKE ME ANXIOUS	—	0·90	0·71	—	0·71

of these constructs were and how the idea of looseness versus tightness is not a trait of an individual, nor of specific constructs, but is related to the person's construction of events occurring at a particular time.

The second feature to be noted about the construct *likely to improve* is that at the first testing such people were regarded by the psychiatrist as being DIFFERENT FROM THE REST ($r_s = 0.92$). Perhaps a note of pessimism here. But, by the second test occasion, the sign had changed to a negative one. And it stayed that way. After three months the psychiatrist seemed to come to the conclusion that those who were likely to improve were those who were *not* different from the rest.

Next it was considered whether a measure of process (Intensity) might be related to the therapist's construction of "improvement". From Occasions 1 to 5 the correlations between the patients' total Intensity scores and the psychiatrist's ranking of these patients in terms of their likelihood of improving were:

$$-0.57, \qquad -0.19, \qquad -0.43, \qquad -0.24 \qquad \text{and } 0.24$$

On the first four test occasions he tended to see tight construing as contraindicating future improvement.

A somewhat similar relationship was found with the "concordance of person perception" scores. Except that this time there was a *significant* overall negative tendency. Those who were *inaccurate* in judging how others saw them were construed by the therapist as being likely to improve. The correlations range from 0·26 on the fifth Occasion to -0.93 on the second Occasion.

The relationship between Intensity and being viewed as likely to improve would be predicted from most theoretical therapeutic standpoints. But there seemed to be no reasonable grounds for predicting a relationship between likelihood of viewed improvement and accuracy with which we see ourselves as others see us. Intensity and "concordance of person perception" scores were not related for this group of patients but perhaps they are in the mind of a therapist. Perhaps it is considered that there is more room for manoeuvre in those who are at sea when seeing themselves mirrored in other eyes.

A therapist-patient interaction was demonstrated at Occasions 1 and 4. The therapist saw as being like him those who wanted to be like him. That is, the patients' correlations between constructs LIKE THE THERAPIST and LIKE I'D LIKE TO BE IN CHARACTER were ranked and correlated with the therapist's own rankings of those he thought were most like him in character. The resulting mean correlations for the five test occasions were:

$$0.83, \qquad 0.10, \qquad 0.10, \qquad 0.88, \qquad -0.05$$

The emergence of this type of construing again at the fourth Occasion might be seen as a desperate attempt on the part of the therapist to impose structure when he sensed that he was in danger of losing control of the situation, possibly as a defence against anxiety in himself. Table IV shows that for the therapist there was a significant positive relationship between the constructs MAKE ME ANXIOUS and LIKELY TO IMPROVE on Occasions 2, 3 and 5 but not 1 and 4.

(iv) Changes in group construing

Although it is not profitable to discuss details of the construct relationships, a few were supplied to test specific hypotheses. One concerns the notion that there are stages through which ideas concerning the group go. The argument is that the "ideal self" is first related to THE THERAPIST but not to ideas of THE GROUP; then the "ideal self" is related to both THE THERAPIST *and* THE GROUP: finally the "ideal self" is related only to THE GROUP—in other words the group takes over the role of the therapist. These stages did not occur in this study as measured by the correlations between the relevant constructs as can be seen in Table VI.

TABLE VI. *Mean correlations for patient group members between "ideal self", therapist and group-related constructs*

	LIKE I'D LIKE TO BE		
	correlated with		
	THE THERAPIST	THE GROUP NOW	THE IDEAL GROUP
Stage I	0·74	0·45	0·78
Stage II	0·46	0·34	0·69
Stage III	0·58	0·36	0·69

The therapist did lose a certain amount of his attraction in the eyes of the group, but nothing else changed very radically. There are several possible reasons why this hypothesis was not supported. The predicted relationships may be susceptible to week-to-week mood changes of the group and the testings may not have coincided with their presence. This is not a very sound argument since the relationship between group and therapist image is supposed to be a fairly fundamental one. A more likely reason for the failure was that the measures were not a fair test of the hypothesis. A better test would have been to include each member's constructs concerning parent figures and to predict that these would be transferred from THE THERAPIST to THE GROUP.

Lastly, as would be expected from small group research, people who were seen as talkative were seen as contributing constructively to the group and as leaders, as is shown in Table VII.

TABLE VII. *Mean correlations for patient group members between the constructs TALKATIVE, LEADER, and SAY USEFUL THINGS*

TALKATIVE correlated with:	Occasions				
	1	2	3	4	5
LEADER	0·86	0·94	0·87	0·83	0·70
SAY USEFUL THINGS	0·59	0·77	0·81	0·70	0·64

(v) Comment

What *did* bring about this radical change in the construing process of the group? What invalidated who? Maybe there was no invalidation. Loosening is certainly regarded by all psychoanalytically-orientated psychotherapists as a desirable event. If the members saw that this form of behaviour was expected and was regarded as desirable, did the behaviour of each one provide validating evidence as to its desirability? Did they start to indulge in creative thinking? Did this get out of hand because they perceived that the psychiatrist was indulging in it as well? If this were so, then they might have been overwhelmed by anxiety since an expectancy would be that the therapist knew what was happening and had everything under control. If he were perceived as exhibiting some confusion as to the group goals, then this expectancy of theirs would be invalidated. One thing is certain, a considerable amount of reconstruing of elements occurred following the loosening apparent on Occasion 4. Of course, when talking about changes in construing, it must always be borne in mind that this only refers to the constructs used in these grids and that everything said is an inference from these. Be that as it may, construct theory does state that loosened construing is a necessary fore-runner of construct change, be it for better or worse.

What must not be overlooked is that not all ten people behaved identically in terms of loosened construing at the fourth Occasion. There was one man who *tightened* his construing system and two who showed no effect at all along this dimension. It will never be known what caused the man to tighten his system, perhaps something happened to threaten him, or maybe it was his form of defence against anxiety. All these questions raised by this study of one group do suggest that here is a way in which the group process and various group phenomena can be studied.

Outcome

On measures of anxiety and depression, the group of patients as a whole improved significantly ($p < 0.05$). But when it comes to the social adjustment measures, the picture is less encouraging. Sticking to the letter of the statistical law, it was decided that psychiatrists do not make open-ended bets on the future mental health of their patients—they do not countenance their patients getting worse. Therefore, a one-tail test of significance was applied to changes in rating measures.

As it turned out, this statistical precision did not matter, since no category of improvement for the group as a whole scraped into significance on the basis of a one-tail five percent probability. According to the psychologist's assessments, no one social adjustment category yielded a significant difference between the start and end of treatment, either on the basis of informants' information or on the patients' own assessment. However, using the written notes of the psychologist, the assessing psychiatrist came up with two categories of improvement for the group as a whole, informants opinions about "non-family social adjustment" and the patients' own assessment of sexual behaviour.

The psychologist however assessed the group as a whole to have become *worse* in two categories based on informants reports and two based on the patients' own reports. For the informants, these were the categories of "leisure" and "social adjustment with the family" and for the patients self reports, "work" and "social adjustment with the family". The "work" category was significantly worse at the 1% level. The assessing psychiatrist found one category in which there was significant worsening—"social adjustment with the family" as assessed by the patients themselves.

These results suggest that overall measures of "improvement" so often used in assessing therapeutic outcome may well hide improvement occurring in certain areas of functioning and not in others. No doubt they also reflect the assessor's own bias; he looks for changes in one or two specific aspects of behaviour and, if they are not present, the patient is judged as "no change". The point hardly needs underlining that when those who are not involved in the treatment of patients do the assessing, as in this case, therapeutic change really can be for worse as well as for better.

Looking at the judged differences for the individual patients instead of the adjustment categories, only two patients had improved significantly in any area of adjustment. One was Person 8 who, on his own assessment, had improved in matters of sex, and the other was Person 3 who had improved, in her own estimation, on sex as well as in "non-family social adjustment".

Patients 3 and 8 have been different from the others on a number of measures. They were the two who showed no significant fluctuation in Intensity as compared with eight people who did. They were the two who showed most awareness of or willingness to acknowledge how others saw them. Person 3 showed the most evidence of construct change or, rather, had the least stability between the grid comparisons. Lastly, they were the only ones to show *any* significant improvement. It was as if they were able to "resist" the group process and instead use it to help with their own reconstruing. This is not a very encouraging explanation as it would imply that the majority in a group of this sort would not be expected to improve, since they would be serving as foils for the few. The position is obviously infinitely more complex than this and it is not intended to make any sweeping generalizations from the results of this one study. But the persistent deviationism of these two people is interesting and could form the basis on which to derive hypotheses for testing in future group work.

Construct Theory Group Psychotherapy

I have discussed the application of construct theory and grid methodology to the study of group therapeutic processes in connection with a psychoanalytically-orientated group. I want to finish by giving an outline of one way in which Kelly considered that reconstruction for the individual may be achieved through the group situation.

Kelly sees the group developing in six phases. These are not necessarily discrete but often overlapping. First, there is the *initiation of mutual support*. The basis of this is acceptance, or "readiness to see the world through another person's eyes". To feel supported a person must be aware that at least one other person is trying to see matters as he does. Only when this happens will he feel safe enough to experiment. Kelly himself prefers to encourage the development of support by the use of role playing, but, of course, there are other ways of getting the same result.

The second phase in the development of the group is that of *initiation of primary role relationships*. He thinks that it is at this stage that group therapy has the advantage over individual therapy. When some enactment has taken place between two or three members of the group, the non-participants are asked to say what the participants may have felt at certain stages of the enactment. This is asking them to subsume the constructs of the others and so play a role in relation to them. The participants can say how accurate they think these interpretations of their feelings are and so give immediate validation of the non-participants' role construing. By careful allotment of roles to members and the interpretation of these roles by the others, the therapist can begin to show the group members alternative ways of construing areas in which they are having difficulties.

The third stage is the *initiation of mutual primary enterprises*. In this stage the group members start to act together and think up and execute their own enactments and experiments based on their understanding of each other. At this stage there is no attempt to experiment outside the group, everything is initiated and completed within the group setting.

Next comes *exploration of personal problems*. This does not differ greatly from what occurs in individual therapy except that here it is a group enterprise. The members all feel well supported and understood by this time and so threat is minimized. *Exploration of secondary roles* is the fifth stage. In this the members enact situations that are related to outside events and outside persons. They will be encouraged to expand the role relationships they have developed within the group to people outside the group and to humanity at large.

The last stage is concerned with the *exploration of secondary enterprises*. Here each member experiments with his new roles outside the group and, if the validational answers he gets are satisfactory, he is considered able to stand on his own feet without the group support.

A Final Word

The aim of this essay has been to show some ways in which Personal Construct Theory and repertory grid technique can be applied to increase our knowledge about the group process. Not only does it enable one to quantify some of the changes occurring in what group members think about and how they think, but it suggests ways in which these processes and the conceptual content may be linked with outcome measures in a meaningful way. But perhaps most important, Personal Construct Theory can be applied to the treatment of patients in a group setting just as it can be for the individual. The constructs of invalidation, loosening, anxiety and so forth as defined are applicable to both the individual and group setting, but some of the construing processes that have been described are solely group phenomena—perhaps they occur in non-therapeutic groups as well.

References

Argyris, C. (1969). The incompleteness of social-psychological theory: examples from small group, cognitive consistency and attribution research. *Am. Psychol.* **24,** 893–908.

Bannister, D. (1960). Conceptual structure in thought disordered schizophrenics. *J. ment. Sci.* **106,** 1230–1249.

Bannister, D. (1965). The genesis of schizophrenic thought disorder: re-test of the serial invalidation hypothesis. *Brit. J. Psychiat.* **111,** 377–382.

Bannister, D. and Fransella, Fay (1967). "A Grid Test of Schizophrenic Thought Disorder: A Standard Clinical Test", Psychological Test Publications, Barnstaple.

Bannister, D. and Mair, J. M. M. (1968). "The Evaluation of Personal Constructs", Academic Press, London and New York.

Bernardez, Teresa. (1967). The role of the observer in group psychotherapy. *Int. J. Group. Psychother.*, **19,** 234–239.

Fransella, Fay and Joyston-Bechal, M. P. (1970). Investigation of conceptual process and pattern change in a psychotherapy group over one year. *Br. J. Psychiat.* (In Press).

Kelly, G. A. (1955). "The Psychology of Personal Constructs", Vols. 1 and 2, Norton, New York.

MacLennan, B. W. and Levy, Naomi (1968). The group psychotherapy literature 1967. *Int. J. Group. Psychother.* **18,** 375–401.

Marcia, J. E., Rubin, B. M. and Efran, J. S. (1969). Systematic desensitization: expectancy change or counterconditioning? *J. abnorm. Psychol.* **74,** 382–387.

Parloff, M. (1967). A view from the incomplete bridge: group process and outcome. *Int. J. Group. Psychother.* **17,** 236–242.

Rogers, C. A. (1958). A process conception of psychotherapy. *Am. Psychol.* **13,** 142–149.

Slater, P. (1965). "The Principal Components of a Repertory Grid", Vincent Andrews and Co., London.

Slater, P. (1968). "A Summary of the Output of DELTA", *Unpublished MS.*

Truax, C. B. and Wargo, D. G. (1966). Psychotherapeutic encounters that change behaviour: for better or worse. *Am. J. Psychother.* **20,** 499–520.

Walker, A. M., Rablen, R. A. and Rogers, C. A. (1960). Development of a scale to measure process changes in psychotherapy. *J. clin. Psychol.* **16,** 79–85.

The Game of Personal Constructs

Dennis N. Hinkle

Introduction

"Seek to understand a man's questions, not simply his answers" advised George Kelly. And when I asked what questions he was exploring by writing "The Psychology of Personal Constructs" he said—with that twinkle of aggressive enthusiasm (fr. *entheos*—the god within—divine inspiration)— "American psychologists have seemed like such a sorry lot; imagine being that cut off from an understanding of the wonder of people and the truth of human relationships! I wondered in writing construct theory if I could devise a way to help them discover people and yet still feel scientifically respectable in doing that." In 1966 I asked him how he would have changed those two volumes, now that he had the perspective of over a decade later. After indicating that he probably would delete the section on the repgrid, because it seemed to him that methodologically-oriented researchers had let it obscure the contribution of the theory, he added wistfully "At the time I was already concerned that it might be too far from the mainstream to be recognized as psychology, but now—yes—I think I would have written it more honestly."

More *honestly?* And what was he getting at when he said (G. A. Kelly, personal communication):

> "Johann Herbart's work on education and particularly mathematical psychology influenced me. I think mathematics is the pure instance of construct functioning— the model of human behaviour." "I didn't advocate the abandonment of sequential explanation in Ontological Acceleration, but I'm not so sure about that now."
>
> "I imagine a society truly based on psychology—a society in which each person's experience, creativity and human relationships are the central issues."

And finally:

> "Personal Construct Theory is fundamentally a theory of human action."

These have been bits of a fascinating puzzle about the questions of a great man. They have also been the points of departure for this essay and the lands at the outreach of the magical Personal Construct Theory telescope—with

91

kaleidoscopic attachment! A fine companion and frequent navigator on this voyage—for which the essay is a position report—has been my good colleague Dr. Peter G. Ossorio.

Is Construct Theory Reflexive?

Kelly liked to point out that most psychological theories fail to account for the behaviour of those who devise and use such theories. He regarded construct theory as a theory about theorizing and recognized that a sufficient account of human behaviour would necessarily include (1) the behaviour of the observed person (subjects), (2) the behaviour of observing (scientists), and (3) the behaviour of observing observers (philosophers of science). This self-reflexive requirement of an adequate behaviour theory means that whatever apparatus is proposed to account for a subject's behaviour must itself also be *sufficient* to account for the activities of persons in the number two and three positions. (Note that a fourth position would simply be the conceptual duplicate of the third position—observing an observer; thus regress would be redundant.) While championing this brave new non-hypocritical psychology, Kelly—it seems—missed the reflexivity mark. Consider the following quotations from Kelly, 1955:

> "But we should like, furthermore, to make clear our conviction that people's thoughts also really exist, though the *correspondence between* what people really think exists and what really does exist *is a continually changing one*." (p. 6; italics mine.)
>
> "Life, then, to our way of thinking, is characterized by its essential measurability in the dimension of time and its capacity to represent other forms of reality, while still retaining its own form of reality" (p. 8).
>
> "Man looks at his world through transparent patterns or templets which he creates and then attempts to fit over the realities of which the world is composed. The fit is not always very good" (p. 8–9).
>
> "But we have already said enough to indicate that we consider a construct to be a representation of the universe, a representation erected by a living creature and then tested against the reality of that universe. Since the universe is essentially a course of events, the testing of a construct is a testing against subsequent events. In other words, a construct is tested in terms of its predictive efficiency" (p. 12).
>
> "We have long since committed ourselves to a point from which we see the world as being real and man's psychological processes as being based upon personal versions of that reality. The personal versions are personal constructs" (p. 135).
>
> "A construct, in turn, is an abstraction. By that we mean it is a property attributed to several events, by means of which they can be differentiated into two homogeneous groups. The invention of such a property is the act of abstracting. To construe events is to use this convenient trick of abstracting them in order to make sense out of them" (p. 120).
>
> "Validation represents the compatibility (subjectively construed) between

one's prediction and the outcome he observes. Invalidation represents incompatibility (subjectively construed) between one's prediction and the outcome he observes" (p. 158).

And additionally:

"Theories are the thinking of men who seek freedom amid swirling events. The theories comprise prior assumptions about certain realms of these events. To the extent that the events may, from these prior assumptions, be construed, predicted, and their relative courses charted, men may exercise control, and gain freedom for themselves in the process" (p. 22).

Now, given only the equipment postulated by Kelly in building Kellian Man (those transparent patterns or templets), how would it be possible for George Kelly—as a Kellian Man—to be in a position to knowingly make those assertions? Given his apparatus, *how* could *he* know that?

The explicit semantic model (Korzybski's influence is acknowledged in "The Autobiography of a Theory") of the relation of language and reality with concepts somehow corresponding to, representing, or fitting reality does lead to the curious requirement of being able to peek around—or through—our concepts in order to check their "goodness of fit" with reality. Why one would ever bother with these "templets," "abstractions," "representations," "maps," when one presumably has a direct, prelinguistic pipeline to the real stuff, the territory, is of course a mystery. Kelly emphasized that we can only "successively approximate" reality with our construct, but how could Kellian Man *know* this?

It is altogether understandable that objectivity occupies a somewhat ambiguous position in Construct Theory given that the theory is in so many ways the dialectical contrast to the reductionistic "objectivity" of the behaviorism of that era. Yet the Scylla of the naive realist's objectivity has the contrasting Charybdis of phenomenology's subjectivism. Kelly, aware of the issue, nevertheless veers dangerously close to that whirlpool as evidenced by his troubled acknowledgment (personal communications) that the "events" we so assiduously construe are themselves constructs. It appears that there are two types of constructs—those that we invent, modify and contrive to suit our human purposes, and those that constrain us by their reality. In this hide-and-seek game of objectivity and subjectivity he achieves an uneasy accommodation of philosophical nominalism on one hand and realism on the other—at the expense, it seems, of an adequately reflexive theory.

Bambrough (1960) in discussing Wittgenstein's approach to the problem of universals presents an alternative having important ramifications for both Personal Construct theory and methodology. He writes:

"There is no limit to the number of possible classifications of objects. (The nominalist is right about this.) There is no classification of any set of objects which is not objectively based on genuine similarities and differences. (The realist is right about this.) The nominalist is so impressed by the infinite diversity of possible classifications that he is blinded to their objectivity.

The realist is so impressed by the objectivity of all genuine classifications that he underestimates their diversity.

Because the nominalist and the realist are both right and both wrong, each is driven into the other's arms when he tries to be both consistent and faithful to our language, knowledge, and experience. The nominalist talks of resemblances until he is pressed into a corner where he must acknowledge that resemblance is unintelligible except as resemblance *in a respect*, and to specify the respect in which objects resemble one another is to indicate a *quality* or *property*. The realist talks of properties and qualities until, when properties and qualities have been explained in terms of other properties and other qualities, he can at last do nothing but point to the *resemblances* between the objects that are said to be characterized by such and such a property or quality."

Wittgenstein, he points out, was neither a realist nor a nominalist:

"He (Wittgenstein) asserts at one and the same time the realist's claim that there is an objective justification for the application of the word "game" to games and the nominalist's claim that there is no element that is common to all games. And he is able to do all this because he denies the joint claim of the nominalist and the realist that there cannot be an objective justification for the application of the word "game" to games unless there is an element that is common to all games (*universalia in rebus*) or a common relation that all games bear to something that is not a game (*universalia ante res*)" (Bambrough, 1960).

Do Constructs Cause Behaviour?

Kelly takes the position that "psychological response is initially and basically the outcome of a construing act" (Kelly, 1955, p. 171). "Psychological response" is admittedly an ambiguous term *vis-a-vis* behaviour. However, expressing his concern about the relation between thought and action, Kelly once said "Perhaps I've emphasized too much the intellectual vantage point at the expense of human participation. Personal Construct Theory is fundamentally a theory of human action." He writes:

"A theory provides a basis for an active approach to life, not merely a comfortable armchair from which to contemplate its vicissitudes with detached complaisance. Mankind need not be a throng of stony-faced spectators witnessing the pageant of creation. Men can play active roles in the shaping of events. How they can be free to do this and still themselves be construed as lawful beings is a basic issue in any psychological theory" (Kelly, 1955, p. 18–19).

That last sentence is a key one and evokes not only the freedom-determinism issue, but also the complex issues of "behaviour" and its "explanations." Kelly's elaboration of the man-scientist analogy and his emphasis on behaviour as our means of inquiry, while providing a welcome relief from the established systems of human abasement, tends to leave obscure important relations between knowledge and action.

The persistent dialectical tension between a man who engages in intentional actions, yet whose behaviour is lawfully locked into an integral universe, permeates Construct Theory. His view that "determinism characterizes the control that a construct exercises over its subordinate elements, freedom characterizes its independence of those elements" (Kelly, 1955, p. 21), reiterates a logical relationship of implication, but does not illuminate the relation between freedom, constructs, causality, and behaviour. A part of the difficulty, I think, resulted because the term "behaviour" for many psychologists had become operationalized to mere muscle movements in order to exorcise all private non-causal, mentalistic, homunculi. But there really is a difference—a public difference if at all—that makes a difference between, for example, enacting the phases of a Grand Mal epileptic seizure and actually experiencing one, or between winking and blinking, isn't there? Actions involve muscle movements, but not all muscle twitches are actions, as we all well know. And my actions, my behaviour, are what I as a person *do;* conversely, what *I* do, in part, characterizes *me* as a *person*. Trying to reconcile the concept of human action with the notion of Man as a lawful cog in the whirling of a deterministic, integral, flowing universe may well be something akin to trying to figure out how to "trump" in chess!

One further point about the relation of constructs to behaviour (action as contrasted to movement). Suppose, for example, that an excited Colorado elk hunter construes his circumstances in such a way that the "elaborative choice" for him is to point his telescopic rifle at those "events" which he construes as an "elk" and to pull the trigger. Upon joyfully running to the spot where his prey fell, with surprise and horror he discovers that he has in fact shot his beloved brother. An observer could truthfully describe what he saw by saying, "He aimed a rifle at his brother and shot him." But that was not the hunter's behaviour. The action *he* initiated was that of shooting an elk. On the other hand, had our hunter danced with ecstasy and celebration around his brother's body, then the action *he* had engaged in becomes more ambiguous for the observer. The observer's description could only be a partial description of the hunter's actions, because he lacks knowledge of the hunter's perception of his circumstances and his intentions given those circumstances. Did the hunter's concepts, his knowledge and intentions, "cause" his behaviour? Well, if it is *behaviour* we're talking about, then isn't it the case that his knowledge of his circumstances and his intentions in those circumstances *define*, rather than "cause", what *he* did? (Does being a male sibling "cause" one to be a brother?) If it is clear that knowledge and motivation are several of the defining parameters of action, then let me conclude this brief preview by noting that Ossorio (1966, 1970) in his monumental delineation of the concept of a person relates this concept to intentional action—the paradigm case of the behaviour of persons. Intentional action, in addition to the motivational and cognitive parameters, is parametrically delineated in terms of the identity of the person engaging in the action; competence or know-how, performance or procedure, achievement or outcome, and individual difference functions—traits, interests, attitudes, ability, value, knowledge, state, status, and style. But that remarkable story is his to tell and need not concern us in this examination of Personal Construct Theory. It is sufficient to note that the explanation of behaviour presupposes the description of behaviour and that with the glib operationalism of positivism, human action is sometimes lost in the reductive translation. (How would you "operationally define" the concept of addition, for example?)

Explanation and Intelligibility

George Kelly was a man who agonized about the growing spectre of a generation of social scientists who seemed to be more committed to controlling behaviour than to making sense out of it. Yet causal explanation also held its appeal for him as evidenced by his model of man-as-scientist seeking his freedom through prediction and control. R. S. Peters' (1958) explication of the purposive, rule-following model of explanations and his clarification of the circumstances in which behaviour requires an explanation in his book "The Concept of Motivation" and the classic article *Personal Constructs, Rules, and the Logic of Clinical Activity*, by Theodore Mischel (1964) in addition to the works of an increasing number of authors in philosophy and psychology who are spelling out the logic of Man's rational, recursive, generational, and calculational functioning for the social sciences will, hopefully, provide the foundations for a new era of psychological investigations. Kelly may well yet be vindicated in his assertion that mathematics is the model for human behaviour, but that's jumping ahead of the story.

An instance in which the distinction between predicting and controlling behaviour in contrast to "making sense" of it was made vividly apparent to me upon seeing my first cricket match. I was painfully an alien in this community of players and spectators, who quite evidently shared a common system of intelligibility and who understood the significance of that form of life. [I am reminded of Arthur Murphy's (1964) observation that the "community" exists only in the heads of its members. Like a game, its successful performance depends upon common understanding of the principles and rules of a way of life having significance for participants in those circumstances.] In fact, while watching the match, I found myself frantically casting empirical dragnets hoping to catch some kind of correlation between the fragments of behaviour that I was able to identify. Here I was, a psychologist straight out of the universities of the great American Midwest and I couldn't even predict behaviour! (Visions of my family in rags—my dear wife giving the last few spoons of gruel to the boney boys!) Yet, what had escaped me that day on that English cricket field was that the players and spectators themselves weren't particularly good at *predicting* behaviour there either and it didn't bother them! In fact, had they had this gift, or curse, of prediction, then what possible point—other than ritualistic—could there have been to a game of known performance and outcome? The rules of their game provided the conceptual context for making even the unpredicted and uncontrolled events intelligible, thus permitting them to take a role in this particular form of the human drama. Prediction and control alone are not enough to qualify one as a participant; sense and significance would still be lacking, and much more. (You didn't predict or control this sentence, yet it is intelligible because you too are a participant in our common language game.)

In the chapter, 'Ontological Acceleration,' we find:

> "Explanation in a humanistic or psychological sense seems to me to be a matter of seeing where something fits into a sequence. We can explain events by looking at their antecedents, as the stimulus response psychologists do, or we can explain them by lining them up with their consequents, or we can look at alternative successions to see what would have ensued—or would ensue—if they had been initiated" (Kelly, 1969).

While such a view encourages the exploring of alternatives, Kelly was not altogether happy with this view, as can be detected from the tone of the paper. In latter conversations he indicated his uncertainty about the adequacy of sequential explanation. In my work with him (Hinkle, 1965; see also Bannister and Mair, 1968) extending the ramifications of the Modulation Corollary I had attempted to clarify the meaning of particular constructs by systematically indexing their position in the hierarchical system of constructs of which they were a part. Analogously, particular behaviour can be made intelligible by describing their relation to, or significance in broader courses of action or social practices (e.g., pop fly to right field; Queen to KB4; he got married; you read this sentence). What broader courses of action was reading that sentence a part of in your life? And those actions have significance in what yet larger forms of your life? Where does it all end?—in your way of life, your culture, and perhaps with grace, a bit of divine revelation.

But is this rule-following "embeddedness" approach scientific? As Kelly was fully aware, man does not live by causal explanation alone. (Imagine what a causal explanation of differential calculus "behaviour,"—or baseball, or friendship would be like.) Mischel, I think, was correct in pointing out the rule-following tenor of "explanation" in Personal Construct Theory; and perhaps the term "explanation" should best be reserved for the causal case. However, it is altogether useful for our human purposes to clarify the concepts governing and defining our actions and to delineate the significance of those actions in larger courses of action, social practices, ways of life, and cultures. Such attempts at conceptual clarification would be empirical and subject to falsification. In addition, the conditions of acquisition and the development of such conceptually governed forms of life could keep psychologists usefully occupied for some time to come. I even imagine a time when those noblest of souls who have toiled in the vineyards of the humanities to preserve and cultivate the significance of our human endeavours will be regarded as valued colleagues in this enterprise. They might even get funded!

George Kelly was keenly appreciative that mankind had always been more audacious and inventive than "respectable" science and the "theories" of academics would have allowed. Always encouraging this magnificent audacity, he once began, with a look of gentle, teasing enthusiasm, an address (unpublished) at Clark University in the drab, gray, mill town of Worcester, Massachusetts in this way:

> "You know, the population of Worcester today is just about the same as it was in another well-known city—the city of Florence as it was at the height of the Italian Renaissance. I suspect that people now are at least as bright as they were then".

Mathematics as a Model

Consider mathematics and friendship for a moment. As it is possible to make errors in arithmetic, so are errors made in the practice of friendship—not simply "unreinforced responses," but rule-violating errors. Likewise, as people differ in their mastery of mathematical concepts, so too do they differ in their mastery of interpersonal concepts. And as a mathematical calculus permits the generation of infinite numerical sequences, it should not come as a surprise that our non-mathematical calculi are capable of generating unlimited behaviour. Now consider the plight of a hypothetical psychologist who had no knowledge of mathematics. For him, arithmetic behaviour, for example, is inconceivable and simply not in the world of observable behaviours. In response to the unpredictable sequence of "number writing" that he is capable of seeing, let us assume that he industriously launches an "empirical" investigation of mathematics "behaviour" using both the correlational and experimental paradigms. Psychology is sometimes like that.

A Close Look at Personal Construct Theory

Is personal Construct Theory a theory about anything? If so, what?

> "The focus of convenience which we have chosen for our own theory—building efforts is the psychological reconstruction of life. We are concerned with finding better ways to help a person reconstrue his life so that he need not be the victim of his past" (Kelly, 1955, p. 23).

Is the theory *about* the psychological reconstruction of life, or a set of instructions, guideline, for accomplishing that end? Consider the central part that the philosophy of constructive alternativism plays—the view that all of our present interpretations of the universe are subject to revision or replacement. Is this a truth statement? Could it be falsified? Perhaps then it should be regarded as a prescription: "If you want to reconstrue your life, then act as if you had reason to revise or replace all of your present interpretations of the universe." Notice the non-reciprocal logic here. Not following this instruction is one of the ways that the reconstruction of life could go wrong; following it, however, is not a sufficient condition for success. This logical form is characteristic of much of the theory. The man-as-scientist theme, for example, points out that one of the ways that making sense out of people can go wrong is to neglect the importance of prediction, control, and experimentation in their lives. The view of the universe as changing, integral, and real serves much the same purpose. Look at the fix we would be in if we didn't play the game this way! (I am reminded here of the literary view of life as the Game of games.)

THE FUNDAMENTAL POSTULATE

A person's processes are psychologically channelized by the ways in which he anticipates events.

The object of chess is to capture your opponent's king. The remaining rules define the allowable means for doing this. The objective of Personal Construct Theory is the reconstruction of life; the Fundamental Postulate and the Corollaries may be seen as a set of instructions appropriate for avoiding some of the ways the objective could be missed.

Of the Fundamental Postulate, he writes:

"A postulate is, of course, an assumption. But it is an assumption so basic in nature that it antecedes everything which is said in the logical system which it supports . . ."

"Let it be clearly understood that we are not proposing this postulate as an ultimate statement of truth. In modern scientific thought it is always customary to accept even one's postulates as tentative or ad interim statements of truth and then to see what follows" (Kelly, 1955, p. 46–47).

Notice the lingering problem of the semantic correspondence model of truth. From a pragmatic point of view, what is tentative here is the human usefulness of making this the key rule of the Construct Theory endeavour. Capturing the opponent's king is hardly regarded as an *ad interim* statement of truth, yet, since so very few of all conceivable possibilities for games are both playable and significant for humans to do so, there is serious question about which rules can, in fact, constitute *our* games. Let's take a look at the terms of this postulate.

Person

The natural sciences elaborate the concept of "things". In the rush to imitate their honoured, fertile, "big brothers", some psychologists have attempted to view man as a complex "thing", yet the elaborate "thing" rules yielded up only passive organisms—man as a "ping-pong ball with a memory", as Don Bannister once phrased it. And looking reflexively with the thing conception—aside from the fortunate conceptual impossibility of doing this—promised only endless reflections and counter-reflections of despair and fatalism in reflexive use. Is it any wonder that those who speak of human life as an activity are listened to today? Piaget's stature, for example, is not likely to level off for quite some time to come, and for good reasons. The point here is simply that the concepts of "thing" and "person" are not identical, and that the individual circumstances of their acquisition and development differ (examples from Nathan, my three-year-old: "Roads are where cars like to live?"; "Does the ground not hurt when I jump on it?"; "What does the moon do?"; "Do television sets die?" and touchingly, "If little boys be dead, they can't play anymore?"). The growing theory of action in philosophy and Ossorio's delineation of the concept of a person in terms of his paradigm of intentional action at a minimum will provide the foundations for a vital assessment of the role that the complex concepts of "thing" and "person" play in our current forms of life. If the ability to engage in actions distinguishes us as "persons", then becoming a person is a considerable attainment and not a birthright (e.g. consider the commonsense expression "What a person!")

Processes

In attempting to move away from the man-as-thing orientation, Kelly stresses process.

> "But our emphasis, if anything, is even more strongly upon the kinetic nature of the substance with which we are dealing. For our purposes, the person is not an object which is temporarily in a moving state but is himself a form of motion" (Kelly, 1955, p. 48).

Unfortunately, "kinetic nature," "motion," and "substance" are part of the object language system. Consider the difference that this rephrasing would make:

> "But our emphasis, if anything, is even more strongly upon the changes of the person with which we are dealing. For our purposes, the person is not an object which is temporarily in a moving state but is himself—as a person—a form of action."

But what about this word "process"? It implies a continuous change in time from state to state—a sequential change of events (growth, the erosion of mountains, travelling from A to B). Now, from the viewpoint of a sufficiently reflexive psychology, such processes—the event structure between events—must be public. Isn't, for example, the description "He is in the process of playing a game of chess" a behavioural observation and a description, in part, of him as a person? Granted the unfortunate reductive implications that "behaviour" had acquired by the early 1950's, I think we can now safely speak of "a person's processes" as his behaviour, unless, of course, we still want to figure out how to "trump" in chess by locking action description into the integral flow of a deterministic universe, an easy trick from the vantage point of an omnipotent God, who, by definition, experiences no reality constraints!

Psychologically

Here the "behaviour as muscle-movement versus action" issue comes into sharpest focus in his writing.

> "A person's processes are what they are; and psychology, physiology, or what have you, are simply systems concocted for trying to anticipate them. Thus, when we use the term 'psychologically,' we mean that we are conceptualizing processes ina psychological manner, not that the processes are psychological rather than something else . . .
>
> Psychology refers to a group of systems for explaining behaviour, all of which seem to offer similar coverage. Thus, when we identify our system as psychological, we are loosely identifying it with certain other systems because it has a similar realm and range of convenience" (Kelly, 1955, p. 48).

As we have seen, "explaining" behaviour by showing its rule-conforming nature is not the same as giving a causal explanation. Further, the distinction between intentional or "voluntary" action and movement is important. (Interestingly, "action" does not even require muscle movements; e.g., (P. G. Ossorio, personal communication) "Noticing that his wife had accidentally put cyanide in her tea, he did nothing"—and doing nothing would be an appropriate thing to do for a man with those intentions.) Recent work on the autoconditioning or volitional control of various body functions, heart rate, for example, is instructive. I, as a person can perform certain actions that will alter my heart rate: running around the block, injecting epinephrine, thinking depressively, etc. A psychological investigation involving a bodily function would consist of showing the effects of my actions on this function and, conversely, the effects of the function on my actions (e.g., his heart was pounding so wildly that he decided to stop running). Now, all of this suggests an incredible definition of psychology; namely, *psychology is the science of behaviour*!

Channelized

> "We conceive a person's processes as operating through a network of pathways rather than as fluttering about in a vast emptiness. The network is flexible and is

frequently modified, but it is structured and it both facilitates and restricts a person's range of action" (Kelly, 1955, p. 49).

How about this version?:

"We conceptualize human behaviour as organized. We perform a variety of actions. Concepts parametrically define action."

Ways

"The channels are established as means to ends. They are laid down by the devices which a person invents in order to achieve a purpose. A person's processes, psychologically speaking, slip into the grooves which are cut out by the mechanisms he adopts for realizing his objectives" (Kelly, 1955, p. 49).

In the language of action, this points out that behaviour is conceptually organized and has significance.

He

The identification of the person engaging in the action.

Anticipates

"Here is where we build into our theory its predictive and motivational features. Like the prototype of the scientist that he is, man seeks prediction. His structured network of pathways leads toward the future so that he may anticipate it. This is the function it serves. Anticipation is both the push and pull of the psychology of personal constructs" (Kelly, 1955, p. 49).

This keystone concept of the theory may be carrying somewhat too much weight. It is difficult, from a commonsense point of view, to understand how a life of predicting the future can have such inherent motivational significance. (See also the subsequent discussion of the Choice Corollary.) The example of the cricket match points up the fact that many of our forms of participation in life would be rendered inconsequential if such a foretelling ability were realized. As limiting cases, imagine a being whose only ability was that of omniscience; conversely, what possible use would an omnipotent being have for knowledge? I think Kelly's view of Construct Theory as being fundamentally a theory of human action provides a solution. Not being able to anticipate would certainly restrict one's eligibility to be a participant in a wide variety of life forms and courses of action. The inability to anticipate is one of the many ways a human life can go wrong, but reversing the logic here creates the unintelligible view of living for the sake of anticipation— the elaboration of one's construct system. One needs some reason, purpose, want, or intention, perhaps an aesthetic motive, in order to make a life of "anticipating" sensible as human action.

Looking, however, at the theory as being a set of instructions for understanding another as a person points up the role of anticipations in the description of action. When our Colorado elk hunter pulled the trigger, he was not anticipating that this would result in the death of his brother. What he was anticipating can thus be seen as an essential element in the description of what he was doing. If his anticipations had been different, then, descriptively, it would not have been *this* action that he engaged in. (A later discussion of "meaning" and "significance" in behaviour description will develop this point.)

With respect to motivation, what I expect, predict, or anticipate cannot, in itself, provide sufficient reason for doing anything. People who participate in the on-going social practices called "science" do have good reasons for predicting events. Science, however, is but one of the life forms; and Kelly's analogy was offered heuristically, not definitively.

Events

Here he says:

> "Man ultimately seeks to anticipate real events. This is where we see psychological processes as tied down to reality. Anticipation is not merely carried on for its own sake; it is carried on so that future reality may be better represented" (Kelly, 1955, p. 49).

The problem of events as constructs and the nominalism-realism issue has been mentioned previously. Rather than for its own sake, the role of knowledge in human conduct has been emphasized in accord with what I take to be the intent of Personal Construct Theory.

The Fundamental Postulate, then, according to the line of thought being presented in this essay, means, in effect and simply that a person's anticipations constitute a parameter in the description of his actions. Neglecting this aspect is one of the ways that making behaviour intelligible could go wrong.

THE COROLLARIES

In his discussion of the Construction Corollary—a person anticipates events by construing their replications—Kelly writes:

> "Once events have been given their beginnings and endings, and their similarities and contrasts construed, it becomes feasible to try to predict them, just as one predicts that a tomorrow will follow today. What is predicted is not that tomorrow will be a duplicate of today but that there are replicative aspects of tomorrow's event which may be safely predicted" (Kelly, 1955, p. 53).

Consistent with his Heraclitean theme that nothing is, only change is real, that all is a continuous passing away, a ceaseless flux, Kelly speaks of replicas. But his definition of construing as "placing an interpretation upon what is construed" means that I anticipate an event by placing an interpretation upon its replication and this is conceptually confusing. To be sure, we anticipate by construing. I may, for example, anticipate that adding this column of figures will yield the sum 321. Now, what is the "replicative aspect" of the "321" I got to the "321" I predicted? What about anticipating "events" never before experienced, such as those who anticipate heaven? What grounds could I have when I assert that I recognize the mountain I see from my window now as being the one that was there yesterday. If "knowing" requires a correspondence between my concepts and reality, and this reality is ever changing with respect to itself, then as knowers we are embarked on a confusing task at best. On the other hand, my recognizing that mountain is an ability that I repeatedly demonstrate. Wittgenstein, in raising the question of how we are able to recognize instances of games, since they apparently have no common characteristic, remarks that games need have nothing else in common save the fact of their *being games* in order for us to recognize them as games. His paradigm case and family of resemblances clarification of concept use and his view of language as a rule-conforming social practice— the language game, forms of life—are particularly helpful for curing the chronic epistemological condition symptomatized by wondering what concepts refer to or trying to fit "maps" to the "territory".

But all of this is for another time. Let us say here only that a person anticipates events by construing.

The Individuality Corollary—persons differ from each other in their constructions of events—points out that my construction of my circumstances, what I am doing, and the consequences of doing it, are all partial defining characteristics of my behaviour. What I do is, in part, defining of me as a person. Thus, construing "events" differently differentiates persons. More properly, in line with the pragmatic emphasis of this essay, *construing* differently differentiates behaviour, and thus persons.

Each person characteristically evolves, for his convenience in anticipating events, a construction system embracing ordinal relationships between constructs; the Organization Corollary simply points up that constructs are logically organized. Logical relationships need not be limited to the set-subset form, nor, in fact, to the restrictive principles of classical logic. Michael Polanyi puts the point well in writing about the relation of logic to human inquiry—the central theme of Kellian psychology.

> ". . . I call 'logic' the rules for reaching valid conclusions from premises assumed to be true. Currently, logic seems to be defined instead as the rules for reaching strict conclusions from strict premises. I think we should reject this definition. No strict rules can exist for establishing empirical knowledge. Most people know this but would urge us to accept strictness as an unattainable ideal for which to strive. But this is to turn a blind eye on tacit knowing, in which alone lies our capacity for acquiring empirical knowledge" (Kelly, 1955, p. 42).

Kelly's writings and his approach to teaching and psychotherapy demonstrated his clear awareness of this point. He saw Construct Theory as "a relatively content-free vehicle for facilitating human inquiry and adventure" (personal communication). I have suggested that it may be seen as a set of rules for avoiding some of the ways that creativity and making sense of others can go wrong.

The corollary that he found was most difficult for others to accept was the Dichotomy Corollary—a person's construction system is composed of a finite number of dichotomous constructs.

"But are constructs really dichotomous?", goes the objection. A distinction should be made here between (1) the meaning of "constructs" and (2) their use. The limiting case of a construct is that of one permitting only one distinction. To talk of a "construct" making no distinctions is conceptual confusion. Thus, a "construct" *logically* implies at least one "contrast." But do we use constructs dichotomously? It seems to me that we frequently do not. As an example, focus your attention on a single letter, any letter, on the opposite page. Did that letter have a *single* contrast? *All* the other letters on the page? Really? While it is true that the particular letter you selected is in fact distinguishable from other letters and events, did you *use* the concept "letter" dichotomously? Suppose we imagine a worker in a printing factory whose job it is to distinguish between various pictures moving along a conveyor belt and to sort them into their respective boxes. In random sequence, for the last six months only pictures of tables and Tibetan toads have come along the belt. Now, how often do you run across poor souls with a well-used table-toad construct? Just imagine the spree of interpretative ecstasy he would provide for a pathology-hunting Freudian on a word association test!

My point here is that the number of possible contrasts for a given concept is potentially infinite. Kelly's constructs seem to reflect the usual *contexts* of discrimination: the more frequent sets of contrasting concepts *used* by a person. To be sure, this is not how Kelly thought of it, but it is an important point having many theoretical and methodological implications, and worth thinking about!

One final comment about a finite number of constructs; such a finite set of constructs, as in a calculus, is capable of generating infinite sets of infinite behaviours—rather an awesome prospect for the predictors of human behaviour!

The Choice Corollary—a person chooses for himself that alternative in a dichotomized construct through which he anticipates the greater possibility for extension and definition of his system—states that we anticipate for the sake of further anticipating.

"Thus we hope it is clear that what we assume is that the person makes his choice in favour of elaborating a system which is functionally integral with respect to the anticipation of events . . . It must be a system *for something*. From our point of view a person's construction system is for the anticipation of events. If it were for something else, it would probably shape up into something quite different" (Kelly, 1955, p. 67).

We have taken the position that the view of life as anticipation is an inadequate description of human behaviour. Rather, anticipation can be seen as a requirement for participation in an increasing variety of life-forms having significance for us. The extent to which a man engages in action is the extent to which he has actualized as a person in this drama of dramas, this game of games. "To act, or not to act; that is the question", goes this version of the Elaborative Choice Corollary. Decisions, policies, matters of principle, reasons, wants, longings, hopes are not conceptually equivalent to the anticipations that are also parametrically descriptive of action. While it is true that particular actions may be elaborations of broader courses of action and expressions of our ways of life, much that we do, if seen as being done for the purpose of anticipation alone, would not be conceptually intelligible to us as behaviour.

The Choice Corollary is presented as a reminder for appropriate description rather than a truth statement, since there is no way it could be falsified; if he chose it, then, by definition, it seemed "elaborative" to him. It points out that rejecting an alternative a person has reason for choosing, in favour of one he has a stronger reason for not choosing, would not be intelligible to us as human action, in the same way that a "physical object" without mass would not be intelligible as a *physical* object. If I construe an alternative as not elaborative, then that means I have reason for not choosing it. The logic is not reversible, however. I do not choose an alternative "because" it is elaborative. I, for example, do not select Beef Wellington in preference to hamburger for the purpose of elaborating my construct system! Thus, man-as-scientist is a heuristic rule in the game of Personal Constructs.

The Range Corollary—a construct is convenient for the anticipation of a finite range of events only—notes that a person may not use a construct in all of the situations in which it could be employed. Logically, a construct that anticipated everything would anticipate nothing and, hence, would have no use or identity as a construct.

In keeping with our previous discussion of the Construction Corollary, the Experience Corollary—a person's construction system varies as he successively construes the replications of events—can be reformulated in public, behavioural terms: a person's behaviour varies, descriptively, as he successively construes.

In his discussion of this corollary, Kelly uses experience, reconstruction and learning as equivalent terms. Now, since just any change in conceptualizing is not what he is getting at with this difficult term "experience", this "progressive evolution" (Kelly, 1955, p. 72), it suggests that learning refers to acquiring skill in conceptually-governed activities; such an approach would avoid the troublesome phenomenologically "private" connotations of "experience."

As in the Organization Corollary, in the Modulation Corollary—the variation in a person's construction system is limited by the permeability of the constructs within whose range of convenience the variants lie—we see again the idea that a person's concepts are *logically* related. Concepts may be described in terms of the logical relationships of their components; so too with the behaviours they describe. Logically related constructs are "permeable" with respect to one another.

That a person may successively employ a variety of construction subsystems which are inferentially incompatible with each other—the Fragmentation Corollary—indicates that we participate in a variety of actions and social practices; human life has many forms, and these forms are not conceptually equivalent. Taken together, the Modulation and Fragmentation Corollaries state the logical relationships of inclusion and exclusion. The set of superordinate concepts for which all others stand in a "permeable" relationship are those constituting our way of life.

To the extent that one person employs a construction of experience which is similar to that employed by another, his psychological processes are similar to those of the other person—the Communality Corollary—can be stated, in terms of action description, in this way: to the extent that the concepts descriptive of actions are similar, the actions are similar.

The final corollary, the Sociality Corollary—to the extent that one person construes the construction processes of another, he may play a role in a social process involving the other person—states one of the major objectives of the game of Personal Constructs. George Kelly dreamed of a creative society in which an understanding and appreciation of individual human experiencing provided foundations for human relationships and moral reasoning. Once, with a look indicating both his joy of being understood and, yet, his ambivalence about revealing his intentions, he said "Yes, I guess I do think of Personal Construct Theory as an implicit ethical system; just imagine a world in which we understood one another as people!" He believed that our assessments of moral character must include an appreciation for the actual options that a person was able to envision in terms of which he defined himself in action. It is not without reason that Kelly so very often assimilated to the model of the theatre. He went beyond the cue-response notion of role, as a skilled actor must, also, and defined role as "a position that one can play on a certain team without even waiting for the signals," (Kelly, 1955, p. 98). As we saw in the cricket match example, the requirement is not so much one of prediction; rather it is the ability to make behaviour intelligible as behaviour: to the extent that a person is able to describe adequately the behaviours of another (as action), he may participate in actions defined in terms of that person's behaviours. It is in this sense that "sociality" requires the making "sense" of the behaviour of persons; it is also a requirement for becoming one. We might yet have a science of behaviour that facilitates participation and self-actualization. And it is good to be credulous!

Meaning and Significance as Behavioural Concepts

Describing the meaning of a behaviour is to say what it is that a person is doing. Such a description states the implications that a given performance has for a person. If our Colorado hunter knew that by shooting that elk his vegetarian wife would become upset, then, by shooting, he is also engaged in the activity of upsetting his wife; that is what *he* would be doing. Additionally, if he realized that his wife's annoyance would in all probability worry his son to the extent that he would not be able to pass his examinations in school, then that too would be a description of the meaning of what he is doing. Thus it is that particular acts vary in their meaning from person to person; or, to put it somewhat differently, people differ in the extent to which they realize what they are doing. We are not privy to the "flow" of the universe; and this is why we all have good reason to wonder what we are doing. Construing the sequential ramifications of our acts gives them meaning; the meaning of acts, in part, describes action; action, in part, describes people; and so also do we have good reason to wonder who we are in this mysterious pageant.

While a course of action could be quite articulated and extended in time, it could also be a mere "going through the motions", a life of quiet boredom and efficient endurance. What it has in the horizontal structure of meaning, it lacks in the vertical dimensions of significance. "Meaning" is what we are doing, and "significance" comprises our reasons for doing it, the difference it makes to us, the point of our doing it. Behaviour may vary from the highly meaningful but insignificant to the purely symbolic and ritualistic, those acts of utter symbolic significance that are complete in themselves, our moments of revelation and peak experiencing. A particular act is not fully intelligible as behaviour apart from these structures of meaning and significance in which it is conceptually embedded. (I am reminded of a fine line from a novel in which—in response to her daughter's existential despair—a mother offers her a bowl of hot chicken soup. When the daughter complains to her brother that this was hardly an appropriate thing for her mother to do, he says "You mean to tell me you can't recognize holy communion in a bowl of hot chicken soup?") Understanding the meaning and significance of behaviour, then, is to know what it is that one is doing and one's reasons for doing it. Such an understanding is not a requirement for much of our behaviour as we all well realize, but it has been a persistent theme of humanistic psychology, a movement with which George Kelly, though decrying the humanist's failure to apprehend the use of scientific inquiry for their purposes, formally associated himself.

The formal structure of Personal Construct Theory has been presented, invitationally, as a set of rules for making behaviour intelligible; being able to do this, in turn, increases our eligibility as participants in the world of human action. Research based on this orientation, for example, is now in progress and is systematically indexing the structures of significance and meaning of conceptually-governed practices in such fields as vocational decision-making, university education and the conduct and strategies of human inquiry. George Kelly's fertile questions, it seems, have pointed us in the direction of conceptual analysis, the theories of action and description, and the conditions of acquisition and development of the calculi of human behaviour. All that—and the promise of hot chicken soup too!

References

Anscombe, G. E. M. (1958). "Intention", Basil Blackwell, Oxford.

Bambrough, R. (1960–1961). XII, Universal and Family Resemblances, in *Proc. Aris. Soc.*, Vol. LXI, 207–222.

Bannister, D. and Mair, J. M. M. (1968). "The Evaluation of Personal Constructs", Academic Press, London and New York.

Care, N. S. and Landesman, L. (eds.) (1968). "Readings in the Theory of Action", University of Indiana Press, Bloomington, Indiana, U.S.A.

Dulany, D. (1968). Awareness, rules, and propositional control, *In* "Verbal Behavior and General Behavior Theory" (Dixon, F. R. and Horton, D. L., eds.), Prentice-Hall, Englewood Cliffs, New Jersey.

Gustafson, D. L. (ed.) (1964). "Essays in Philosophical Psychology", Doubleday and Co. Inc., Garden City, New York.

Hampshire, S. (1959). "Thought and Action", The Viking Press, New York.

Hinkle, D. (1965). The change of personal constructs from the viewpoint of a theory of construct implications, *unpublished dissertation*, The Ohio State University.

Kelly, G. A. (1955). "The Psychology of Personal Constructs", Norton, New York.

Kelly, G. A. (1969). "Clinical Psychology and Personality: the Selected Papers of George Kelly" (Maher, B. A., ed.), Wiley, New York.

Langer, S. K. (1951). "Philosophy in a New Key", Harvard University Press, Cambridge.

Mischel, T. (ed.) (1969). "Human Action", Academic Press, New York and London.

Mischel, T. (1964). Personal constructs, rules, and the logic of clinical activity. *Psychol. Rev.* 3, No. 3, 180–192.

Murphy, A. E. (1964). "The Theory of Practical Reason", The Open Court Publishing Co., LaSalle, Indiana.

Ossorio, P. G. (1966). "Persons", Linguistic Research Institute, Los Angeles.

Ossorio, P. G. (1970). Syllabus No. 2. 1969. Material prepared for G. S. Reynolds (ed.) "Contemporary Experimental Psychology", Vol. III, Scott, Foresman, Chicago.

Ossorio, P. G. and Davis, K. E. (1968). The self, intentionality, and reactions to the evaluation of the self. *In* "The Self in Social Interaction" (Gordon, C., and Gergen, K., eds.), Wiley, New York.

Peters, R. S. (1958). "The Concept of Motivation", Routledge, London.

Polanyi, M. (1968). Logic and psychology. *Am. Psychol.* **23,** No. 1, 27–43.

Taylor, R. (1966). "Action and Purpose", Prentice-Hall, Englewood Cliffs.

Wittgenstein, L. (1953). "Philosophical Investigations", Blackwell, Oxford.

George Kelly: Constructive Innocent and Reluctant Existentialist

Ray Holland

There is a certain honesty, almost an innocence, in the work of George Kelly, that is difficult to match in an essay that seeks both to understand and to criticise his theory of personality. His writings are so full of the most personal invitations to join in the good life of inventing and exploring different ways of seeing the world, and each other, that he seems to celebrate and exemplify the scientific quest. At the same time his engaging modesty, his constant deflation of his own pretensions by the use of colloquialisms, promises a completely humane, fun-loving irreverence towards the established systems, structures and orthodoxies of that dehumanized *Science* which he obviously despises and frequently attacks.

The attractiveness of his obstinately human voice was brought home to me when I introduced personal construct theory to a group of mature adult students whose critical powers had already been well sharpened over a couple of years of study. In two weeks they seemed to have been converted to Kellyism. What had I done to them? They quickly acquired and positively relished the new vocabulary: it seemed so full of reason and hope after the terrors of Freud and Laing. I wondered if they would ever want to study any other work and I suddenly felt very lacking in either ready counter-arguments or sources of written material that would provide some critical restraint for this persuasive man and his theories. The next step was obvious and not at all novel: it was to take up the challenge and invitation that ran through George Kelly's work: to construe it all in a different way. Why not consider the attractiveness as seduction; the openness to criticism as a sophisticated defence against it; the orderly form of the basic postulate and its corollaries as a rationalization of the trivially obvious?

Clearly to adopt this approach is to treat both the man and his work *very* seriously. Rather than take this or that corollary and subject it to experimental tests of the kind well summarized by Bonarius (1965) and Bannister and Mair (1968), it goes more deeply to the roots of the theory: it tries to discover the assumptions that crept into the theory without its author's

111

knowledge, and the limitations placed on his viewpoint by the particular social and historical location from which he worked. This is not to rule out one method of evaluation in favour of another; it is to state a preference based on limited competence, in this case as a sociologist or social psychologist rather than as an experimental psychologist. Both these approaches, and others, are needed, and all are open to failure if badly done.

There is, however, one characteristic of personal construct theory that positively calls for a broad critical approach and for some attempt to place it in socio-historical context: it is the reflexive nature of the theory—the fact that it incorporates assertions about the conditions under which psychological theories come to be held. Loosely speaking, it is a philosophical theory and it even has political overtones which need to be examined, splendidly democratic though they may be. In other words, personal construct theory proposes a social philosophy which its author has with characteristic honesty tried to make explicit. It asks, therefore, to be evaluated in relation to the history of ideas as well as in terms of its fruitfulness as a source of hypotheses for investigation in the psychological laboratory or in clinical practice. This kind of approach has a fairly close connection to that area of sociological analysis called the sociology of knowledge.

The dangers of tackling personal construct theory at this rather general level are clear. If all that results is a kind of intellectual map showing influences leading up to George Kelly then little understanding will have been gained. But if it is possible to go further and look at the reasons he gave for accepting or rejecting some of the ideas available to him, it may be possible to account for strengths and weaknesses in his theory. One of the most revealing stages in the unfolding of a new theory is that at which the theorist places himself in relation to those who, so to speak, already occupy the field. Any new personality theorist must come up against Freud and the Freudians, the behaviourists, the existentialists and others, and at a certain point it becomes necessary to accept or reject, in whole or in part, the existing work. This is a crucial point for understanding a new theory because it is not difficult to see on close reading whether the acceptances and rejections it incorporates are based on *argument* or on *attitude*.

It could be said that George Kelly escapes this kind of analysis by reason of his declared philosophy of constructive alternativism:

> "Constructive alternativism is therefore an invitation to immediate adventure. By not insisting on disproof as a precondition for initiative it saves a lot of wear and tear on nerves and it should release a great deal of scholarly man-power for more productive and less disputatious occupations" (Kelly, 1970).

But, construing this as unfavourably as possible, one could criticise the unreality—the innocence—of this wish to begin again, out of history, as though nothing had gone before. And although the very innocence of the proposal, that we rise above wasteful disputation, adds a charismatic quality to the man and possibly accounts for some of his attractiveness, he does not actually practise what he preaches. Despite the fact that he declares it unnecessary to disprove earlier theories before entertaining a new one, he does not leave his predecessors alone: he continually swipes at the ogre of the accumulative fragmentalist, the behaviourist who takes his abstractions seriously, the drive theorist, and the rest. It is therefore not only possible but essential, with George Kelly as with any other personality theorist, to look at the pattern of acceptances and rejections and to examine closely the balance of arguments and attitudes in each particular acceptance or rejection.

It must be acknowledged that the approach to Kelly outlined here runs close to the dangerous ground of an argument *ad hominem*. However, the intention is not to discredit the man's argument by reference to his motives for asserting it: it is rather to understand it more fully by assuming, with Kelly, that when a man proposes a theory of personality he inevitably puts a lot of his own self into it. More forcefully than most personality theorists, Kelly refuses to use separate categories for therapist and client: he insists on the image of all men as scientists and that therapist and client share in the basic human enterprise. It follows from this relation of reciprocity that Kelly's self-concept is as good a clue to his concept of personality as the self-concept he attributes to others. Furthermore it follows that Kelly's most fundamental assumptions as to *what it is to be human* are the foundation of his theory and these assumptions are likely to enter the theory implicitly even if they are not fully stated.

The aim of this essay will therefore be to bring out more clearly, by means of a close critical reading, some of the ideas in which the theory is rooted. I shall concentrate on what seem to me to be Kelly's most sensitive points: his reactions to Freud, behaviourism and the existentialists.

The Reaction to Freud

For a one time "Freudian" (although he did feel it necessary to use apostrophes) Kelly says very little about Freud. He speaks more appreciatively of Freud than of Freudianism: Freud was a "great clinician"; there was "so much new truth" in what he said. Freudianism on the other hand is "condemned to end its days as a crumbling stockade of proprietary dogmatism" (Kelly, 1969).

Freud was not blameless however—a leader whose work was completely misused by his followers—because Freud himself had certain faults:

> [Freud] ". . . in the now-fading Nineteenth Century tradition, regarded the scientific enterprise as an effort to discover bits of truth or to uncover things in the mind heretofore concealed" (Kelly, 1969).

Here, it seems, Kelly has decided to cast Freud in the role of the old-fashioned bad scientist—the accumulative fragmentalist—against whom Kelly brings his sharpest criticisms. Freud sought "bits of truth", and not only that but bits of *absolute* truth:

> ". . . like most theories of our times, psychoanalysis, as a theory, was conceived as an absolute truth, and, moreover, it was designed in such a manner that it tended to defy both logical examination and experimental validation" (Kelly, 1969).

And yet, even where Freud was arguing for the scientific spirit as a philosophy of life, and as an alternative to the illusions of religion, he showed himself well aware of the provisional nature of scientific findings:

> "All that it teaches is only provisionally true; what is prized today as the highest wisdom is overthrown tomorrow and experimentally replaced by something else" (Freud, 1932).

Freud may rightly be accused of having many inadequacies; among them his conception of truth as correspondence with external reality, and his great faith in the unifying power of reason, but Kelly's particular criticism seems to derive more from his own construing than from Freud's work.

There is some textual evidence that Kelly is both unfamiliar with Freud's work and rather defensive when trying to assess it. In 'The Autobiography of a Theory' (Kelly 1969) he mentions his early days as an unsupervised "Freudian" therapist in Kansas, where, in the nineteen-thirties, he was attempting to set up clinical psychology services for schools. Completely eclectic and unconventional, he went back to Freud's work and used it to help many clients by providing interpretations at the right time. He was a Freudian by persuasion but not by training. At this point in the paper, Kelly puts down a new heading, "Beware of the Obvious," and begins another of those short two page reflections that characterize much of his theoretical writings. Unlike those people who are tormented by the ambiguities and uncertainties of life he finds himself in trouble over the very opposite—those things he once thought he knew with certainty.

> ". . . a world jam-packed with lead pipe certainties, dictionary definitives, and doomsday finalities strikes me as a pretty gloomy place" (Kelly, 1969).

Given the choice he would prefer a world without hopes to a world without doubts. If he had to end his life on a final note it would be on a question. A final conclusion is like the "stroke of doom; after it—nothing, just nothing at all!"

He then goes on to say that thoughts such as these made him uneasy with

Freudian "insights" so he tried offering "preposterous interpretations" to his clients, some of which worked beyond normal expectations. Over about five paragraphs which begin and end in a joking tone he justifies his rejection of Freud and particularly Freudianism. The first joke likens ideas taken as certainties, to women taken for granted—they turn fickle. The last joke is at the expense of sophisticated clients who, if they can afford the fee, want their lives psychologized, or Freudianized, according to their "preconceived sophistries".

I do not see how a clinician of almost any school can miss the significance of these autobiographical elements around the themes of uncertainty, death, hope and the Freudian picture of the world. The clumsiness of the images, the errors in word choice, the caricaturing of Freud and his doomsday world, the jokes, the ridicule of orthodoxy; all these point to the inability of Kelly to see the world in terms of the Freudian alternative. If only Kelly would follow his own prescription, that disproving the work of others is not a necessary precondition of entertaining a new theory (whether or not this is true), and leave Freud alone. As it is the attitudes that show through the defensiveness may be construed as an anxiety about the adequacy of his theory vis-a-vis Freud's. (It is noticeable that where Kelly is weakest— childhood and personality development—Freud has made the greatest contribution.)

If Kelly's reaction to Freud stood as a single example of misunderstanding it would not be so very important, but when Kelly generalizes his reaction and applies it to "most theories of our times" he shows something basic about his theoretical position. It is his tendency to push his imaginary opponents into extreme positions in order to criticise them: personal construct theory is then made to appear so modest and reasonable (as it is in many ways) by comparison with the others' theories. But theories made only on the basis of comparison with exaggerated or misunderstood versions of other theories are not very strong: they exist not so much in their own right as in assumed contrast with a fictitious alternative. Such theories are not strong enough to have clear and cruciably testable implications and they are not powerful enough to retain a hold on the methods of investigation they propose. If, as Bannister and Mair (1968) suggest, there is a tendency for psychologists to bypass Kelly's theory and simply use his grid methods, it may be due not simply to the empiricist and statistical stockpiling proclivities of many modern psychologists, but to the inherent weakness of the theory. This is a harsh judgment to make even on a tentative basis, but I am sure Kelly would not deny anybody the right to entertain such a possibility. The question is whether this judgment can be substantiated over a wider area of his theory and as a further step towards an answer I now examine his reaction to behaviourism and science.

The Reaction to Behaviourism and Science

There are many important questions that might be asked in relation to behaviourism, and since behaviourism is primarily a programme for a very firmly *scientific* psychology, many of these questions would turn on conceptions of *science*. The unresolved issue of whether there is a human or social science as distinct from the physical or natural sciences would necessarily arise, and immediately several major intellectual positions, each with its tradition and its literature, would be seen as relevant. For example, Popper's (1957) contention that there are no significant differences between the models and methods used in the social sciences and those used in the physical and natural sciences, would be noted as one of the most influential views in Britain and America. Against Popper, and under constant attack from his school, a number of Marxist positions could be defined. Broadly these would take the Popper position as just one more transient ideology, particularly suited to prevailing economic conditions ("economic" having a deep connotation to include social relationships and the distribution of power). The Marxist dialectical method would imply the emergence of an integrated, fully human (as well as physical and natural) science, from a future society in which the economic relationships have been re-ordered so as to remove the conflicts and the knowledge-distorting ideologies.

Another position is that of the phenomenologists and existentialists, coming down from Husserl if phenomenology is emphasized, or from Nietzsche and Kierkegaard if the existentialist theme is stressed. The foundation of this position is the notion of privileged access to human experience which human beings enjoy, or which they can achieve more fully by means of special techniques such as the "phenomenological reduction". As with Marxism, the broad position includes a variety of emphases defined by such modern exponents as Sartre, Merleau-Ponty, Laing and Erwin Straus, among many others.

Other theorists share a common objection to the use of physical and natural science models of explanation for human personal and social events: Dilthey put weight on the unique qualities of historical events and on the essentially *meaningful* nature of human phenomena, and a modern version of this is to be found in the work of Rickman (1968). Wittgenstein has, through Winch (1958), provided a model for social explanation in terms of the explication of meaning rather than the tracing out of cause and effect. MacIntyre (1967) has attempted to resolve the apparent contradictions of explanations in terms of reasons, and explanations in terms of causes.

It is only necessary to set this out at such length (although by no means exhaustively) because Kelly seems to be totally unaware that he has so many allies, who could offer him a range of positions from which to propose well grounded alternatives to behaviourism. As it is, his own attack on behaviourism is relatively superficial: it does not penetrate far enough to really challenge the behaviourists, who seem for the most part to ignore it.

The form of Kelly's attack on behaviourism is very clear because of its sheer repetition in his work. Basically it is an undiscriminating rejection of everything associated with behaviourism, and the features to which he makes most frequent reference are these: it is deterministic; it is the dominant psychology of our time; it is manipulative; it is static and fails to account for or register the explosive change now taking place in the human world; it assumes that the future of all men, except psychologists, must be a repetition of the past; it generally regards a fulfilled prediction as a pinned down fragment of ultimate truth; it is Darwinian; it assumes primordial beginnings and blind drives.

One outstanding deficiency of these characterizations of behaviourism is that they are made in very general and impersonal terms. If Kelly did go into the detail of particular experiments and particular theories presumably he would see the provisional nature of findings, the changing forms of series of experiments which attempt to follow up a particular theme: he would occasionally see creative use made of behaviourist methods, and he would not be able to generalize his criticism so confidently. The effect of his repeated attacks is to set up a category of people who can be identified as the enemies of personal construct theory. This involves Kelly in at least two self-contradictions: firstly he sees his own theory as a way of breaking out of accepted categories and yet in practice he creates that most ossified category of all—the stereotyped threatening group; secondly, he argues for a new conception of man as a scientist but seems to exclude behaviourists from this generously rationalistic image.

In a curious way Kelly inverts the picture he often paints, of a behaviourist treating a human subject as a blindly driven automaton and arrives at a conception of *the behaviourist* as the blind, inhuman one.

If it seems that behaviourism is being well defended here, I intend this only in one important sense: that all scientific programmes and theories need criticism, indeed they are supposed to thrive on it; but the kind of criticism that Kelly brings to bear is counterproductive in that it is largely misplaced.

The textual form of Kelly's (1969) reaction to behaviourism is quite similar to that of his reaction to Freud. When he becomes doubtful as to the viability of his own theory, he goes over to the attack and says that *the others* have set themselves an impossible standard, not he. They are waiting for this moving universe to settle down to a routine before they will be able to understand it.

Frequently there is a mixture of crude imagery which ridicules the opposing position, and then a joke to cover the intellectual aggressiveness of the attack.

> "Simply stated, scientific determination is the belief that one event is bound to lead to another. Put your finger on that event and you are well on your way to the prediction and control of what ensues. Applied to human affairs this means that you look to see what antecedents are necessary and sufficient to make such matters predictable. Applied to psychology this means that you look for the stimulus that accounts for man's response. Punch him here and he jumps there. Tickle her here and she—well! And all that sort of thing" (Kelly, 1969).

Far from providing a good argument against S-R psychology, behaviourism or "determinism" such remarks must help to convince those against whom they are directed that their case is a better one than that of the attacker.

The Reaction to Phenomenology and Existentialism

Kelly takes a delight in telling stories about the labels that have been attached to personal construct theory. There was an occasion on which Gordon Allport explained to some Harvard students that it was not a "cognitive" theory but an "emotional" one. Later the same afternoon, Henry Murray told Kelly (1969) that he was "really an existentialist". In the "Brief Introduction to Personal Construct Theory", he lists a whole range of labels from "typically American" to "Zen Buddhistic", through "pragmatistic", "behaviouristic", "humanistic" and so on. He then disposes of the labels with a joke: since the reader will not be helped by the categorizations perhaps having a whole lap full will suggest what might be done with them. For a man whose whole theory rests on understanding the constructs of other people it seems a quite perverse suggestion. And at the same time he shows no awareness of how much his wish to question existing labels does put him on common ground with the existentialists. For example, Sartre's novel "The Nausea", provides a dramatized paradigm of a man whose experience will no longer stay within conventional categories. The experience, less structured by language than it would normally be, is alarming as well as revealing, and, although Sartre's character does not consciously seek to do so, the implication is that it is possible to break through the labels of the everyday world and explore more directly the experience of being-in-the-world. Existing labels are a liability since they tend to pre-empt the experience.

Nor does he have any conception of the close relation of many cognitive theories to existentialist theories. He can say: ". . . not many theories have been accused of being both cognitive and existential!" and the exclamation mark indicates what a ready response he expects. It is only necessary to mention Merleau-Ponty's "The Structure of Behaviour" and "The Phenomenology of Perception" as evidence of a fundamental link between cognition and existence, and it appears that Kelly misconstrues, or construes in a predominantly American fashion, one or both of the terms "cognitive" and "existential". I will try to show further on just how badly he misunderstands the term existential, but even in his use of the term cognitive I believe he is giving it a narrow meaning so that it refers primarily to studies of perception mechanisms. How else could he be so confident of the assumed contrast between the terms?

Given this great confusion about cognitive and existentialist theories there arises the more general question of how Kelly conceives the other theoretical positions he takes himself to be surpassing in fruitfulness and human sensitivity? In so many cases he seems to have only the haziest impression of what other people are trying to do. For example, Kelly (1969) lectured in Warsaw where he expected his work to be "an open challenge to dialectical materialism". He was surprised to find the Poles saying that personal construct theory was very close indeed to dialectical materialism. The most likely explanation of his surprise is that his notion of dialectical materialism was nothing more than the popular stereotype which presents it as a blindly deterministic, non-humanistic (inhuman!) doctrine, that is only fit to be mentioned as a deplorable inversion of Western pragmatism and democracy. In fact the dialectical method is quite as open to the future and capable of being used to construe change, as Kelly's own approach. Indeed, it was devised for the very similar purpose of avoiding reduction of the distinctively human to the level of the natural and the physical. Once again my aim is not primarily to defend the dialectical method but to show how little Kelly knew of many of the other theories he refers to.

As further evidence of Kelly's misunderstanding of other people, but his willingness to speak for them, there is his reference to what the Russians decided to do in the twenties when they were faced with the task of building an industrial society:

> ". . . Soviet scholars, including psychologists, could find little in the behavioural record and measured aptitudes of the people to support the hope they could ever operate machines and man factories, much less supply the vast needs of an industrialized society for advanced engineering and technical skills. What was the U.S.S.R. to do? The choice was to listen to the experts or throw away the book. They threw away the book" (Kelly, 1969).

Out of this genuine and bravely liberal gesture comes a parody of the U.S.S.R. making a decision, as well as an implied criticism of psychological methods involving "the behavioural record" and "measured aptitudes". Kelly does not seem to realize that the Russians had a book which they did not need to throw away and which told them in terms very similar to Kelly's that it is possible to release human creativity. What the Russians did with their own book, and whether the utopianism of Marx is akin to the utopianism of Kelly are questions that might be followed up, but the certainty is that such questions will never emerge from the kind of superficial illustrative use that Kelly makes of other people's work and of other people's experience.

It would be possible to go on with this kind of analysis, showing *in what sense* Kelly is a learning theorist, pragmatist, etc., etc., and I believe that in each case it would turn out that Kelly would only be able to escape the category by interpreting it in the most crudely inflexible way. But I would prefer to take further the question of whether his theory is phenomenological or existential, because it seems to me that *it is so*, in a more important sense than he ever realized. Was Kelly an unwitting and reluctant existentialist?

Firstly there is the familiar picture of Kelly disengaging himself from the label for various reasons. I shall not put him in the double-bind which accuses him of being an existentialist in virtue of his protestations that he is not such: the real question is whether his characterization of phenomenology and existentialism is correct and whether his reasons for rejecting the position will stand examination.

He has an image of phenomenology and existentialism which fits well into his own way of construing, that is, he takes phenomenology as being concerned exclusively with subjective experience and, as such, it forms a polar opposite to behaviourism, which he takes to be concerned exclusively with external reality. His categorization of both Freud and the behaviourists (they were not allowed to escape a label) was in terms of their search for truth as correspondence with reality. He exaggerated this position by calling it a search for fragments of absolute truth of a static kind. And now in setting up the polar opposite there is a similar exaggeration which appears when he discusses the use of language. In a simple assertion "The floor is hard", the criterion of truth appears to lie in the external world—in the nature of the floor. But:

> "Contrast this with the phenomenological use of language in which it is presumed that such a statement portrays a state of mind of the speaker and does not necessarily represent anything more than that" (Kelly, 1969).

Having set up the objective-subjective dichotomy, Kelly then proposes a new use of language, neither objective nor phenomenological, but cast in the more hypothetical moods of the conditional, subjunctive or imperative. He acknowledges Vaihinger's philosophy of the "as if" and says that he regards it as of particular value for psychology. What Kelly is working towards, apparently, is an open, exploratory way of using language, a use that will not arrest human creativity or fix human nature in predetermined categories. The trouble is that he has to do such violence to the other positions in order to distinguish his own. Against the purely external criterion of the objective school and the purely internal criterion of the subjective school, his own position obviously seems more fruitful.

Kelly's (1969) image of phenomenology is held fairly consistently throughout his work: phenomenology is given to "global phraseologies" it portrays the environment as a figment of men's imaginations; it does not concede an external reality. Most of these remarks are made incidentally in the course of setting up dichotomies or just in passing: where he does describe phenomenology at slightly greater length the accuracy is not significantly better. The phenomenological view gives man "nothing save the image he himself conjures up"; he "experiences the absolute freedom that only utter emptiness can guarantee the human soul"; he is in a state of "encapsulated redundancy"; he has abandoned hope of "finding substantial explanations".

"It is, I suspect, only a once naive realist, now too suddenly disillusioned to cope with his own transition, who ends up with no remaining alternative save the extreme existentialism I have described. He steps into a trap. It is one into which men, who have grown up expecting science or religion to offer conclusions rather than ways of asking further questions, are prone to fall. To be sure, I am such a man, but my biography notwithstanding, I do not choose to stumble into this particular manhole" (Kelly, 1969).

This passage occurs at the end of the two page discussion of phenomenology. Perhaps discussion is too mild a word for what can be more accurately described as a fulmination. It is clearly intended to tell people what Kelly thinks, but I believe it tells much more about *him* in its tone and wording than he was ever aware of.

Firstly, the section started out by referring to the "phenomenological view". By the time he has elaborated its shortcomings in the ways already mentioned, it becomes, without any explanation of the transition, "extreme existentialism". Only a nearly complete unfamiliarity with the varieties of phenomenological positions would enable him to make this shift, the effect of which is to narrow down phenomenology to one of its sub-categories— existentialist literature, and stories are told (D. Bannister, personal communication) of Kelly rushing to attend a lecture on existentialism just to see why it was that some people had labelled him as one. Finding the lecture nearly incomprehensible he concluded that the label was misapplied.

Since attendance at the odd lecture would not in any case enable him to understand a quite unfamiliar and literally foreign philosophy, it seems reasonable to suggest that Kelly knew nothing more of existentialism than the popular stereotype to which Satre has given the appropriately superficial title, "the existentialism of clothes". As James Edie puts it:

"The word 'existentialism' has retained a meaning in American usage which it has practically ceased to have in Western Europe; it is associated with certain beatnik-like phenomena, with cliches about the absurdity of life and despair;

in short it evokes what Sartre is said one day to have called 'l'existentialism vestimentaire' " (Edie, 1964).

Elsewhere in this same review of recent work in phenomenology Edie points out what a slight influence the European phenomenological tradition had exercised on American philosophy, although he detects a subtle change at the time of writing. Judging by the number of publications appearing since 1964, Edie detected, and contributed to, the beginnings of a considerable upsurge of interest in phenomenology, but all this came too late for Kelly.

In the field of psychology, as distinct from philosophy, the situation would be rather similar. Gordon Allport, the great American registrar of personality theories did not mention existentialism in his 1937 book. References gradually appear in the later books until in 1955 with the publication of "Becoming" he appears willing to consider the existentialist movement as bringing a "needed blood transfusion" to personality theories. Allport's own concept of "propriate striving" or "becoming" is similar in some respects to the existentialist conception of man as projecting his future. The most interesting feature of this gradual acceptance of existentialism by Allport is the way in which he attempts to filter out the more radical and disturbing qualities of the European theory. He does this by calling the European theory "pessimistic" and suggesting that the pessimism can be attributed to the influence of sociocultural factors on personality theories:

"When life is a hard struggle for existence, and when, as in war-torn Europe there appears to be 'no exit' (Sartre), then personalities do in fact grow tense and develop a heavier sense of duty than of hope. In America, on the contrary, where the search for a rich, full life suffers fewer impediments, we expect to find a more open, gregarious, trusting type of personality" (Allport, 1955).

I find this idealization of American society very difficult to accept, particularly as Allport's theory is so much a reflection of it. He seems to use sociocultural analysis as a way of rejecting the unwelcome aspects of existentialism, not as a means of criticising his own theory on grounds that it is too optimistic. His sociocultural analysis does not differentiate the effects of social factors on personality *theories*, from their effects on persons; nor does he admit this social influence for long before cancelling it out with the dubious assertion that "it is equally true that we are all rebels, deviants and individualists". In sum, his comments on existentialism are relatively superficial, using and helping to perpetuate the "despair" stereotype.

The other possible local source of information on existentialism that Kelly might have used is the small group of American personality theorists which has been characterized in a very loose sense as existentialist: Carl Rogers, Abraham Maslow and Rollo May. The kind of information gained from this group would not have helped him very much since they too borrow very selectively from the European sources: heavily influenced by Kurt

Goldstein, they stress "self-actualization" as a basic motive and "human encounter" in the therapeutic situation, but their philosophies are only varieties of Oriental mysticism, Nature mysticism or humanism of a quasi-religious kind.

What Kelly does share with the American "existentialists" is a vague optimism about where man is going. It is vague because as usual it is not clearly specified as something desirable in its own right but as something more desirable than the (stereotyped) others can offer:

> "Perhaps if I were a Euclidean psychologist, sharply dividing events into those which do happen before my eyes and those which can never happen, I would be overwhelmed by a growing awareness of man's failure to reach any conclusions about nature. I might then be tempted to throw in the sponge and concede that the lines of human construction and outer reality can never, never touch.
> But I prefer the more cosmic view which supposes these two progressions may ultimately join hands, though that auspicious moment may prove to be an infinity of years away" (Kelly, 1969).

Again and again Kelly uses this technique, which incidentally is commonly used by Allport, of setting up the "wicked other", whose extreme position can be understood as socially determined, or consequent on some other external influence such as the constraints of linguistic forms. The others are simply explained away. Kelly's "explanation" of existentialism suggests that they are disillusioned naïve realists, who despaired of finding ultimate truth and who now fall into the trap to which their disappointment predisposes them. If they had looked for new ways of questioning they would not have been so disappointed. Kelly adds that he was himself such a man, but, "biography notwithstanding" he will choose to avoid the common mistake.

For a man who sees himself as a modest if audacious questioner, and for one who criticized the "global phraseologies" of the phenomenologists and existentialists, there are some sweepingly self-righteous assertions in these few sentences. I wonder why Kelly falls into such a style when dealing with these particular groups of personality theorists; unless he perceives them at some level of awareness as threatening. To turn his theory against him (and it is to his great credit that he positively asks for this to be done even if he did not do it), is it that he dimly perceives in this work an impending change in his core role construct—Kelly, *the existentialist?*

Up to this point I have suggested that Kelly did not know much about phenomenology and existentialism; I have hinted that the stereotyped American view of existentialism available to him was a hindrance towards fuller knowledge and, finally, that Kelly may have had good psychological reasons for avoiding such knowledge as would have brought him an unwelcome identification with a group he regarded as despairing subjectivists.

All this is a kind of negative evidence which is relevant only to Kelly's denials that he is any such thing as a phenomenologist or existentialist, for these will carry less weight if it is established that he did not know what he was denying and if he can be shown to have had a psychological reason, in terms of his own theory, for avoiding the identification. Now I turn to some of the qualities of his theory which place him on common ground with just those people he seems most anxious to dissociate himself from.

The Reluctant Existentialist

Two surface similarities between personal construct theory and existentialism have already been noted: Kelly's attitude toward labels in general (not just his denial that he is an existentialist), and the importance he gives to a person's unique structuring of the world by impressing his perceptions upon it. These two points will be further substantiated, and some other similarities will be explored.

Kelly's conception of the other personality theories currently available stresses their inadequacy; their incapacity to deal with the creative human being in an explosively changing social and physical world. Not only does he complain about the static, deterministic nature of these inadequate theories, he also tries to explain why they have become what they are, the implication being that if he knows where the others have gone wrong he need not fall into the same mistake, or as he likes to say, same "manhole". He accounts for the present form of other personality theories by saying that they rest upon the logic of our times: they suffer from the limitations of inflexible categorization to which we have rarely given thoughtful consideration. The main task is to "break out of our categories" because

> " '. . . hardening of the categories', a common affliction among scientists, usually marks the end of the creative phase of a distinguished career" (Kelly, 1969).

But why did the categorical logic of our time come to dominate science? And here Kelly widens his scope even further: it is because Western thought has been influenced by the subject-predicate form of the language on which it is built. He refers to Korzybski's book "Science and Sanity" which seemed to suggest that the words men use hold the structure of their thought, and he says that the "dogmatism of subject-predicate language" is a feature of Western thought which has gone unchallenged for two thousand years.

There are three levels of assertion in his explanation. Firstly, that words hold the structure of men's thought; secondly, that the grammatical forms of languages influence the structure of thought; and thirdly, that knowledge in the Western world has been limited by both the foregoing factors. Having seen all this, Kelly will provide a way of breaking out from these linguistic and cultural restrictions on man's creativity. The audacity of this, is not in doubt, but it is doubtful whether he would dare to put it forward if he had any real acquaintance with the work that has gone into this general theme of the linguistic and cultural limitations on thought (cf. Hotopf, 1965), or the related sociological theme usually called the "sociology of knowledge" (Mannheim, 1952). All three levels of Kelly's explanation depend on assertions that, on the evidence available, can only be made with the greatest caution and in a much qualified form.

Yet Kelly, in his concern for the "sickness of the language" (cf. Murdoch, 1967) brings to mind none other than Sartre and more particularly, Roquentin, the hero of Sartre's novel "The Nausea". Roquentin, who, according to Iris Murdoch, might be taken as "an aspect of an immature Sartre" saw the world breaking through the labels and categories that had so long served to order and structure it in men's minds. The words, labels and slogans will no longer go out from the man and rest upon the object. The world has become separated from a language that cannot deal with or contain the overflowing and frightening reality.

If Roquentin's response was to seek a literary solution by writing a novel in which he hoped the words would follow with the beautiful order of notes in a melody, Sartre's mature response was to take a new grasp of the sick language; not to deplore its inadequacy or play with its aesthetic forms, but to use it actively and committedly in the fight for new meanings and new human values. So many of these characteristics have a clear counterpart in Kelly's personal construct theory. The very idea of a construct, as distinct from a concept, is that it introduces criteria of relevance *and responsibility* (Kelly, 1969). Actions can only be subjected to moral judgment in the context of what a man might have done, as a field of choice around what he did, and perceptions, being selective, negate certain possibilities. We are, then, responsible for our construing since this is the formative structure of our choosing. Thus Kelly shares with the existentialists the theme of "responsibility". He is conscious that it is a big burden for a scientist to carry and that there is "little elsewhere in science that goes as far as that". But he does not seem to see the contradiction of telescoping perception and action in this way, and of subjecting both to moral judgment. It assumes that perceptions *dictate* actions whereas a constructive alternativist would surely say that perceptions explore ranges of possible interpretations of a situation. Only the extreme behaviourist, an absolutist (and this creature Kelly does not think to be anything more than a reification of the experimentalists' abstractions) would need to carry *such* a load of responsibility. The interesting point is, however, that Kelly attracts just the criticism which is commonly directed at the existentialists—that they put too much responsibility on the individual person.

Another similarity between personal construct theory and existentialism is the paramount importance attached to human experience, and particularly to the need for radical examination of it.

> "The task of man, emerging psychologically in this Twentieth Century, as never before, is to pull his innermost experience apart and then to put it together again . . ." (Kelly, 1969).

And again, in Kelly's essay on Mozart's "Don Giovanni,"

> ". . . imagination put to the test, becomes the key to realization. The world of reality has no other key. Nor does truth have any other access" (Kelly, 1969).

Further similarities are: the rejection of a disease entity, classificatory approach to mental abnormality, the adoption of a spiraliform model for interpersonal perception (Kelly, 1955), and the rejection of motivation as a misleading concept in psychology (Kelly, 1969). On this last point, and because it is crucial in relation to the human freedom and responsibility which is fundamental to both approaches, Merleau-Ponty might be allowed to speak:

> "Once I am free, I am not to be counted among things, and I must then be un-interruptedly free. . . . if, as is often said, motives incline me in a certain direction, one of two things happens: either they are strong enough to force me to act, in which case there is no freedom, or else they are not strong enough, and then freedom is complete, and as great in the worst torments as in the peace of one's home. We ought, therefore, to reject not only the idea of causality, but also that of motivation."
> "The alleged motive does not burden my decision; on the contrary my decision lends the motive its force" (Merleau-Ponty, 1962).

And finally, if it is felt that the element of anguish, which goes along with freedom and responsibility in existentialist thought, is entirely missing from Kelly, consider this passage:

> "Thus, the experience of tragedy, and not the sense of certainty, is the basis of all hope, and is indeed the most essential step in the bold pursuit of better things" (Kelly, 1969).

On just one occasion that I am aware of, Kelly shows some willingness to stand on existentialist ground. In the paper he presented in 1964 at Brunel College, [subsequently published in the *Bulletin of the British Psychological Society* and now in Kelly (1969)] he explores the notions of personal involvement, and commitment. Possibly his entry into Britain, the lion's den of logical positivism and "Darwinian" psychology, brings out the fighting existentialist in him, but even then he proves to be a clumsy ally of existentialism and eventually backs off from the identification.

Firstly he explores personal involvement: it takes courage to wholly involve oneself in therapeutic or research undertakings—to risk one's constructs in new experience—but it is essential for anything other than "academic" theory. A researcher should put himself in the concrete circumstances he wishes to investigate, otherwise he cannot hope to conceptualize their real dimensions. Kelly then mentions his visit to Haiti where the smell of the Port au Prince market brought poverty stricken people into "deep perspective". This kind of involvement:

". . . if I understand them correctly, is what the existentialists mean when they talk about being 'in the world' " (Kelly, 1969).

Once again a popular and exotic image is associated with existentialism, and then to cap this he manages to confuse going out to see how others live, with the technical but clear sense in which existentialists use the term "being-in-the-world".

Secondly he looks at "commitment": he accepts that committing oneself to a course of action involves personal aggression and the risk of being seriously wrong. This is existentialism all right; but then he tries to outbid them:

"But even commitment is not enough; and here we part company with the existentialists. There must be appraisal and reconstruction. A commitment is not a blind undertaking—at least it should not be" (Kelly, 1969).

Again the popular stereotype: existentialists are committed to a doctrine; they are engaged in a blind undertaking which rules out appraisal and reconstruction (as usual there are no references or quotations to support his assertions), and he then goes on to describe his own theory of continuous reappraisal and reconstruing, in terms which echo the existentialists in almost every detail. The pity is that, by reading commitment in this superficial way, as a commitment to revolution or some political programme, Kelly misses another sense of the word which might please him greatly, namely, Merleau-Ponty's sense, which brings out the meaning of commitment to what Kelly would call the "Human enterprise".

"I do not understand the gestures of others by some act of intellectual interpretation; communication between consciousnesses is not based on the common meaning of their respective experiences, for it is equally the basis of that meaning. The act by which I lend myself to the spectacle must be recognized as irreducible to anything else. I join it in a kind of blind recognition which precedes the intellectual working out and clarification of the meaning" (Merleau-Ponty, 1962).

Personal Construct Theory

In the earlier sections of this essay I have tried to follow George Kelly's exhortation to "construe alternatively" views and theories with which we are confronted. By picking out the weakest points of his theory and by interpreting every lapse of tone or style in the most unfavourable way I have attempted to show that he misunderstood much of what he criticized: so much so that his work can be most adequately identified by reference to an area of theory that he was amused, if not reluctant, to be associated with— existentialism. But since it is possible in principle to distinguish a theory from either the way in which a theorist comes to hold it (a reason for rejecting the argument *ad hominem*), or from the theorist's own misunderstandings of the implications of his theory, the question of evaluation of personal construct theory still remains. What then is the value of this theory?

Some preliminary distinctions must precede a clear answer. Firstly, as to the kind of theory Kelly presents, it is not so much a set of assertions from which falsifiable implications can be drawn as a recommendation in general terms for the most fruitful way of regarding men (as scientists). Like many other successful practitioners he attempted, later in his life, to give an orderly exposition of his assumptions, aims and practices, and the result is something closer to a philosophy of life than to a theory in any strict sense. (When the theory is called "Kellyism" by its detractors this, presumably, is what they are getting at.) This means that two kinds of evaluation are possible, the first a strictly logical and empirical assessment, the second a more general appraisal of the kind of "philosophical" approach he recommends. Of course the two are not completely separable, although they can be distinguished, but Kelly's formal style fights against the ambiguity of the content: in a sense he invites strict evaluation without providing the means to it.

Take as an example the sociality corollary which reads "To the extent that one person construes the construction processes of another, he may play a role in a social process involving the other". Although it appears to contain a predictive assertion it is actually tautologous since construing the construction processes of another, or taking the attitude of the other as G. H. Mead might have expressed it, is itself the definition of a role-based social process. Then again, by including the quantitative phrase "to the extent that" Kelly implies that full participation in a social process involves complete ability to construe the construction processes of another. This is clearly not so because many social processes depend on one person *not* being able to construe the construction processes of the other—for example, the various non-reciprocal and sometimes exploitative relationships, legal and illegal, which are commonly found in the social processes which now exist: doctor-patient, confidence trickster and victim, dictatorial ruler and duped subject. However undesirable some of these relationships may be they cannot simply be defined out of the social process. There is another limitation of the corollary, which is that it invites analysis of social processes in terms of individual meeting individual. Even G. H. Mead was aware of the limitations of this one-to-one model and tried to overcome these limitations by use of his concept of the "generalized other", a concept that, for all its inadequacies, certainly brings out the fact that a person meets single others, groups of others, a society and a culture, all in the same social process.

What is missing from the sociality corollary is an awareness of *the social* as a distinctive set of normative pressures or external constraints, on the role player. This is not to propose a flight into the "oversocialized" conception of role where persons are the passive incumbents of fully prescribed roles. For it is easy to see that people help to create their roles. The aim is rather to avoid the other individualistic extreme:

"At the other extreme, a role may be seen as the personal creation of the individual who occupies it, a product of both personal and social forces (Kelly, 1955). This extreme psychological position throws out role as an explanatory concept. The way the person behaves *is* the role. Expectations may develop, but there is no normative element; deviation from the role merely changes its characteristics. The role of the wife in the Davis household is merely another name for Mrs. Davis's behaviour, providing a satisfactory concept only for those unable to recognize a tautology" (Dornbusch, 1967).

The individualist tenor of Kelly's theory shows through when he says of a person's constructs, "He devises them." Surely it is closer to the truth to say that constructs are for the most part given to people—even imposed upon them—through socialization. (Indeed, Kelly implies a very widespread imposition of this kind when he attributes the inadequacy of most available psychological theories to the subject-predicate form of Western language).

Pushing even further towards the kind of individualist subjectivism of which he accused certain nameless existentialists, Kelly asserts that constructs are "imposed *upon* events". In arguing against an extreme view he has shot over to the opposite extreme.

One thing might have saved Kelly from the extreme individualism of his position; that is an ability to see the social process in a less benign way. He underestimates the extent to which conflict, domination and alienation are a "normal" part of the social processes we know, even though they may not be a necessary part of social processes we might imagine or work towards. If he had enjoyed any closer contact with the work of Hegel, Marx and the existentialists he would have produced, in my view, truer models of the psychological social processes he wanted to explain, and this is my justification for pushing him hard towards these unwelcome colleagues. Without the constraint of this more negative view of the social process Kelly produces descriptive models which are useful for describing a utopian creature—the man as scientist, testing, modifying and elaborating his constructs; communicating with and understanding others by construing their construction processes—but he misses those very powerful psychological and social forces which make men terrorize, dominate, misunderstand, mystify and kill each other.

As a final example of the looseness and ambiguity of the actual content of the theory take the "choice corollary". (Incidentally this concern for choice is another feature in common with existentialism.) When first formulated this read, "A person chooses for himself that alternative in a dichotomized construct through which he anticipates the greater possibility for the extension and definition of his system." In 1966 the words "extension and definition" were altered to "elaboration". The first version could be understood as highly ambiguous since extension of a construct system might be the very opposite of making it more definite. However, the revised wording only saves the internal consistency of the corollary at the cost of greater generality and ambiguity. It is, finally, so general an assertion that it is difficult to see ' what evidence could possibly be brought against it, even though a more pessimistic interpretation of people's choice-making seems equally plausible. Could it not be said, for example, that many people give such priority to short term accuracy in anticipating events that they are continually falling into crises of reconstruing brought about by their blindness to the longer term patterning of events? Although this is only slightly more specific as an assertion it does move towards testability.

To sum up this attempt to test the theory in a strict way, by forcing through its logical implications and pointing to inaccuracies in its basic assumptions, I think it does not stand up at all well to such rigorous testing. It appears to be a set of corollaries with varying degrees of specificity and varying degrees of accuracy but with very little in the way of connective assertions which relate the corollaries to each other. As such it is the ideal framework for "accumulative fragmentalism" that is, for an accumulation of illustrative, demonstrative, validating evidence around single corollaries without much possibility of crucially testing the basic theory, and from reviews of experimental work so far published this pattern does seem to be emerging (Bonarius, 1965; Bannister and Mair, 1968).

If one may dare to *label* Kelly's theory I would suggest that it be called "metaphysical or programmatic". Such a description would take account of the untestable aspects of the theory at the same time as acknowledging its real value as a guide to research, for, as Cohen (1968) has said, such theories may be "highly suggestive".

The possibility of a second kind of evaluation of Kelly still remains. Reading his "theory" in much more general terms, what is it that he is recommending as a line of approach to the study of personality? Is it likely to be productive?

Within the confines of a formal specification, Kelly draws attention to certain distinctive qualities of the human being which had long been noticed by the phenomenologists: (that man has a sense of time, that he is open to the future and projects himself towards it, that he uses his experience as a unique base from which to construe future possibilities, and that he enjoys a remarkable degree of flexibility in dealing with events) Kelly's determination to put these human qualities at the very centre of his theory, rather than try to build a model out of the non-human contexts of animal behaviour, is rare enough in American social sciences to provide a useful counterweight to the predominant style of a natural science approach. That he should manage this without the backing of an alternative tradition is a tribute to his enormous bravery and practicality. Not knowing an alternative, Kelly invented his own. His quality of constructive innocence is just this willingness to look for himself and say what he sees, and the peculiar tactics he uses to escape a label are attempts to preserve the purity of his vision. The price of this fresh individuality of his approach is a failure to link up with and benefit from the work of other theorists who have solved many of Kelly's problems without needing to adopt his extreme position. The best example of this is the phenomenology of Alfred Schutz.

Schutz's language bears an uncanny resemblance to personal construct theory. For example:

"The individual's common-sense knowledge of the world is a system of constructs of its typicality" (Schutz, 1953).

Schutz gave clear expression to "constructive alternativism":

"If I assert with respect to an element of the world as taken for granted: 'S is p', I do so because under the prevailing circumstances I am interested in the p-being of S, disregarding as not relevant its being also q and r" (Schutz, 1953).

He dealt with motivation not by rejecting the concept but by differentiating "because" motives (causal in form), from "in-order-to" motives (intentional in form). He provided a model of interaction which takes full account of the social constraints and context of the action and particularly of the presence of language as a social institution. Finally he solved the problem of the social scientist's relation to his subject by differentiating scientific accounts from common-sense accounts, not by promoting every man to the status of scientist.

The prospects of advancing our understanding of social action in fully human terms are very good if we can now make the links with phenomenology that Kelly was unable to make.

There is one last label that I would risk putting on Kelly's theory. Is it not an ideology? As MacIntyre has said, "A successful ideology tends to make true that which it asserts to be true", and Kelly does so much want men to be more like (good) scientists, more rational, more human. We have heard so much in recent years of possible consequences of the behaviourist programme —"The danger is not that it is true, but that it may become true"—so perhaps it is not too fanciful to see in personal construct theory a counter-ideology. If this is so then merely by realizing it we are insulated against the self-deception that goes with perpetuating an ideology. What is more we can see the implicit values that much more clearly, and recognize that Kelly was trying to create for his fellow men a human science. I know of no more admirable intellectual aim.

And finally I suggest that Kelly in trying to look without preconceptions at human experience, exemplified the phenomenological method which is the basis of existentialism, even though we can see with hindsight how many mistakes he made, and how nearly inevitable these mistakes were, given the intellectual environment in which he worked.

References

Allport, G. W. (1955). "Becoming", Yale University Press, New Haven, Conn.

Bannister, D. and Mair, J. M. M. (1968). "The Evaluation of Personal Constructs", Academic Press, London and New York.

Bannister, D. (1969). Personal communication.

Bonarius, J. C. J. (1965). Research in the Personal Construct Theory of George A. Kelly, *In* "Progress in Experimental Personality Reseach", (Maher, B., ed.), Vol. 2, pp. 1–46, Academic Press, New York and London.

Cohen, P. S. (1968). "Modern Social Theory", W. H. Heinemann, London.

Dornbusch, S. M. (1967). *In* "The Development of Sex Differences" (Maccoby, E. E., ed.), Tavistock Press, London.

Edie, J. M. (1964). Recent Work in Phenomenology. *Am. Phil. Quart.* **1**, 2.

Freud, S. (1932). "New Introductory Lectures on Psychoanalysis", Hogarth Press, London.

Hotopf, W. H. N. (1965). "Language Thought and Comprehension", Routledge and Kegan Paul, London.

Kelly, G. A. (1955). "The Psychology of Personal Constructs", Norton, New York.

Kelly, G. A. (1969a). "Clinical Psychology and Personality: the Selected Papers of George Kelly" (Maher, B. A., ed.), John Wiley and Sons, New York.

Kelly, G. A. (1970). "A brief introduction to personal construct theory", *in* "Perspectives in Personal Construct Theory" (Bannister, D., ed.), Academic Press, London and New York.

MacIntyre, A. (1967). The Idea of a Social Science, *Proc. Aristotelian Soc.* **LXI**.

Mannheim, K. (1952). "Essays on the Sociology of Knowledge", Routledge and Kegan Paul, London.

Merleau-Ponty, M. (1962). "The Phenomenology of Perception", Routledge and Kegan Paul, London.

Murdoch, I. (1967). "Sartre: Romantic Rationalist", Fontana Books, New York.

Popper, K. (1957). "The Poverty of Historicism", Routledge and Kegan Paul, London.

Rickman, H. P. (1968). "Understanding and the Human Studies", W. H. Heinemann, London.

Schutz, A. (1953). Common Sense and Scientific Interpretation of Human Action. *Phil. Phenomenol. Res.* **XIV**, I.

Winch, P. (1958). "The Idea of a Social Science", Routledge and Kegan Paul, London.

Words and Worlds

Grahame Leman

George Alexander Kelly, in the first chapter of his "The Psychology of Personal Constructs," suggested that it might turn out to be more useful to talk about people as if they were scientists than to go on talking about them as if they were something quite different from scientists (adjustable machines, perhaps, or general systems).

What I want to do here, is (1) to accept this encouragingly parsimonious suggestion, and (2) then to take off from it in a direction rather different from the direction Kelly himself took.

In describing scientists, for the purpose of encouraging us to talk about people as if they were scientists, Kelly affected to swallow whole the going description of the characteristically scientific things scientists were supposed to do: he assumes for the purposes of his argument, that scientists are people who seek to predict and control the course of events; who, to this end, hold and up-date theories, frame and test hypotheses, run experiments, and judicially weigh experimental evidence.

For the purposes of my own present argument, I shall assume that the characteristically scientific activity is an operation with language, or occasionally *on* language; and that the scientist's most important problems have to do with the relationship between language and extralinguistic reality, between what is said to be so and what is so when nobody is talking about it. When I have explained more or less what I mean by that, I shall then pursue my imitation of Kelly by suggesting that it might be helpful to talk about people, or to talk about some people some of the time, as if they were scientists in my present sense.

Given current concern with the information explosion, pressures to publish or perish, and so on, it should not really be necessary to point out that most scientific work is work with language; but it does indeed seem to be necessary. The descriptions of characteristically scientific activity most often encountered, suggest either that the scientist is set apart because he shoves his hard nose into tangible things on the near side of language (he observes, he experiments, ideally with the help of instruments) or that the scientist is set apart because he applies his honed mind to *in*tangible things on the far

133

side of language (numbers, invariants, propositions, fields, neutrinos, behaviour, and so on.) Sometimes the descriptions suggest that the real scientist is set apart from the less real and from everybody else because he does *both:* because he shuttles back and forth between the tangibles on the near side of language (observations) and the *in*tangibles on the far side of language (theories, hypotheses, deductions, inductions, reductions, demonstrations, and the like). The language in the middle, between the tangibles on the near side and the intangibles on the far side, is customarily left out of the accounts. If we had nothing but these commonly encountered descriptions to go by, we would have to suppose that it really is possible (say) to observe without using language, to hypothesize without using language, to move back and forth between hypothesis and observation without moving through language: all without making use of systems of sentences, composed of words, numbers, logical particles and other symbols and signs, and ordered by some kind of grammar.

Such commonly encountered descriptions of characteristically scientific activity sometimes seem to some people to have a mildly programmatic or public relations flavour, as if they had been drafted by a committee of experimentalists, a committee of theorists, and a committee of grandees capable of moving freely from theory to experiment and (chastened) back to theory, all in hot competitive pursuit of funds, floor-space, machine time, or glory. An ordinarily sceptical outsider, with some experience of eavesdropping in the laboratory or intruding at the symposium (especially when people are making real or pseudo science on their feet) will often feel that the neat bisection of the universe into hard tangibles on the near side of language and high (or deep) *in*tangibles on the far side of language is rather too tidy to be altogether true. He will want to insist that language is mixed into experience on the near side and into thought on the far side, even perhaps to suggest that scientists are very likely to get mixed up if they avert their eyes from the immixture of language into experience and the immixture of language in thought. What I am going to talk about next, in that order, is precisely (i) the immixture of language into experience, and (ii) the immixture of language in thought about experience.

Perhaps the best way to get into a useful discussion of the immixture of language into experience, is to begin by introducing (to anyone who has not yet come across it) the important notion of *terministic screens* introduced by the American generalist Kenneth Burke (1966). Burke was once shown some photographic prints made from colour separation negatives, of the kind used in process engraving or photographic astronomy. These, of course, are made by using narrow-pass colour filters (or screens) to prevent light of any colour but one reaching the negative, and a set of prints made from a set of colour separation negatives consists of a number of *different* pictures of the *same* object: for instance, a monochrome photograph of a red rose made through a narrow-pass red filter will show in the print a pale flower with dark leaves, and substitution of a green filter for the red (without any other change in the conditions) will give a print showing a dark flower with pale leaves; similarly, a print from a telescopic plate of the planet Mars, made through a filter which passes only infrared light, will show the relatively smaller disc of the solid Martial globe, with surface detail, while substitution of a filter which passes only ultraviolet light (without any other change in the conditions) will give a print showing the relatively larger disc of the Martial atmosphere, with no detail. Burke suggests that the ordered sets of terms used by scientists and others act in much the same way as these colour filters or screens: rather as a red filter stands between the object and the film, allowing only red light to pass through, so the *terministic screen* constituted by an ordered set of terms stands between observer and observed, preventing him from "seeing" most of what is there to be seen and allowing him to "see" only a small part of what is there to be seen.

One of Burke's own examples of a terministic screen in operation is especially apt and illuminating (Burke, 1966). While working on the use of language in St Augustine's *Confessions*, he happened to read a paper by the child psychologist John Bowlby, called "The Nature of the Child's Ties to its Mother". In this paper, Bowlby describes observations of what he calls "five instinctual responses of infants", constitutive of reciprocal social relations between child and mother, namely: crying, sucking, smiling, clinging, and following. Burke noticed that Augustine uses, in describing what small children do, one term not used by Bowlby: *resting*, to describe a small child resting in the mother's arms, or on her lap. This is evidently just the sort of thing Bowlby was ostensibly looking for, something importantly constitutive of the mother-child relationship: it is strange that he did not see it. If we imagine two research assistants, one briefed by Augustine, the other by the Bowlby of this paper, both observing the same mother and child, we have reason to fear that Augustine's assistant would "observe" a lot of resting, whereas Bowlby's assistant would "observe" none: perhaps, because of a difference in the layout of record sheets (or more likely because of a difference in something in the minds of the two assistants corresponding to the layouts of the record sheets). Click Augustine's terministic screen into its place in the apparatus between your ears, and you see small children "resting in" their mothers; substitute Bowlby's terministic screen for Augustine's, and you see no such thing.

Before Bowlby started this particular series of observations of small children with their mothers, he may (or will) have had very much in mind more than one problem involving use of language. He may have had to write up proposals, in order to get permissions and resources for the work.

For the work, he may have had to specify routines in writing, provide for recording observations in writing in a standard form, and so on: so that assistants or remote collaborators would know just what to do, and so that the work could be repeated as required by sceptical strangers. He will have had in mind the limits on the kinds of papers he wished to write and publish after the observations had been completed. His attempts to solve these problems involving the use of language may (or will) have determined the precise character of his terministic screen. For instance, the little phrase "instinctual responses" suggests decisions (among others) at least about an audience and about a method, or the superficies of a method. It suggests choice of an audience which prefers its psychology assimilated to biology, rather than (say) to philosophy: this is not to say that Bowlby's relationship to his chosen audience is necessarily simple or supine; the British Ambassador in Paris may talk French without being a Frenchman; and there are those who refuse to believe that people are human unless you can show, precisely by assuming that they are not human, that they must behave as if they were. For method, it suggests a concentration on *automatic* responses, and a concentration on *responses* to something, calculated to make observation, recording, and reporting as clear cut and simple as possible. Bowlby's five "instinctual responses" (crying, smiling, sucking, clinging, following) are convenient: we need make no doubtful guesses about what is going on inside the child's head; it is impossible to confuse one response with another of the five; and the child is either making one of the five responses or not. Augustine's *resting* is very much less convenient. If a child is crying, it is crying; if a child is smiling, it is smiling; but, if a child is doing nothing, what kind of nothing is it doing? and how can you be sure? Bowlby's responses can be seen as responses *to* something the mother does, so that there can be manifest stimulus and response dialogues between mother and child: the child cries, the mother opens her dress, the child sucks and smiles; the mother goes off to do the washing up, the child cries and follows, clinging to her leg while she stands at the sink, and so on; but, if mother and child are both doing nothing, who is responding to whom? to what that who does? and how do you know? Some people would argue, that a small child can "tell" from subtle changes in his mother's body (musculature more or less tense, and so on) whether or not she is relaxed, and that the mother can "tell" the same thing about the child: when the child is "resting in" the mother, a form of non-verbal dialogue may in fact be going on; each "mind" keeps "asking" the other body if all is well, and each body keeps "answering" (simply by not being tense) that everything is fine. A small child's "resting in" its mother, understood in this way, would be well suited indeed to Augustine's metaphorical use of it, when he writes afterwards of "resting in the Lord"; and it is hard to see that it can be any less instinctual, any less an affair of responses, than Bowlby's pentad of crying, smiling, sucking, clinging, and following; all we can say, is that this kind of dialogue between a small child and its mother would be relatively much more difficult to observe, record, report, and write about without muddles and misunderstandings. If we decide to rule out Augustine's resting, it will not be because resting is known not to happen, nor because resting is not the sort of thing a reputable scientist may traffic in, but rather simply because (in the context, including the context of situation) resting is very difficult to talk about without getting into one or more kinds of trouble.

On an earlier page, with malice aforethought, I included *behaviour* (along with numbers, invariants, propositions, fields, neutrinos, and so on) in a list of examples of those interestingly *in*tangible things that are accessible, apparently, only to the honed mind of the scientist. This may look like wilful clowning with paradox: for many people are tempted to argue, that *behaviour* (a philosopher kicking a stone, for example, or his wife) must make better hanging evidence than can anything like the rest mass of the photon; and simply because behaviour is tangible (or otherwise sensible), whereas anything like the rest mass of the photon is no more than a logical construction or other instrumentally useful myth. According to such people, I may ask my witnesses whether or not Professor Hardnose kicked a stone (or Mrs. Hardnose) outside the Corrupt University computer centre on Saint Swithin's Day, 1984; but I may *not*, because it "calls for a conclusion of the witness", ask whether or not Professor Hardnose was refuting Berkeley (or "really" kicking the Vice-Chancellor of Corrupt University) on that occasion. But, as I shall show, *behaviour* is itself an instrumentally useful myth, on a par with the rest mass of the photon, and calls as loudly as the act of refuting Berkeley for a conclusion of the witness.

It is customary in philosophical anthropology to distinguish between the *motions* of matter and the *actions* of men, or (better) between the language of motion and the language of action. A stone falling through the air is matter in motion; Galileo rolling balls down inclined planes and timing their descents with a water clock, in a deliberate attempt to establish some of the laws of motion, is a man in action. We can say such things as a physicist would wish to say about the fall of the stone, entirely in the language of motion introduced by Galileo and refined by Newton; but we cannot say much to the purpose about what Galileo was doing (not even, if that happens to be what we want to say, that he was a fumbling pioneer of the hypothetico-deductive method), without using the language of action. Throughout the recorded history of thought (which goes back only five or six thousand years), there have been two perennial and opposed tendencies in description and explanation: one party tries to describe and explain motion in the language of action (the stone falls because it wants to, or because a God is pushing it, and so on); the other party tries to describe and explain action in the language of motion (by a happy chance, there happened to happen to the atoms constituting Galileo's inner economy such happenings as eventuated in the array of marks on paper that we call his "Dialogues on the New Sciences," helping to make the future safe for the pursuit rotor). In ages when the language of motion is more than ordinarily useful in its own proper sphere and sounds extraordinarily well at the important dinner tables, this second party is more than usually hot and noisy. The classic case history is that of the English natural philosopher Thomas Hobbes, who was born in the Spring of the year 1588 (prematurely, when his mother heard that the Spanish Armada was on its way) and lived in the first great age of the language of motion, opening with Copernicus and closing in Newton's synthesis. Hobbes worked with Sir Francis Bacon, visited Galileo in Italy, and was intermittently a member of Mersenne's brilliant circle in Paris, which included Descartes. Galileo had, of course, transformed the language of motion (or stood it on its head) by taking *motion* rather than *rest* for granted, so that it became possible to talk about the motions of bodies in the modern terms of inertia and acceleration.

Hobbes was moved by Galileo's achievements to try to explain everything that seemed to him to need explaining in the language of motion. He even made an interesting attempt to reconstruct geometry as a deductive science of motion (defining the circle, for instance, as the path traced by a moving point remaining equidistant from a fixed point). Since Hobbes' major interests were anthropological and political, rather than physical, he above all his contemporaries was especially eager to describe and explain human action in the language of motion: in 1637 (the year in which Descartes published his "Discourse on Method"), Hobbes projected a universal system of philosophy grounded in his theory of motion: the first part was to set out the metaphysics and physics of natural bodies; the second was to show how human feelings, sensations, thoughts, and desires could be explained in terms of motions inside the human body in contact with motions of other bodies; the third (and final) part was to show how society could be described and explained in terms of the motions of the individuals constituting society. In other words, his programme was to show that psychology can be constructed from physics, and then that anthropology (in the largest sense) and prescriptive political science can be constructed out of the psychology so constructed. Quaint survivals or revivals of the Hobbesian metaphysics and programme may, of course, be seen in the writings of Auguste Comte, John B. Watson, Clark L. Hull, and B. F. Skinner. It is perhaps worth remarking that Hobbes was a circle-squarer (his mathematics was not as good as he thought it was, and he made himself ridiculous trying to defend his circle-squarings in public controversy with Wallis and other able enemies in the

Royal Society, to which he did not belong): in Hobbes' day, of course, it was not as rash as it would be today to try to square the circle, since no rigorous proof that it could not be done had been discovered, and it was Hobbes' faulty proof that he had done it (rather than folly in trying to do it) that got him into trouble; but it makes me feel that, perhaps, trying to describe and explain the actions of men in the language of motion is a kind of circle-squaring, or something like trying to find an integral ratio of the diagonal to a side of the square. In any case, Hobbes never realized his programme in performance, and nor have the latterday Hobbesians. Hobbes, it is true, convinced himself, by uncontrolled metaphysical speculation, that everything everybody does *must* somehow be reducible to a very large number of extremely small motions inside each body; but he never went so far as to carry through a convincing reduction of action to motion in a case (say, the case of his friend Descartes' own impressive reduction of geometry to algebra). Our own Hobbesians, to be sure, have persuaded themselves, by recapitulating Hobbes' flights of metaphysical fancy, of the very same thing; but, again, none has yet published a convincing reduction of action to motion in a case (say, a case of goosing through a grant of funds for research, or a case of fixing a rival for a chair with tenure). To assert that action *is* motion, in the perennial and prevailing absence of such convincing reduction of cases of action to motion, is not physics: it is bad metaphysics (and worse metapsychology).

Behaviour is a fuzzy category of events or processes or something, lying vaguely between the category of motions and the category of actions. It is not difficult to describe the doings of Professor Hardnose in the pure language of motion: I can say, for instance, that S's right toe-cap moved from x_0, y_0, z_0, t_0 to x_1, y_1, z_1, t_1 and came into contact with a stone; this is clear enough as far as it goes, and of course very much the sort of thing that can be instrumentally recorded (say, by a suitable motion picture camera). Nor is it much more difficult to describe the same doings in the language of action: I may say, for example, that Professor Hardnose was discussing the ontological status of middle-sized, middle-distance physical objects with a group of students who had done a year of philosophy, and that he silently kicked the stone to remind them of Samuel Johnson (who kicked a stone when he was asked what he made of Berkeley, saying "I refute him thus"); this goes some way further; and it too is clear enough, always provided that I know how the conversation was going before the kick and how it went on after the kick, and always provided that both I and my audience know enough about the histories of the culture and subculture in which the Professor and his students swim, and enough about their biographies; but it is not, of course, the sort of thing that can be recorded by any instrument other than a whole, well-informed, well-read, and able person of the same culture and subculture.

What *is* impossibly difficult, is any attempt to use a language of behaviour which floats between the language of motion and the language of action: there is a tendency to do this, and simply because the language of motion seems to offer tangible (or otherwise sensible) data, while it is nevertheless impossible to say anything worth saying about the doings of human beings without shifting into the language of action. This floating vagueness inherent in the language of behaviour is distilled and immortalized in the priceless phrase *verbal behaviour:* anyone who says anything to anyone else is assuming common knowledge of the natural world, the culture and subculture, the social reality, and the language, of the context (including the context of situation) in which he is using the word, the sentence, or some longer segment of discourse; and if he is trying to persuade, or to produce action, rather than merely to convey information, he will be taking into account his own best estimate of the perceptions and purposes privy to others; so, if we want to define behaviour, for scientific purposes, as that and only that which can adequately be described in the pure language of motion, then anything anyone says (as distinct from any series of noises some S has been heard to emit) certainly cannot be counted into the data bank as behaviour. If, on the other hand, we want to define behaviour, for scientific purposes of a larger kind, so as to include human action (Galileo contriving and testing a new theory of motion, Descartes achieving the reduction of geometry to algebra, or Professor Hardnose refuting Berkeley by silently kicking a stone), then we should surely come right out and use the language of action; instead of covertly stretching our language of behaviour (of behaviour just now defined, for convenience in the gathering of data, *as motion*) and continuing to use it when we have shifted into talking about action (bad), so as to let it be understood, or to reassure ourselves, that we are somehow still *really* talking about motion (good). If we go on insisting, that refuting Berkeley *is* motion, then we may be smiled upon by the existentialists (they approve of people who lighten their darkness by rolling their own metaphysics from nothing); but frowning empiricists will go on asking, and waiting, to be *shown* (preferably some time before the great neurophysiological breakthrough of 2184) that it *is* more useful to talk about action in the language of motion than it is to talk about action in the language of action.

Proponents and exponents of the strategy of using the language of motion to describe and explain action do commonly, it is true, confuse this strategy with empiricism itself: it is supposed to be hard-headedly empirical to traffic in small motions, soft-headedly metaphysical or mystical to traffic in larger actions; but the appeal here is to a primitive empiricism, enshrining an unsatisfactory logic of bits; and motion men seem to be unaware that the resounding failure of primitive empiricism and its logic of bits has led to the rise of a chastened empiricism, grounded in a logic of wholes. A potted history of the decline and fall of primitive empiricism and the logic of bits may help to clear up this confusion of empiricism with the metaphysics of motion.

Common sense and formal science alike amount, for all practical purposes (and I do mean, practical) to a *prudential* use of language. Ordinary language or some special language is used as a working model of extralinguistic reality or of some part of extralinguistic reality: so that, instead of waiting to see what happens, we can foretell what *will* happen; or so that, instead of doing something to see what happens, we can foretell what *will* happen if we do it. So far as our working model is complete and accurate, just so far do we have a measure of control over our own fate and that of spaceship Earth. As matters stand, it must be said, the only reliable prediction we can make is that novel actions will have unforeseen consequences (as, notably, when we interfere with the ecology of the biosphere); nor is control strictly entailed by prediction (we seem to be able to predict the consequences of technological progress without being able to control them, and there is no reason why we should not become able to predict a collapse or explosion of our sun without becoming able to control it).

Naturally enough, this important prudential use of language gives rise to grave questions about the relationship between language and extralinguistic reality. Very early in the pre-history of man, hard practical problems must have thrust forward urgent questions about the *fit* of language to extra-linguistic reality, the accuracy of the working model: the sentence "tigers don't eat people", for example is a part of a working model of the ecological relations linking tigers and people, and it could seem usefully complete and accurate to a band of migrant hunters new to tiger country, who had not so far come across a crippled or senile tiger; an indigenous informant might offer, as a more complete and more accurate model, the sentence "tigers don't eat people unless they have become too slow to catch the animals they prefer to hunt and eat"; and the decision-maker of the immigrant band would be faced with the grave question, which of the two sentences is the more complete and the more accurate model? Such first-order questions about the fit of language to extra-linguistic reality in particular cases must very soon thrust forward serious second-order questions: the decision-maker will want to know how best to tackle and answer questions about the fit of language to extralinguistic reality, about the relative accuracy of competing word models of the world outwith words; and this, naturally, involves trying to be sure just what he means by "complete", "fit", and "accurate", by what tests he would accept a word model of the world as "complete", "accurate", or "a good fit", or reject it as "incomplete", "inaccurate", or "a bad fit".

There are, evidently enough, two possible ways in which a word model of the world could be a good fit to the world itself, in which language could be a good fit to extralinguistic reality: (i) bit by bit and bit *to* bit (bit of language to corresponding bit of the world); and (ii) as a whole, and whole to whole (whole language to whole world).

Now, at first sight it seems both obvious and also encouraging, that language and extra-linguistic reality fit one to the other bit by bit and bit to bit. It seems to be unmistakably given in our everyday experience *of* the world and in our everyday use of ordinary language *in* the world, that both world and language come in bits (or kinds of bits), and that to each bit (or kind of bits) of the world there corresponds a unique bit of language: thus, there are unique individuals in the world about us, and each unique individual has a corresponding unique name; there are different kinds of individuals in the world about us (for example, biological males and biological females of the human race), and each kind has a unique name (for instance, "men" and "women"). It seems as clearly given, that there are also kinds of words we use to fit the first kinds of words together according to rules (rules we may know, without being able to make them verbally explicit after the fashion of a grammarian or logician): such words as "not", "and", "or", "all", "some", and "none"; thus we know, for instance, that it makes sense to say "a person must be male *or* female", but not to say "a person must be male *or* male". Indeed, if we heard someone say "a borogove must be mimsy *or* mome", we might very well suppose that he was talking perfectly good sense about things we happened not to have heard of, whereas we could hardly suppose any such thing if we had heard him saying "a borogove must be mimsy *or* mimsy". All this looks encouraging, as well as obvious, because it suggests that the rules we use to fit together words of the first kind (with the help of words of the second kind) *represent ways in which the bits of the world fit together*, just as words of the first kind *represent bits of the world:* if this were only true (or if we had contrived, by improving language, to make it true), then we could foretell events we had not so far experienced by combining words of the first kind (representing bits of the world) according to the rules for combining words of the first kind with the help of words of the second kind (representing ways in which bits of the world do combine); and this, of course, would be *just* what we want for successfully prudential use of language.

Up to a point, this procedure does work quite well. The leader of the immigrant band new to tiger country, for example, might argue somewhat as follows after his first sight of a whole tiger: "This is a large animal with whiskers; some large animals with whiskers eat people; *ergo*, this large animal with whiskers may eat us". A defence of this reasoning (perhaps, to a scoffer, who wanted to save time by pushing on through the woods regardless) would be rather straightforward, and it might go something like this: "You will agree that x is an *animal,* because x goes on four legs and is covered with a coat of hair; you will agree that x is *large,* because x stands more than knee-high to a grown man at its fore-shoulders; you will agree that x *has whiskers,* because it has bristles sticking out to either side of its muzzle, just like the bristles we call 'whiskers' to be seen on the large animal y we have in our own country; you will agree that there are at least two kinds of large animal with whiskers in our own country, because we have both seen a sample of each kind more times than we can easily count; you will agree that some of these large animals with whiskers eat people, because we have both (and more than once) seen a person being eaten by each of the two kinds; surely, if *some* large animals with whiskers indubitably eat people, then this new large animal with whiskers x might very well eat us?—because it just can't make sense to say, in one breath, both that *some* large animals with whiskers eat people and also that *no* large animals with whiskers eat people". The leader, in making such a defence of his reasoning, is inviting the scoffer to check his prudential use of language in one or the other of only two ways, and not otherwise: (i) by checking *world-bound* bits of language (such as the words "large", "animal", and "whiskers"), bit by bit and bit *to* bit, against corresponding bits of the world (a bit of the world with four legs and fur, standing more than knee-high to a grown man, and with y-like bristles prominent at the muzzle); or (ii) by checking *rule-bound* bits of language (such as the words "some" and "no" meaning "none") against the rules for putting world-bound bits of language together with the help of rule-bound bits of language (for example, the rule that it makes no sense to say "*some x* is F and *no x* is F").

A checking procedure of this kind may be called *primitive empiricism.* The primitive empiricist holds that a bit of language is prudentially useful *only* if it is: (i) demonstrably world-bound (directly referable to sense experience of a bit of the world), or (ii) demonstrably rule-bound (tautologous), or (iii) demonstrably assembled according to the rules from world-bound bits and rule-bound bits only.

Early primitive empiricists (such as Locke and Hume) were interested chiefly in *very small world-bound bits of language,* typically single words. Confronted in their clinic by some suspect sentence, say the sentence "unicorns eat clover", they would characteristically embark on an empiricist critique of the sentence by fastening on the single word "unicorn": the sentence is prudentially useful, they would argue, only if there corresponds to the single word "unicorn" a bit of the world of which one could have immediate sense experience, and otherwise not—(and they would, of course, when being very thorough and explicit, apply the same test to the single word "eats" and to the single word "clover"). Their assumption was, to put it crudely but not unfairly: sentences are made of words; *ergo,* if your words are all right, then your sentences must be all right too. The unit of empirical significance, for them, is the *word*.

This word by word empiricist critique of language turned out to be unsatisfactory, for very many more good reasons than can be adduced in a short essay. One important reason is this: in real life (and no matter how you choose to understand or define the word "meaning"), a word standing alone has no definite meaning at all; a word has *a* meaning only in use, and *the* meaning varies with the use. Since you have to know what a word *says* is in the world, before you can satisfy yourself that there is a corresponding bit of the world of which you could have sense experience, this one good reason is alone enough to make the word by word empiricist critique of language unsatisfactory.

Later primitive empiricists (such as Bentham, Russell, the early Wittgenstein of the *Tractatus*, and the early Carnap) were, accordingly, chiefly interested in *rather larger world-bound bits of language*, typically whole sentences. Confronted in *their* clinic by the suspect sentence "unicorns eat clover", they would characteristically embark on an empiricist critique of the sentence, *not* by breaking it down into bits, but rather by expanding it into a longer and less confusing sentence or string of sentences: Russell, for example, would characteristically expand the sentence "unicorns eat clover" into some such string as "there exists at least one thing x, such that x is a white horse and x has one, long, spiraliform horn; and x eats clover". Wittgenstein, too, would at one time have argued that *all* suspect uses of ordinary language are in effect labour-saving abbreviations (arrived at by complicated and subtle "silent adjustments") of wholly explicit strings of sentences. Russell, if I read him aright, argues that the one-word sentence "Fire!" is really the name of a class of sentences, including such sentences as "There is a fire which will kill you if you don't get away from here" and "There is a fire here: you are needed to come and help put it out": evidently, such one-word sentences are useful only in a *non*-verbal "context of situation" (Malinowski*); this first class of sentences named by the one-word sentence "Fire!" could, without a context of situation, be mistaken for a second class of sentences so named, including such sentences as "Ten rounds rapid: fire!" But, by these later primitive empiricists, single words are, on the whole, seen as *names* of implicit sentences or strings of sentences. The assumption of the later primitive empiricists, to put it roughly but not too unjustly, was: prudential discourse is made of sentences; *ergo*, if your sentences are all right, then your discourse must be all right too. The unit of empirical significance is now the *sentence*.

This sentence by sentence empiricist critique of language didn't work out much better (or any better) than the word by word critique attempted by earlier primitive empiricists: again, for very many more good reasons than

* See Ogden and Richards (1949).

can be given in the compass of a short essay. One instructive instance is provided by the gallant failure of Rudolf Carnap: before Carnap came along, empiricists had merely *asserted* that you could build up a useful word model of the world, using only world-bound words or sentences, put together with the help of rule-bound words; no empiricist had gone so far as to try to demonstrate conclusively that this could indeed be done. Carnap tried to do just this in his *Der Logische Aufbau der Welt*, first published in 1928: he used only sentences that could be checked against immediate sense experience, fitting them together with the help of a rather rich logic (some empiricists would say, *too* rich: because he allowed himself to talk about classes, even classes of classes, as if they were "real" in the same way as a kickable stone is "real"—technically, he quantified over abstract entities); but, even with the help of this lush logic, he was unable even to show that the thing could in principle be done. In his later writings, Carnap does not even try to maintain that sentences about the world outwith language can be translated into less suspect sentences about immediate sense experience. However, since it is at all times regrettably easy to mistake programme for performance, there has lingered an unjustified dogma that this *is* possible (for some reason, especially among experimental psychologists). One major difficulty for the sentence by sentence empiricist critique of language, of course, is that even a *sentence* standing alone has no definite meaning at all: a sentence, a string of a few sentences, even a rather large segment of discourse (such as a chapter of a book, or a volume of an encyclopaedia), has *a* meaning only in a given verbal context and non-verbal "context of situation", and *the* meaning varies with the context. Such a sentence as "the rest mass of the photon is zero", for instance, has the meaning it has only as an integrally meshing component of the whole coherent system of sentences constituting our natural science in our corner of the natural universe. In the words of the Harvard philosopher Willard Van Orman Quine (1961, p. 42): "The unit of empirical significance is *the whole of science*."

The attempts of the earlier primitive empiricists to make the *single word* the unit of empirical significance were so unsatisfactory, that later primitive empiricists felt obliged to see what could be done by taking the *sentence* as the unit of empirical significance. It soon became clear, that the sentence is of very little more use for the purpose than the single word; and this suggested that language and extralinguistic reality, words and world, can after all *not* be fitted together bit by bit and separate bit of language to corresponding separate bit of the world. There remains, then, only the second of the two possibilities we started with: that language fits extralinguistic reality only as a whole, and whole language to whole world (*without* minute correspondences between separate bits of language and separate bits of the world). The resolute empiricist arrives in this way at something like Quine's position, that the unit of empirical significance is *the whole of science*—or, as I would personally prefer to say, the whole prudential language.

This shift in focus from bits to wholes, quite unlike the earlier shift in focus from very small bits of language (single words) to rather larger bits of language (sentences), is a marked change of direction rather than a mere change of pace. Empiricists who have found themselves obliged to make this change of direction, may be called *chastened empiricists*.

In philosophy, the change of direction from the line of march of primitive empiricism (enshrining a logic of bits) to the line of march of chastened empiricism (grounded in a logic of wholes) seems to have come about for purely technical reasons, internal to philosophy: primitive empiricism can't be made to make enough sense even in the philosopher's study, leaving aside the question, whether or not primitive empiricism works in practice as the best way of coping with the world outwith language.

At the same time, and interestingly, a comparable shift in focus from focus on bits to focus on the whole has been going forward outside the philosopher's study. Those who manage (or try to manage, or try to appear to be managing) the world outwith language, or chunks of that world, have for some time been obliged to try to think in terms of progressively larger volumes of space and progressively longer spans of time. For instance, many gaseous wastes of industry are distributed by the winds throughout the *whole* atmosphere of spaceship Earth and remain afloat in it, neither falling to the ground nor escaping into space, so that what comes out of the chimneys in Sheffield or Pittsburgh affects the *whole* world, not just Yorkshire or Pennsylvania; some of these wastes (carbon dioxide, for instance) build up cumulatively in the atmosphere, and (if we go on as we now go) the atmosphere will be so changed in composition that consequent changes in the secular climate will eventually ensue, with such further consequences as the melting of all the ice around the two poles—which may be expected to raise the mean sea level enough to drown all the major cities of the world, along with a large part of the fertile and populous lowlands. It is no longer quite as easy as it was to argue, without fear of contradiction (save by negligible cranks), that a man or woman suffering from tunnel-vision complicated by extreme short-sightedness is *therefore* admirably and usefully hard-headed and down-to-earth: unless, of course, you want to argue only, that such people make more tractable liveware.

The whole, bitty, language of primitive empiricism itself may function (and commonly does function) as a *universal terministic screen*. The appropriate analogy here is the half-tone screen used in making engravings for letterpress printing, from continuous tone originals (such as wash drawings and photographs). The half-tone screen is a transparent glass screen engraved with a grid of fine lines, which is interposed between the continuous tone original on the copyboard and the plate in the process camera, in such a way that the image of the continuous tone original is coded into a pattern of dots of only one tone and of varying sizes, ordinarily spaced at equal intervals of around sixty dots to the linear inch. In newspaper reproduction especially, the range of tones apparent in the final printed picture on the newspaper page (compared with the range of tones apparent in the original photograph) is drastically compressed: a photographer working for newspapers must bear in mind, when he is deciding how to interpret the subject before his camera, that the picture the reader sees will ordinarily be made up of solid black, empty white, and about three steps of grey in between. This has a very interesting effect on the way we see original photographs: newcomers to photography simply do not see the full range of grey tones present in a properly graded monochrome print; they have to be taught to do so, with the help of such aids as abstract grey scales; until they learn (and some photographers never do learn), they tend to prefer and produce original prints with the severely limited grey scales of newspaper reproductions (which is very easy to do, simply by giving the negatives a little too much development or by printing properly developed negatives on a too contrasty grade of paper). The new photographer has seen an enormous number of newspaper cuts, very few good, original prints: he therefore sees original prints, so to say *through* newspaper cuts; and he sees *in* original prints only that which newspaper cuts have prepared him to see. In much the same way, the language of primitive empiricism codes a whole, continuously varying world outwith language into patterns of a severely limited number of discrete bits, drastically compressing the apparent range of variation. The tendency to suppose (as Hobbes did), that the world outwith language *must* be constructible, like a model gantry crane built by a boy with a constructor set, from a few kinds of bits, is no doubt the result of seeing the world outwith language *through* the terministic screen of the language of primitive empiricism: just as the new photographer's inability to see the full range of grey tones present in a good, original print is the result of seeing original prints *through* half-tone newspaper cuts.

It may be objected, that there is little point in going on so about language, on the grounds that we can, after all, so easily set language aside and open ourselves to direct experience of the world outwith language: once alerted to the danger of taking words for world, it may be said, we shall at once be able to see the world as it is.

This is a dangerous mistake. Any event which is past, future, or outwith the range of our five senses in the passing instant, must clearly be *mediated* to us by symbolic processes, by way of systems of symbols, of which the most important is ordinary verbal language. *Im*mediate sense experience constitutes only a vanishingly small fraction of the world we *live* in (as opposed to the local environment we momentarily *exist* in): the world in which we try to apply the lessons of the past to the moulding of the future, in which we try to provide against the actions of people (remote from us in various ways: overseas or in the hiding places of power) whom we cannot have continuously within range of our five senses; *this* world, whether we like it or not, *is effectively made of language;* there is no least possibility of ducking past words to the world itself—the world itself *is* words (and word-like things). Even the natural universe, as distinct (so far as the distinction has meaning) from social reality, is itself (as we experience and manipulate it) mostly made of words: what, after all, are these scintillating points of light on the under-surface of the blue-black bowl of the night sky, without talk including talk about the speed of light in a vacuum, the red shift, galaxies, and big bangs or steady states?

It is true, as Quine has pointed out (1962), that some strings of words seem to stand somehow closer than other strings of words to extralinguistic reality, or at any rate to *im*mediate sense experience or to possibilities of *im*mediate sense experience. Thus, we feel this kind of difference between saying, that wet soil is harder to shovel than dry, and saying (with Aristotle), that some men are by nature users of tools, other men by nature tools to be used: in the first case, we feel that changing the words won't change the world, while in the second case we feel that the words *are* the world, which can therefore be changed by talking about it in a different way. But the prudential uses of language I have uppermost in mind—(shall we call them, using language to write the operating manual of spaceship Earth, or perhaps using language to contrive a personal operating philosophy for you or for me?)—involve a relationship between words and world outwith language much more like that of the second case than like that of the first case. For instance, I touched earlier on the strong possibility, that waste carbon dioxide produced by burning fossil fuels will accumulate in our atmosphere, to the point at which the "greenhouse effect" of carbon dioxide will lead to undesirable changes in the secular climate: it is not *proven* beyond doubt, that this and its consequences will happen, and the only way of proving it beyond doubt would be to go on as we now go and see what *does* happen. Now, our present approach to such problems assumes that anybody is entitled to go on doing anything that will add a dollar or a rouble to the gross national product in the short run, just so long as nobody else can prove beyond doubt that harm *will* come of it: it may well be, that we should stand this permissive approach on its head, assuming that nobody should be allowed to do anything (however productive in the short run) unless *he* can prove beyond doubt to the rest of us that *no* harm can come of it. The question, whether or not we should stand the prevailing permissive approach on its head, is not one we can settle by using only a special language, such as the special language of natural science, still less by using a special language (like the language of primitive empiricism) constructed exclusively of world-bound words or sentences (directly referable to *im*mediate sense experience of the world outwith words) and of rule-bound tautologies (such as the self-evident falsity of flat self-contradiction): we have, as it seems to me, to appeal to our *whole* word model of our *whole* universe extended in time. It is difficult to discuss such large questions with decent economy, without modulating into poetic language, and what I mean is something like this: it may be, that our whole programme of *mastering* Nature (so well figured in certain science fiction writers' dreams of cosmic conquest—as especially in an unintentionally disturbing story by Arthur C. Clarke, which admiringly has our own remote descendants burn up the entire local galaxy to fuel a voyage of emigration into the unknown, or to nowhere in particular), which dates back at least to the Neolithic Revolution of a few thousand years ago, is simply a dangerous mistake, a major mis-match between our word model of the universe extended in time and extralinguistic reality; and perhaps our programme ought to be rather to learn, if we can, how to *live with* Nature, a programme of *symphusis* as opposed to the *antiphusis* of orthodox Marxism (or, so to say, a matriarchal rather than patriarchal marriage with Nature). Again, it may well be that our notion (important in the theology of scientism), that the scientific enterprise must lead to a progressive increase in our knowledge of Nature and in our power over Nature, is just another dangerous mistake, mere *pi* in the sky: Albert Einstein told the publisher Harry Kessler, in 1924, that it would always be possible to advance science by mere reflection upon what is accepted as scientific truth—since every scientific proposition, without exception, is incorrect; moreover, it seems to me clear enough, that, if the number of answers to old questions is increasing arithmetically, then the number of new, unanswered questions increases geometrically, so that the net tendency of the advance of science is an exponential increase of ignorance; also, that our vaunted power to *control* local events therefore increases at a much greater rate than our mere programmatically envisaged power to *predict* all the remote consequences (remote, in time and space) of our exercise of local control, so that the net tendency of the advance of science is also an exponential increase in the weights of the risk factors in decision and action situations. The Mediaeval cosmos, or its word model in the experience of most, was small, closed, and fully understood; now we find ourselves talking about a cosmos in which there are around 1000 million galaxies, each containing at least 100 million stars; it would not be at all difficult for us to pollute the entire biosphere of our own planet with radioactive materials, but only a fool or a knave could pretend to know even how to begin to predict the evolutionary consequences after a thousand years.

Thus far, I have been talking about the relationship to extralinguistic

6

reality of *public* or third-person language: this relationship seems to me to pose the major problem for natural philosophy and the special natural sciences—how *do* we go about writing a reliable operating manual for space-ship Earth, the fragile vessel upon which we find ourselves embarked? But I have been mindful all along, that George Alexander Kelly spent a great deal of his time considering the problems of individuals: a person may, of course, face comparable personal questions, involving his whole private word model of the world outwith words he lives in—if you like, he has the problem of writing an operating manual for flesh ship Me, the lump of meat in which he finds himself (as language develops) self-consciously embarked as Captain and Navigator.

It is interesting, that "The Psychology of Personal Constructs" begins, in the very first chapter, with a discussion of overarching natural philosophy, (*not* some parochial "methodology"), as an indispensable prolegomenon to the discussion of psychology as a special natural science and of the perplexities of individuals as clinical problems. In the particular things Kelly has said in this first chapter (or, perhaps, only in the particular ways in which he has chosen to say them), I find much to disagree with. One major theme of this essay, is that it is a mistake to talk about thought, or about the world outside thought, instead of talking about language and the world represented in language: natural philosophy is a public, third-person activity, and what people *think* cannot be known, only the way they use a shared language; and it seems to me a disgracefully neglected fact, that clinical treatment of people without any discoverable organic disease is entirely a matter of *talking* (and of symbolic action of other kinds), that is to say, of use of verbal and non-verbal language. Another major theme of this essay, is that the rhetoric of *prediction and control* is in some ways perilously misleading, that we can in fact control very little and predict even less—certainly not the remote consequences of exercising our growing, if still puny, ability to control local events—, and I cannot altogether agree with Kelly's stated view (shared with the Marxians and the pragmatists), that philosophy can and should be reduced to a kind of fumbling forward through the encircling darkness, to find out what open trapdoors we shall fall through; if Kelly had not been interested, here, chiefly in turning the rhetoric of prediction and control back upon those psychologists within the parish who had decided to resign upwards from the human race, he would no doubt have agreed with me—although, it must be said, there were moments when he said rather grand things about Man's duty to prepare himself for the task of taking over charge of the universe from God.

What does seem to me magnificent and inescapably right, is the insistence on beginning with overarching natural philosophy (". . . man might be better understood if he were viewed in the perspective of the centuries rather than in the flicker of passing moments", Kelly, 1955), and the insistence on regarding individual men as individual natural philosophers (". . . might not the differences between the personal viewpoints of different men correspond to the differences between the theoretical points of view of different scientists?", Kelly, 1955). The expression "natural philosophy" is carefully chosen: the change of direction discussed earlier, from the line of march of primitive empiricism with its logic of bits to the line of march of chastened empiricism with its logic of wholes, removes the imagined barrier between speculative metaphysics and natural science, leaving us with natural philosophy as a seamless way of coping with the world outwith words (" If we examine a person's philosophy closely, we find ourselves staring at the person himself. If we reach an understanding of how a person behaves, we discover it in the manner in which he represents his circumstances to himself", Kelly, 1955).

What I have tried to suggest here, is that we (collectively and individually) live, not so much in the world, as in a model of the world made of words and word-like things; that it is this, rather than the world outwith words (whatever that may be), that we experience and try to manipulate. Collectively, as "Man", we have to try to correct and complete this linguistic model of extralinguistic reality into a comprehensive and reliable operating manual for spaceship Earth, which we did not build, whirling through a cosmos we did not design; individually, as you or me, we have to try to complete and correct our individual linguistic models of our own extralinguistic realities into a comprehensive and reliable operating manual for flesh ship Me, which we did not mould, "thrown" (as the existentialists say) into a world we did not make. In this, as in other ways, ontogenesis recapitulates phylogenesis: and all the more so, since we have to write our own manuals largely in the language of the big manual, for fear of ending up in the sickbay or in the brig. It seems to me sufficiently clear, that there is no way in which we can duck through or past language (in the largest sense) to *im*mediate experience of extralinguistic reality: if, after all, the operating manual of spaceship Earth was not in its current edition, or present state of revision, we could have no way of knowing that we *are* on a spaceship, drifting in a universe large beyond the imaginings of any mystic of the recent past; and one lately arrived on board a spaceship of any size would be unable to grasp it as a functioning whole, without access to a comprehensive operating manual.

Quine, in discussing the relationship between words and things, likes to quote Otto Neurath's characterization of the natural philosopher trying to correct and complete the language he has inherited:

"Wie Schiffer sind wir, die ihr Schiff auf offener See umbauen müssen, ohne es jemals in einem Dock zerlegen und aus besten Bestandteilen neu errichten zu können."

In English (my translation), this goes:

"We are like sailors obliged to rebuild our ship on the open sea, without ever being able to knock it down completely in dry dock and build it anew from the best of replacement parts."

The scientist, the philosopher, the natural philosopher who combines the two, has nothing to float him on his voyage through extralinguistic reality extended in time (whatever *that* may be), save an encapsulating shell of words and word-like things, *which also represents extralinguistic reality to him:* he cannot get out of this shell—neither of us will have seen anybody walking on the water lately; all he can do, is try to improve the fabric (including the terministic screens in the windows of the bridge) from within, as best he may.

If this is the situation of the scientist (as seen, what is more, by Otto Neurath, the most enthusiastic destroyer of metaphysics of all the Vienna Circle), then perhaps the patient, the client, the subject, perhaps even the albino rat, are no better off; or, for that matter, no worse off.

Acknowledgement

The short account of the development from "primitive empiricism" through "chastened empiricism" is adapted from part of a study prepared for the British Bureau of Television Advertising.

Select Bibliography

(Anybody who is attracted by the approach taken in this essay, will find much to attract him in the books listed here.)

Alston, W. P. (1964). "Philosophy of Language", Prentice-Hall, Englewood Cliffs, New Jersey.

Ayer, A. J. (1956). "The Problem of Knowledge" (available as Pelican A.377), Macmillan, London.

Bachelard, Gaston (1963). "Le Matérialisme Rationnel" (second edition), Presses Universitaires de France, Paris.

Bachelard, Gaston (1966). "La Philosophie du Non: Essai d'une Philosophie du Nouvel Esprit Scientifique" (Fourth Edition; First Edition, 1940), Presses Universitaires de France, Paris.

Bachelard, Gaston (1967). "La Formation de l'Esprit Scientifique: Contribution à une Psychanalyse de la Connaissance Objective" (fifth edition), Librairie Philosophique J. Vrin, Paris.

Bannister, D. and Mair, J. M. M. (1968). "The Evaluation of Personal Constructs", Academic Press, London and New York.

Barker, S. F. (1964). "Philosophy of Mathematics", Prentice-Hall, Englewood Cliffs, New Jersey.

Barthes, Roland (1953). "Le Degré Zéro de l'Écriture", Editions du Seuil, Paris.

Barthes, Roland (1957). "Mythologies", Editions du Seuil, Paris.

Barthes, Roland (1964). "Essais Critiques", Editions du Seuil, Paris.

Bartlett, F. C. (1932). "Remembering: a Study in Experimental and Social Psychology", Cambridge University Press, Cambridge.

Berger, P. L. (1966). "Invitation to Sociology: a Humanistic Perspective", Penguin, Harmondsworth (Pelican list number A.841; first published in the U.S.A. by Doubleday Books, New York, 1963).

Berger, P. L. and Luckmann, T. (1967). "The Social Construction of Reality: a treatise in the sociology of knowledge", Allen Lane, The Penguin Press, London (first published in the U.S.A. by Doubleday Books, New York, 1966).

Berger, Peter L. (1969). "The Social Reality of Religion", Faber and Faber, London (first published in the U.S.A. as "The Sacred Canopy", SBN: 571 08865 1).

Bloomfield, L. (1935). "Language", Allen and Unwin, London.

Boulding, K. E. (1956). "The Image: Knowledge in Life and Society", University of Michigan Press, Ann Arbor, Michigan.

Brown, Roger (1958). "Words and Things", The Free Press, New York; Collier-Macmillan, London.

Burke, Kenneth (1962). "A Grammar of Motives" and "A Rhetoric of Motives", World Publishing Meridian Books paperback series, list number M.143, Cleveland and New York (2 books in 1, first published separately in hardback by Prentice-Hall, Englewood Cliffs, New Jersey in 1945 and 1950 respectively).

Burke, Kenneth (1966). "Language as Symbolic Action: Essays on Life, Literature, and Method", pp. 44–62, University of California Press, Berkeley and Los Angeles.

Burke, Kenneth (1967). "The Philosophy of Literary Form" (Second Edition; first edition, 1941), Louisiana State University Press, Baton Rouge, Louisiana.

Carroll, J. B. (ed.) (1956). "Language, Thought, and Reality: Selected Writings of Benjamin Lee Whorf", The M.I.T. Press, Cambridge, Massachusetts.

Carroll, J. B. (1964). "Language and Thought", Prentice-Hall, Englewood Cliffs, New Jersey.

Cherry, C. (1966). "On Human Communication: a Review, a Survey, and a Criticism" (second edition with important revisions), The M.I.T. Press, Cambridge, Massachusetts.

Chomsky, Noam (1957). "Syntactic Structures", Mouton, The Hague.

Chomsky, Noam (1965). "Aspects of the Theory of Syntax", The M.I.T. Press, Cambridge, Massachusetts.

Collingwood, R. G. (1924). "*Speculum Mentis:* or the Map of Knowledge", Clarendon Press, Oxford.

De Cecco, J. P. (ed.) (1967). "The Psychology of Language, Thought, and Instruction: Readings", Holt, Rhinehart, and Winston, New York.

Douglas, Mary (1966). "Purity and Danger", Routledge and Kegan Paul, London.

Empson, William (1961). "Seven Types of Ambiguity", Penguin, Harmondsworth (Peregrine list number Y.2; first published in hardback, 1930).

English, Horace B. and English, Ava Champney (1958). "A Comprehensive Dictionary of Psychological and Psychoanalytical Terms: a Guide to Usage", Longmans Green & Co., London.

Evans, R. M. (1948). "An Introduction to Color", John Wiley, New York.

Evans, R. M. (1959). "Eye, Film, and Camera in Color Photography", John Wiley, New York.

Fodor, J. A. and Katz, J. J., (eds.) (1964). "The Structure of Language: Readings in the Philosophy of Language", Prentice-Hall, Englewood Cliffs, New Jersey.

Fraser, J. T., (ed.) (1968). "The Voices of Time: a Cooperative Survey of Man's Views of Time as Expressed by the Sciences and the Humanities", Allen Lane, The Penguin Press, London (first published in the U.S.A. by George Braziller, 1966).

Gellner, Ernest (1964). "Thought and Change", Weidenfeld and Nicolson, London, SBN: 297 16997 1.

Gellner, Ernest (1968). "Words and Things", Penguin, Harmondsworth (Pelican list number A.926; first published in hardback, 1959).

Gerth, H. and Mills, C. Wright (1954). "Character and Social Structure: the Psychology of Social Institutions", Routledge and Kegan Paul, London.

Greenberg, Joseph H. (ed.) (1966). "Universals of Language: Report of a Conference held at Dobbs Ferry, New York, April 13–15, 1961", The M.I.T. Press, Cambridge, Massachusetts (Second Edition, with important revisions).

Hempel, C. G. (1966). "Philosophy of Natural Science", Prentice-Hall, Englewood Cliffs, New Jersey.

Henry, J. (1966). "Culture Against Man", Associated Book Publishers, London (Social Science Paperbacks series, list number SSP.2; first published in the U.S.A. by Random House, New York, 1963).

Humphrey, George (1963). "Thinking", John Wiley, New York (Science Editions paperback series, list number 305-S; first published in London by Methuen).

Hymes, Dell (ed.) (1964). "Language in Culture and Society: a Reader in Linguistics and Anthropology", Harper and Row, New York.

James, William (1950). "The Principles of Psychology", Vols 1, 2, Dover Publications, New York (Dover paperback series, list numbers T.381 and T.382; first published in 1890).

Kelly, G. A. (1955). "The Psychology of Personal Constructs", Vols 1, 2, Norton, New York.

Kelly, G. A. (1969). "Clinical Psychology and Personality: The Selected Papers of George Kelly" (Maher, B., ed.), John Wiley and Sons, New York.

Lévi-Strauss, Claude (1955). "Tristes Tropiques", Plon, Paris.

Lévi-Strauss, Claude (1962). "La Pensée Sauvage", Plon, Paris.

Lévi-Strauss, Claude (1964). "Mythologiques: le Cru et le Cuit", Plon, Paris.

Lévi-Strauss, Claude (1968). "Structural Anthropology", Allen Lane, The Penguin Press, London (first published in the U.S.A. by Basic Books, 1963, in translation).

Lewis, C. S. (1961). "An Experiment in Criticism", Cambridge University Press, London (paperback list number CAM.350).

Mandelbaum, David G. (ed.) (1949). "Selected Writings of Edward Sapir in Language, Culture, and Personality", University of California Press, Berkeley and Los Angeles.

Mannheim, Karl (1936). "Ideology and Utopia: an Introduction to the Sociology of Knowledge", Routledge and Kegan Paul, London.

McCulloch, Warren S. (1965). "Embodiments of Mind", The M.I.T. Press, Cambridge, Massachusetts.

Merleau-Ponty, Maurice (1945). "Phénoménologie de la Perception", Editions Gallimard, Paris.

Merleau-Ponty, Maurice (1960). "Signes", Editions Gallimard, Paris.

Merleau-Ponty, Maurice (1966). "Sens et non-sens", Editions Nagel, Paris.

Merleau-Ponty, Maurice (1969). "La Prose du Monde: Texte Établi et Présenté par Claude Lefort", Editions Gallimard, Paris.

Mills, C. Wright (1959). "The Sociological Imagination", Oxford University Press, New York.

Minsky, M. L. (1967). "Computation: Finite and Infinite Machines", Prentice-Hall, Englewood Cliffs, New Jersey.

Morris, Charles (1964). "Signification and Significance", The M.I.T. Press, Cambridge, Massachusetts.

Ogden, C. K. and Richards, I. A. (1949). "The Meaning of Meaning: a Study of the Influence of Language Upon Thought and of the Science of Symbolism" (Tenth Edition; First Edition, 1923), Routledge and Kegan Paul, London.

Passmore, John (1968). "A Hundred Years of Philosophy", Penguin, Harmondsworth (Pelican list number A.927; Second Edition with important revisions).

Peters, Richard (1967). "Hobbes", Penguin, Harmondsworth (Peregrine list number Y.66, second edition).

Quine, W. Van O. (1960). "Word and Object", The M.I.T. Press, Cambridge, Massachusetts.

Quine, W. Van O. (1961). "From a Logical Point of View: 9 Logico-Philosophical Essays", p. 42 (Second Edition, with important revisions), The M.I.T. Press, Cambridge, Massachusetts.

Quine, W. Van O. (1962). "Methods of Logic", pp. xii–xiii (Second Edition, revised; reprinted with corrections, 1966).

Reid, Leslie (1962). "The Sociology of Nature", Allen Lane, The Penguin Press, London (Pelican list number A.556, first published as *Earth's Company* by John Murray, London, 1958).

Richards, I. A. (1926). "Principles of Literary Criticism" (Second Edition with two new appendices; First Edition, 1924), Routledge and Kegan Paul, London.

Ruesch, J. and Bateson, G. (1951). "Communication: the Social Matrix of Psychiatry", Norton, New York.

Ruesch, J. and Kees, W. (1956). "Nonverbal Communication: Notes on the Visual Perception of Human relations", University of California Press, Berkeley and Los Angeles.

Russell, Bertrand (1962). "An Inquiry into Meaning and Truth", Penguin, Harmondsworth (Pelican list number A.590; first published in hardback, 1940).

Ryle, Gilbert (1963). "The Concept of Mind", Allen Lane, The Penguin Press, London (Peregrine list number Y.29; first published in hardback, 1949).

Sapir, Edward (1921). "Language: an Introduction to the Study of Speech", Harcourt, Brace and World, New York.

Sartre, Jean-Paul (1943). "l'Être et le Néant: Essai d'Ontologie Phénoménologique", Editions Gallimard, Paris.

Sartre, Jean-Paul (1965). "Esquisse d'une théorie des Émotions", Hermann, Paris (first published in 1939).

Saussure, F. de (1966). "Cours de linguistique générale" (Third Edition), Payot, Paris.

Sorokin, P. A. (1963). "Modern Historical and Social Philosophies", Dover, New York (Dover paperback series, list number T.1146, first published by Beacon Press, Boston, as "Social Philosophies of an Age of Crisis", 1951).

Smith, Frank and Miller, G. A. (eds) (1966). "The Genesis of Language: a Psycholinguistic Approach", The M.I.T. Press, Cambridge, Massachusetts.

Stebbing, L. Susan (1950). "A Modern Introduction to Logic" (Seventh Edition; First Edition, 1930), Methuen, London.

Suttie, Ian D. (1963). "The Origins of Love and Hate", Penguin, Harmondsworth (Peregrine list number Y.31; first published in hardback, 1935).

Taylor, Charles (1964). "The Explanation of Behaviour", Routledge and Kegan Paul, London (SBN: 7100 3620 5).

Toulmin, Stephen (1953). "The Philosophy of Science: an Introduction", Hutchinson, London.

Touraine, Alain (1965). "Sociologie de l'Action", Editions du Seuil, Paris.

Tylor, E. B. (1958). "The Origins of Culture", Harper and Row, New York (Harper Torchbooks paperback series, list number TB.33; first published in 1871, as Chapters I–X of "Primitive Culture").

Vaihinger, H. (1935). "The Philosophy of 'As If': a System of the Theoretical, Practical, and Religious Fictions of Mankind", Routledge and Kegan Paul, London.

Vygotsky, L. S. (1962). "Thought and Language", The M.I.T. Press, Cambridge, Massachusetts (first published in Russian in 1934).

Wann, T. W. (ed.) (1965). "Behaviorism and Phenomenology: Contrasting Bases for Modern Psychology", University of Chicago Press, Chicago and London (Phoenix paperback series list number P.192; first published in hardback, 1964).

Wellek, R. and Warren, A. (1963). "Theory of Literature" (Third Edition), Penguin, Harmondsworth (Peregrine list number Y.28).

White, Leslie A. (1949). "The Science of Culture: a Study of Man and Civilization", Grove Press, New York (Evergreen books paperback series, list number E-105).

Whitehead, A. N. (1964). "The Concept of Nature", Cambridge University Press, Cambridge (first paperback edition; first published, 1920).

Psychologists are Human Too

J. M. M. Mair

When I hear people accuse psychologists of being isolated from the real world, small minded, hidebound by doctrine and method, incapable of learning from experience, I have to laugh. After all, I know, personally, half a dozen (well at least three) psychologists who, after only a few years of dedicated experimentation in their discipline, and despite very expensive and lengthy training to the contrary, have been forced to change some of their fundamental professional beliefs and accept that the subjects they have been herding through their laboratories *are human* after all. Not that mere personal experience is enough in such matters and thankfully they have had moderate support from *the literature* to sustain their struggling, new-born beliefs. Recent papers attesting to the same view have appeared under such titles as "The human subject in psychological research" (Schultz, 1969) and "The human person in modern psychological science" (Rychlak, 1970).

This would be enough of a change to digest, but further murmurings of unrest have been heard recently in the psychological world. Both arguments and evidence have been presented in recent years to leave little doubt that almost all methods of psychological enquiry—interviewing, testing, experimentation—are forms of human *relationships*. If even half the results reported by Rosenthal (1966) are confirmed, there is enough to suggest that certain characteristics and expectations of experimenters interact with characteristics and expectations of subjects in ways which can significantly and systematically affect the outcome of experiments. When the work of Friedman (1967), Orne (1962), Milgram (1965) and others is also considered, there seems little reason for rejecting the central fact that psychological experiments are social events not "pure" situations in which a detached scientist observes subject-beings who react only to the things prescribed or noticed by the experimenter.

Those who are not steeped in the ideals and traditions of psychology may consider it evidence in support of their views of the pettiness of much psychology that these two considerations—that subjects are human and that psychological investigations involve social relationships—should only now be recognized as possibly affecting experimental psychology. They may also find it difficult to understand why these two "discoveries" should cause any alarm or uneasiness among scientific psychologists. Though one might readily sympathize with this outsider's view, I think they would be very wrong in supposing that no fundamental issues are involved. Indeed I want to suggest that it is some awareness of the basic reorientations involved in recognizing these two features as part of scientific psychology which accounts for their general neglect and any present uneasiness now they are being forced more directly on the psychologist's attention.

The Psychologist's Dilemma

Many psychologists are dissatisfied with the fragmented and limited nature of their discipline in face of the rich subtle diversity of their subject matter—man. Many also feel that the present limitations of psychology are merely the inevitable hallmarks of a young science and, if we continue as we have done, we will, in time, increase the effective relevance of our findings. While I readily agree with this in part, it may also be that alteration of some basic assumptions in psychology will open up some paths for exploration which the recipe "more of the same" may not do. It is this alternative which I wish to follow here in an attempt to undo some of the straps on the straight jacket of traditional scientific methodology within which psychologists have long struggled.

Why then might psychologists find it hard to accept the humanity of their subjects within the experimental situation and why might some find it disturbing to acknowledge that the results of most forms of psychological enquiry are determined in part by the sort of relationship existing between scientist and subject? To understand the psychologists' dilemma here a little consideration needs to be given to what might be meant by *subjects being human* and *experiments involving relationships*.

Now, of course, psychologists have never been any less likely to regard other people as human than anyone else when they have been dealing with them in their everyday lives. It is only when they adopt their professional roles and place people in their experiments as subjects that they temporarily act as if these people, within that context, were less than human—in fact *subjects*, ready to do their master's will. In suggesting that we as psychologists now need to recognize more often the humanity of subjects what is implied is that we come to regard people who take part in our experiments as human beings *just like us*, the experimenters, *even while they are helping us with our research*. This really can be alarming because it means accepting that subjects, like experimenters, can and do continuously think, theorize, anticipate, experiment, react, create, rebel and comply just like everyone else—and what is more, they can and often do all these things in any experiment the psychologist designs. Since there are virtually no theories which can adequately account for this sort of behaviour in subjects or experimental designs which begin to offer us means of controlling and partialling out these many activities, this recognition of humanity *is* professionally disquieting.

These problems multiply when we consider the question of *relationships* and their possible effects on results. The problems here, as with so many in psychology, can be traced back to the fact that modern scientific psychology is based essentially on a "physical science" model, on the pattern found so successful by those involved in the natural sciences at the end of the last century. In these "hard" sciences, experimenters were dealing with *things*. It mattered not a jot if the experimenter smiled, shouted, sang or danced a jig as he poured acid A into acid B or mixed a quantity of element X with compound Y. He could do any of these things in the experimental situation in the happy knowledge that the actions or properties of the acids, elements and compounds would be quite unaffected. Clearly then the experimenter did not have to be conceptualized as an integral part of each experiment. His personal characteristics did not have to be recognized as variable modifiers of the action of the elements or acids on each other. Psychologists adopted the same position and viewed experimenters as quite interchangeable "Es", assuming that as long as you had one it didn't really matter who or what he was, provided he adhered to a loosely defined policy of pseudoself-effacement. Each E was then required to adapt his own person to the roles of all-knowingness and anonymity at the same time.

Recent research on the social nature of psychological research casts all these practices into doubt. Now we find, whether we like it or not, that experimenters are after all, all different, because they are different people and they form different relationships with each of their subjects whether they intend it or not. While it must be the case that this matters more for some kinds of experiments than others, it does seem likely that the more the focus is on probing factors felt to be of some significance to each subject's view of life, the more his relationship with the experimenter and the whole experimental situation will affect how he responds.

If we, then, consider confrontations between experimenters and subjects in order to try to specify what sorts of relationship they generally involve we may note some interesting things which could be disquieting if we took them seriously. We note that, as a rule, the experimenter makes use of people to help him answer questions which *he*, not they, raise; more frequently than ever (Seeman, 1969) he makes use of some form of deception, misinforming subjects about what they are doing or about what this indicates about themselves; often he takes little care, or exercises little responsibility, concerning the effects which stressful experimental tasks or conditions have on subjects, other than as regards his interest in the experiment, in short or long term; seldom does he give subjects much opportunity to express their concerns or ideas relating to the experimental experience; seldom does he engage in repeated encounters with subjects, mostly preferring single or few meetings with naïve subjects.

While I am intentionally painting a rather lurid picture, there are perhaps enough grains of truth in it to be recognizable. This present tendency to set up psychological experiments in which the experimenter quickly "grabs" some data from subjects and then makes off with them with relatively little concern with the subjects he leaves strewn in the path behind him seems to rest on the fairly pervasive belief in science generally (though it is now more often being challenged) that the scientist has no direct social responsibility concerning his scientific commitments. This position can be questioned in all sciences, but surely most of all in psychology where the subject matter is people. When we try to unearth their secrets and use them to predict and control behaviour we are engaging directly in social manipulations for which we are surely obliged to take full responsibility. Otherwise, in many areas of investigation, we may end up only with the sorts of information which people who distrust and deceive us are prepared to provide (*see* Kelman, 1967; Stricker, 1967; Stricker *et al.*, 1969).

So experiments seem to involve relationships and the sorts of relationships implied by common experimental practices are sometimes rather unsavoury. This presents real problems for the psychologist who wishes to respect his subjects' humanity. He may feel obliged to try to change features of the relationships traditionally established and avoid deception, give more to his subjects for their help, take more responsibility for their reactions and welfare, make more long-term engagements with them so that they and he have more opportunity to ensure that the "results" obtained are in some way meaningful. Each of these possibilities creates severe problems for psychology, but none so great as the central problem inherent in acknowledging that experiments involve relationships; namely, that we do not know how differences in relationships have influenced the kinds of facts we have already collected or continue to affect those now being gathered. Our first response is likely to be to seek ways of ruling out or controlling for this "source of error". This will certainly be necessary, useful and even possible in some circumstances, but is it enough, and is it wise to treat this ever present phenomenon as an enemy to be defeated whenever possible rather than an ally to be recognized and used?

The dilemma for psychologists is then two sided: if we accept that our subjects are human, just like us, do we have to do the impossible and become super-human in order to study them as scientists, trying to predict and control their theorizing, questioning, experimenting and all the rest? If we accept or find that experimental results are often determined in part by the sorts of relationships existing between experimenter and subject surely we have to abandon all claims to objectivity and detachment as investigators and even to the possibility of ensuring replicable results in some areas of enquiry. Have we not then to abandon claims to being or becoming a science at all?

My own answer to both of these questions is a firm "NO". What follows is an attempt to give some grounds for this belief.

Subjects as Scientists

"The Psychology of Personal Constructs" outlined by George Kelly in 1955 seems helpful here. Kelly's theory is liberating in a way that no other psychological theory seems to be because his is an elaborated theory about the "theorizing" and "experimenting" of ordinary people. He suggests that everyone makes sense of the world in terms of personally learned interpretations, or *personal constructs*. For each person these personal dimensions for *discriminating between* events and *anticipating* new events are organized to form different, more or less coordinated systems—their personal construct systems. No two systems are then exactly alike (though there are similarities because we inhabit similar external and internal worlds) and no two constructs refer to exactly the same discriminations (though again there are greater or lesser similarities between people, depending partly on which subsystem the constructs belong to). While Kelly assumes there is a real world around us, he assumes that we *never* at any time in our lives come into direct, naked contact with it. All our contact with reality, he suggests, is by means of our interpretations, our constructions.

He suggests that it may be advantageous not to view man only in terms of certain common problems, experiences or drives, but to look at men in their efforts at trying to make sense of themselves and their worlds; to look at their personal ways of giving meaning to events and their constant engagements in the world in testing out, modifying, defining or elaborating their ways of experiencing the world. Kelly turns the tables on psychologists by suggesting that it may be profitable for us to look at people in the ways in which they are somewhat like scientists; to look at them as if we were of the same breed and not some different species. So he here directly faces us with the inevitability of psychologists using their own *personal* construct systems to make sense of the sense-making systems and actions of others. The psychologist, like everyone else, can only give meaning to events within the limits of his own system and when he studies other people it is likely to be they who are the informed experts on their own personal construct systems, not himself.

So right away this view of man in relation to the psychologist who studies him looks unusual and challenging. Here in one blow the subject, patient or anyone else is seen as sharing some of the essential skills and limitations of those who call themselves scientists. Furthermore, Kelly specifically designed his theory to have central relevance to the problems of interpersonal interactions. In this connection one of his most useful concepts is that of *role* which he redefined in relation to the main features of construct theory, making it a distinctly psychological, rather than a social or economic notion. He described it thus—"In terms of the theory of personal constructs, a *role* is a psychological process based upon the role player's construction of aspects of the construction systems of those with whom he attempts to join in a social enterprise. In less precise but more familiar language, a role is an ongoing pattern of behaviour that follows from a person's understanding of how others who are associated with him in his task think. In idiomatic language, a role is a position that one can play on a certain team without even waiting for the signals" (Kelly, 1955).

A *role* in Kelly's system, then, is based on the sense you make of the sense being made explicitly or implicitly by others with whom you are engaged. This concept clearly provides a useful context within which problematic notions like deception, lying, social desirability and other biasing of responses can be given psychological rather than moralistic interpretations. According to how one person construes another, he will modulate his own thinking and action in relation to that other person. Here we are back with something very relevant to the second part of the psychologist's dilemma.

For the sake of what follows, two other features of Kelly's theoretical position will be mentioned. Unlike many other theorists, Kelly insists that man be viewed as an *essentially* active creature. By being alive he is in constant motion and even to stay in some respects the same in a changing world he has to keep on moving. Of course he is not all moving all the time in just the same way. Some aspects of his construct system are seen as changing more obviously and quickly than others, but we are encouraged right from the beginning to change our minds about the inevitability of finding good solid stabilities in man's personality; change, Kelly suggests, is of the essence and stabilities may better be viewed as regularities of movement or methods of controlling movement than as static traits.

Kelly also clearly recognizes that many of our constructions of events are outside consciousness. Many of our most important ways of dealing with events, he suggests, are by means of constructs which are non-verbal constructs, acted out rather than specified by language. Many of these non-verbal constructs may have been acquired in infancy before language was developed and have since remained outside our awareness. Constructs are therefore recognized as being at different *levels of awareness*, some being clearly articulated and tied to words while others are more vaguely appreciated, being manifest in action and feeling only.

Many aspects of construct theory seem very like common sense, but it would be unwise to suppose that the theory is no more than this. Kelly has, I think, provided a "new look" for psychology which could transform not only how we view those we study but also our ideas about experimenters and about the nature of the discipline psychology may become. A fruitful science of man may begin to look very unlike what we presently recognize if some of Kelly's fundamental ideas can be worked out in practice. And this is where difficulties begin to arise; can they be worked out in practice or has he left us with a heightened desire for a more human perspective on our subject matter without the means of doing much about it? Many psychologists with very un-Kellian theoretical positions will readily admit that much of what Kelly says makes a great deal of sense. But in a practical world, seeming sensible, even exciting, is no substitute for *being* useful.

A Methodological Theory Without Adequate Methods

At first glance these doubts seem unfounded. Kelly has, after all, provided novel and exciting *methods* for studying the nature and functions of personal constructs. Perhaps more than any other personality theorist he has enriched our stock of tools for psychological enquiry. The Role Construct Repertory Test and the better known extension of this, the Repertory Grid (Kelly, 1955; Bannister and Mair, 1968) are both means of eliciting from individuals some of the personal constructs they use to structure their worlds. Something of the sorts of things they are concerned to make sense of and how they order the sense they make—the personal meanings they erect and use—can be grasped and systematized within these methods.

The Self Characterization Sketch (Kelly, 1955) is an additional, simple yet subtle, means of obtaining from any individual something of his constructions about how he views himself, his strengths and weaknesses, methods and missions. These sketches were often used by Kelly as the first stage in designing new role sketches for patients to use in the course of Fixed Role Therapy. This form of treatment can also be viewed as a tool of enquiry whereby the patient in adopting a new, temporary view of himself (defined in terms of a role sketch which he will try to act out in life) may find new perspectives on the world and new modes of enquiry and action coming within his grasp because he is approaching the world differently.

Surely these are innovations enough? Well, for our present purposes I think not. Over the course of some years of making some use of most of these methods I have repeatedly been forced to recognize that Kelly, while enormously extending the sorts of subtle things about people we can systematically study, still left us in the dilemma outlined earlier. He himself was not so trapped, I am sure, but he has not provided the necessary means for others to transcend the usual subject/scientist roles and make full use of the scientist-like qualities of man which his theory encourages us to explore.

The Role Construct Repertory Test, the Repertory Grid and the Self Characterization Method all give freedom to the person studied to express something of his own personal achievements and concerns as regards sense-making. They all allow him to make use of and express some of his personal means for structuring events and anticipating the future. None, however, take much note of the fact that the poor experimenter, therapist or tester has to make some sense of what has been presented to him. Remembering that Kelly suggests that we *all* make sense of things by means of interpretative constructs, surely an adequate methodology for a science of personal constructs would have to take intimate account of how the psychologist is to interpret the interpretations of others. Within Kelly's theory there is just no escape from your own construct system. Yet, as in virtually all psychology to date, psychologists doing work with grid methods or in relation to construct theory make pronouncements about their subjects on the basis of their test results just as though we should accept the sense they make as the inevitable end points in their enquiries rather than any statements made by those they have studied. Surely the sense they make is their achievement or failure and their sense-making equipment would have to be understood to know what conclusions we should draw from it; and of course, we, in drawing our conclusions are aware, not of naked truth, but only of those things which our own systems allow us to entertain.

Remember Kelly suggests that no construct dimensions used by different people are quite the same and no two construct systems have been put together with quite the same pattern or logic. So the possibilities of one person misunderstanding the concerns or intentions of another are likely to be quite great even where no active deception is practised. How we jump the gap of personal knowledge would seem to be something deserving study and requiring incorporation into the methodology of a discipline based on the use of personal constructs.

Kelly was well aware of the central importance of his idea of *role* to his theory and methods. His theory focuses on interpersonal role construing and his methods all make reference to the term *role* in their titles. Yet it seems to have been only in Fixed Role and other forms of therapy that he approached an adequate use of his own novel definition of role as *a course of activity* carried out in the light of your understanding of another. So this central construct in Kelly's theory which indicates how a man can enter into meaningful social interaction and understanding with others is only fractionally developed within the formal methods suggested by him. Even in Fixed Role

Therapy little formal account is taken of the fact that in any interaction both or all participants are engaging in a series of developing role relationships of various kinds. Attention is focused most directly on the means whereby one individual—the patient—can make use of a new role sketch and by trying to adopt it begin to understand himself and others in a new light.

As we have noted, Kelly stresses that "man is a form of motion", but we find that movement is only awkwardly incorporated in the methods he outlined. Only by testing and retesting with grid measures (as in most traditional methods of measurement in psychology) can some idea of movement be gained. Hinkle (1965), in his discussion of *Resistance to Change* and *Implication* grids introduced a more direct concern with change, but still he only dealt with some aspects of change *thought* possible by the subject. The processes and paths whereby a person in fact changes are still not tapped. In Fixed Role Therapy, as in any therapy, change is of course central, but Kelly functioning as a clinician does not provide an explicit framework within which personal and interpersonal changes can be systematically noted and explored.

Finally, although Kelly stressed in his therapeutic work the importance of pre-verbal (acted out rather than conceptualized) constructs and other constructs (whether *submerged* or *suspended*) which were outside the person's normal levels of awareness, these constructions find relatively little place in his more formalized methods of enquiry. Certainly it is possible to guess and to enquire into what is being denied by a person on the basis of what he is affirming (through the idea of *contrast* implicit in any construction); certainly in a Repertory Grid it is possible and not unusual for a person to reveal relationships between constructs of which he was previously unaware; certainly it is possible in some Implication Grids to note second and third order implications of which the person himself is in ignorance; and additionally in Self Characterization Sketches it may be possible to get some ideas about some of the enterprises a person may be engaged in without full awareness. But all of these only touch the edge of the vital range of centrally important constructions which are acted rather than stated, felt rather than thought. While Kelly himself found great scope for detailed study of these constructions in his therapeutic work (as evidenced by many parts of Volume 2 of "The Psychology of Personal Constructs") and in his dealings with students in research and teaching, they eluded any adequate inclusion in his formal methods of enquiry.

The psychology of personal constructs can be considered a *methodological theory*. It does not preempt any particular problems or characteristics as being of fundamental and universal importance to all men but rather focuses on *how* people give meaning to their lives, act on and test the sense they make.

It is a framework within which to explore *how* people "theorize" and "experiment" in their own continuing concerns with pinning down their lives or broadening their horizons. This makes it a unique theory in psychology and of importance because it raises the whole enterprise onto a higher level of abstraction (*not* vagueness) thus enhancing its generality (because it gives freedom to explore and fill in the contents and structure of each person's life within the framework provided) and its *potential* usefulness. The word "potential" has to be insisted on here because, to date, the theory has excited many people but left most baffled as to *how* to make real use of it. Although this is potentially a revolutionary theory, most research using its ideas or the methods associated with them still looks remarkably like much traditional research in many respects. The experimenter still tends to remain outside most studies in grand omnipotence and isolation. True he more often affirms his common humanity with his subjects in the opening paragraphs of his research reports, but somehow he manages, none the less, to remain in the end aloof from the common herd.

So, with Kelly's theoretical contribution, the psychologist's dilemma seems theoretically soluble, but generally *in practice* it remains stubbornly unresolved.

Bringing the Experimenter in from the Cold

Without doubt, concern with bringing experimenters in from the cold is hotting up. Schultz (1969) observes that because of a changed view of the capacities and functions of the scientist, there has been a "closing of the gap between the observer and the observed, and the change of focus of scientific enquiry from an independent and objectively knowable universe to man's observation of the universe. No longer the detached observer, the modern scientist is now cast in the role of participant-observer. The process of observation becomes an interaction, with both sides contributing to the observational transaction". He argues further that a "change in experimental technique is called for on empirical, ethical, as well as philosophical grounds". What sort of change this is to be remains the crucial question.

The fascinating work by Rosenthal (1966) is clearly one approach to the study of experimenters which merits much attention, but from the point of view being discussed here this is still essentially a slightly modified use of traditional methods where the *real* experimenter takes one step backwards and studies as his *subjects* both experimenters and subjects. Other approaches have been indicated by Kelman (1967) focusing on various forms of Role playing exercises. These also seem in varying ways promising in that they may reduce active deception and perhaps allow more co-operation rather than competition or conflict between experimenters and subjects. However for present purposes, they still leave the experimenter on the side-lines to some extent, though of course he may participate in some experiments in various subject-roles. Even then, the end would be to gain co-operation and reduce distrust so that this and other experiments can continue to draw on a willing group of subjects; the experimenter is not here woven into the fabric of the experiment in much more than a make-believe manner.

Also of considerable interest is the approach to this problem being investigated by Jourard (1968) and his students. They seem concerned with factors which affect "disclosures" between subjects and experimenters and the effects of mutual disclosure on people's readiness to open themselves further to study and understanding. His concern with "dialogue" between subjects and experimenters and the "dyadic" effect ("disclosure begets disclosure") resulting from dialogue provides a more integral involvement of experimenters in experiments. Without intending my comments as criticisms, I am personally unhappy with the passivity of the language Jourard uses to describe interactions; using terms like "disclose", "uncover", "reveal" and "unveil". His belief here seems to be that in mutual, trusting relationships the *real* person is "revealed", while it may be that to a considerable extent people are created and developed in relationships and not just uncovered. But more important in the present context, Jourard's immediate concerns seem to be in exploring the benefits to be gained once people are prepared to reveal more about themselves. This is certainly of great interest but in exploring the strategies and tactics people employ in developing relationships of different kinds it will be important to be able to study the ways people create and use fictions, keep and reveal secrets for personal and interpersonal reasons, not just to know what happens at some point late in the process when trust has been achieved.

The Cycle of Enquiry

My own suggestions for a general model for psychological enquiry which may come a little nearer to solving the psychologist's dilemma noted earlier have been outlined elsewhere (Mair, 1970). At this stage it must be regarded as essentially speculative. What follows may be more intelligible if read subsequent to that other account. Here I want only to present a very brief outline of some of the main features of the approach and will concentrate more on specifying some of the reasons why various aspects of the methods so far conceived in relation to the model seem important and necessary.

Experiments involve relationships and relationships generally involve some form of interaction. One of our commonest forms of interactions which we use to build and develop relationships is *the conversation*. What I'm suggesting is using *a model for enquiry patterned on some of the important features of the sorts of activities which constitute conversations; what leads up to them and what results from them.* I am *not* suggesting a directly literal use of the term and finding out about people just by chatting to them. Making the assumption, like Kelly, that people are always actively going about the business of living their lives, I'm supposing they actively theorize, speculate, experiment and explore on their own account; they don't just do these and other things when "pushed" by other people.

But before pursuing this further some orienting comments concerning the possible relationship between this approach and current methods of investigation and legitimate topics of concern in psychology may be useful.

In psychology most studies involve the experimenter in putting a subject in a specified situation and observing what he does, or doing things to a person within some prescribed context and recording how he responds; or getting him to do certain specified things and seeing what happens to him as a result. There is generally little or no concern with incorporating *as part of the study* the ways in which the experimenter makes something of what he thinks the subject is doing or how the experimenter goes about adjusting or making up his next moves on the basis of what he thought happened in the initial phase of the encounter. Neither is much attention paid to what the subject makes of what the experimenter thought he did to him, nor of the use to which he puts the sense he makes nor of how he may then variously act or experiment on his own account to see what he can make of what he thinks the experimenter suggested or to see how the experimenter will respond if he does one thing rather than another. Again, most experiments only exist within the prescribed laboratory situation and what happens beyond these bounds is presumed generally to be irrelevant. But accepting that people may by now often have developed quite special ways of responding in any situations they view as psychological experiments (e.g. Orne, 1962; Milgram, 1965) it may be particularly important to try to change some of their characteristics and broaden their relevance to normal living.

What I am suggesting may direct attention to aspects of the process of interaction or *the cycle of enquiry* which have received relatively little attention. This in no way detracts from the necessity and importance of work on observation, manipulation and control which at present occupies such a central position in much of psychology. If anything, I hope that some attention to the other aspects of the process of enquiry may allow us to develop further skills in these presently popular parts of the process and open up new possibilities of understanding people which exclusive focus on these aspects alone would not readily allow.

As psychologists it would seem important, if we wish to understand and use more about the whole process of interaction, not only to be able to make predictions about others but to explore how people in general make use of anticipations in their normal lives; not only to be able to carry out experiments on others to see what results we get, but to appreciate that everyone can be seen as an active agent and to explore the diverse ways they and we as people, all the time, are constructing and executing "experiments" to confirm old answers or raise new questions. Not only do psychologists need to be able to define the criteria they use in accepting new evidence as proof, but we could also be concerned to specify the diverse ways in which we and others, as people, set up and use (mostly implicitly) criteria to allow us to convert personally appreciated possibilities into usable beliefs; not only do we as psychologists need to be able to create and use theories to organize our actions, but we have to be able to examine how we and others as people create and organize our ideas and the range of uses to which ideas of different kinds can be put; not only do we professionally need to be able to modify our theories in the light of new evidence and create new ideas and frames of reference for future action, we also need to recognize how people generally also have to abandon present beliefs and develop means of "riding with the punch" in creating new possibilities for thought and action to meet changing circumstances; not only do we as psychologists have to recognize that people often don't know at all fully what they think, feel or do, we need also to recognize that we, like everyone else, are in the same boat and that our control over ourselves and our subject matter might well be extended by the introduction of methods whereby our personal limitations of awareness could be partly overcome and we thus extended.

Everything the psychologist does as a scientist is part of his capacities and skills as a human being and is therefore by definition part of the subject matter which, as a psychologist, he claims to study. While psychologists as scientists no doubt have a lot to teach themselves and others as people; psychologists as people have a lot more to teach themselves and others who study people, because they are and will always be the subject matter which by their discipline they seek to understand a little further.

A Conversational Model for Psychological Enquiry

In using the term "conversational model", I wish to define a contrast to the more usual "physical science" or "observational" model on which much of psychology has been based. In some ways the term "role" model would have been as appropriate (using "role" in something like Kelly's sense) but this was avoided because "role" means so many different technical things to different people, because I wanted to stay close to common language and because I did not want the model to be tied only to Kellian theory. The term "conversational cycle" or "experiential cycle" model might have been more adequate, if a bit clumsy, because what I am concerned with is the complete cycle of how we create, test and modify our experience of the world,

especially our interpersonal world. Though accepting the term "conversational" model at present to refer to this cycle of events, the term may also
be slightly misleading because I am certainly not interested only in what
people say to each other, but also with what the other person is not saying or
"saying" by his actions and what each thinks and does as a result of what they
have made of everything gathered from their encounters and how they again
go about changing themselves in anticipation of and as a result of further
encounters.

Consider a practical situation. Mr. Rogers and Mr. Skinner sit down
together to undertake an exploratory study of how they each and together
"theorize" and "experiment" about themselves, each other and others in
general. Mr. Skinner writes *two* brief character sketches of Mr. Rogers
(following, perhaps, similar instructions to those used by Kelly for Self
Characterizations). One of these sketches is written *only for himself;* a
completely private view of Mr. Rogers which no one else will see. The other
sketch is written *specifically for* Mr. Rogers to read. This latter one is couched
in terms and touches on topics which Mr. Skinner will feel *quite comfortable*
about telling Mr. Rogers, he is not required to "bare his soul" or "tell all",
but just to give a picture of his view of Mr. Rogers which he will feel quite
able to take (one participant must not traumatize the other or others since
each needs everyone else to stay around so that the enquiry can continue).

Mr. Rogers also writes two equivalent sketches about Mr. Skinner, one
private one for his own eyes only and the other a more public one specifically
for Mr. Skinner to read.

Messrs. Skinner and Rogers now *pass to the other* their "public" sketches.
They read them, then systematically take turns at questioning the other to
clarify points in the sketch they received which they understood little or not
at all. They then take time to *note down* their initial reactions to the new
information which has been given them about themselves; what they feel,
think, want to do, say, reject, accept, avoid or welcome about it.

Next, in turn, each questions the other in detail about what *evidence* he
has for each of the statements he has made about the other; about his
grounds for believing the things he does and for saying the things he has;
about the criteria he may be functioning in terms of, in accepting the evidence
he has done and about the criteria and evidence he would use if he were to
become more certain yet of the validity of the statements he has made.
In addition, at this stage, they may then examine the description of themselves
presented to them by the other and analyse it in terms of what it seems to
suggest about the interests, ideas, strengths, limitations, tactics and such
like *of the person who wrote it*. Each will then also take turns in questioning
the other concerning the evidence which justifies the conclusions he has
reached regarding the characteristics and concerns of the writer. (Here, as at

any other point in the entire investigation, each may write both public and private versions of conclusions reached, the evidence he has used, the assessments he has made, and so forth).

At this point the first face to face encounter might end and each withdraw to continue their normal lives, arranging to meet again in an hour, day, week or month (whatever their purpose in the enquiry) to continue the face to face part of the study. As they go, however, the study goes with them. In the encounter just completed many personal issues will have been touched on and stirred; each participant (and there could easily be more than two) may find, whether he wishes it or not, that he continues to ruminate on, act out, experiment with, attempt to disconfirm or confirm in a variety of imaginary or practical ways some of the issues and possibilities raised. Each participant must be vigilant to note down at any time how he goes about dealing with these matters (and this is likely to require considerable training in sensitive, detached self-awareness).

The cycle of encounter and withdrawal for personal exploration can be repeated indefinitely or terminated at any agreed stage, depending on the main point of the study or the concerns of those involved.

Why?

Why participate in such a procedure? Why is it structured in this form? Some possible answers to these questions can now be considered.

WHY INVITE "PRIVATE" AND "PUBLIC" STATEMENTS?

Although some people, sometimes, in relation to some topics will not wish or need to present a different assessment to others from the one they entertain privately, this aspect of the design is very important. It is a direct affirmation that it is acceptable, expected, humanly necessary, frequently personally or socially laudable and always of some use to think more than you say or to modulate the expression of your beliefs according to the context within which you are placed. Instead of constantly urging people to a spurious ideal of "pseudohonesty", participants are here encouraged to recognize and take for granted that on both or all sides of any interaction other people and they themselves have a right to *privacy* and quite legitimately use and need to use "fictions". What is here prized more highly than "instant honesty" is the development of *skill* in recognizing and expressing for your own use, and for scientific purposes, the diverse ways in which ideas can be held for use within oneself rather than jettisoned carelessly in the outside world. It is here that study of the nature and purposes of secrets (Bakan, 1967) finds a proper and useful place in general psychology.

Now perhaps people will not believe you when you say the "private" sketch is really private. This is however a matter of increasing trust between participants and is exactly the kind of issue which can readily be seen not as a limitation or problem but used as a topic for investigation. As the cycles of encounter and exploration continue people's views of the situation and the relationships involved will change. The manner and pattern of these changes would be the subject of enquiry. Further, it does not really matter if a person keeps out of his "private" sketch some of the concerns of which he is fully or only partially aware. Sometimes we cannot afford to admit what we suspect we feel, at least at some times and in some contexts. By recognizing the necessity of privacy and by encouraging people to record, even partially, their private views, they may more readily develop their *awareness* of what is unsaid, not fully conceptualized but real none the less.

Hopefully, these "private" and "public" versions may serve other purposes. Their use seems directly relevant to Kelly's concept of role. As we all know, we are prepared and able to say different sorts of things to different people depending on what we think of them and what we want them to think of us. This is really what Kelly's idea of role is about. But full understanding of the explicit line of action a person follows in relation to another often cannot be gained from examining his expressed words or deeds in relation to that other person. The posture one person takes up towards another may be more readily clarified (even for the person himself) when he compares what he would say and what he would not say to the other person. *By examining the similarities and differences between one's private and public views of a person* one may be able more surely to define his assumptions about that other person in relation to himself. He may then be in a better position to *choose* to adjust or maintain that stance once it has been spelled out so clearly. The participants in so examining the differences between their public and private versions and systematically questioning themselves as to "why?" each difference and similarity exists for them (in a "laddering" process like that for eliciting superordinate constructs outlined by Hinkle (*see* Mair, 1969; Wright, 1969, 1970) are likely also to extend their awareness and skills in conceptualizing the sorts of needs or concerns they have regarding self-maintenance or self-development in many of their relationships with others.

Of course, what is kept private and what is made public will change in a variety of ways as different relationships progress. Throughout the course of any investigation of this sort repeated comparisons would be made by each participant between public and private statements (though what these statements were about would differ according to the purpose of the study) made at any particular time *and* between private or public versions used at different stages. The analyses of the latter might indicate something of the changing nature of the role relationships involved.

But surely it is ridiculous in something calling itself research, or even science, to encourage people to produce and use material which they may never divulge to the other participants? Certainly this seems a bit unusual, but the problems may be more apparent than real. If a person is unwilling to communicate the concrete details of any secrets this may matter little since, after all, virtually no secret in itself is likely to be very surprising and any specific kind of secret is likely to mean different things for different people. What may be of more importance in understanding a person are the *implications* of particular secrets for him; what functions they serve in his personal and interpersonal affairs. These functions may sometimes be more easily admitted than specific secrets and they may be explored in comparisons *between* public and private views. Even if *they*, initially, are not made available to the other participants, remember the investigator is an involved participant and will be developing his own insights into such issues. He can choose to communicate his discoveries whenever he wishes. Furthermore, we are here dealing with the study of *developing* relationships, continuing interactions, and what seems "unmentionable" at one stage is likely to seem like mundane "past history" at a later date and easily divulged.

This approach to psychological investigation is not intended as an exercise in psychic "strip tease" or "self revelation" or "confession". It is rather a mode of enquiry into the *processes* of interaction, enquiry and change which aims to make use of and develop *all* a person's psychological skills. Each participant also has the opportunity to extend his understanding, conceptualizations and means of finding out about himself, others and relationships between them.

WHY WRITE FORMAL SKETCHES?

This whole set of engagements is intended as a *disciplined* research enquiry, not a casual chat or a mini-encounter group. Because of this it seemed important to have opportunities at repeated encounters to record considered, organized ideas about the present position reached by each person regarding the topic of the enquiry. Without such firm, considered statements it would be difficult to trace the processes of change involved since each person would readily lose sight of his earlier positions. These "set pieces" may fulfil a number of purposes. They may provide each person with a means of expressing his present position regarding himself or others in relation to the topic under investigation; they provide a way of conveying convincing, genuine, personally relevant information to the other person or persons involved; they give an opportunity for each to develop his skill in specifying characteristics of himself or others. In the terms used by Fingarette (1969) in his penetrating analysis of self-deception, they may provide an opportunity for each to develop the "skill of spelling out his engagements in the world". In this procedure each is not only describing aspects of himself or others, but is given the opportunity to discover and create further possible ways of adequately capturing in words the sense he can make of psychological issues.

More formal analyses of these character sketches using Kelly's method of analysing Self Characterizations or Murray's system of need analysis or psychoanalytic ideas or any other, could also be used if required. But in the first instance the participants' own means of analysing and conceptualizing the information may be of particular importance.

WHY MAKE INFERENCES ABOUT THE WRITER OF THE SKETCHES?

There is still sometimes in psychology a tendency to think that when a description of someone is made it can in some sense be quite "objective", implying that personal limitations have somehow been by-passed in reaching conclusions. I do not see such a view as *generally* realistic. Consequently in this part of the procedure of enquiry it may be possible to find out about the varying ways and degrees to which people formulate their descriptions or judgments of others in terms which can be viewed as "projections" of themselves. In addition, it seems important to seek some rules concerning how people's evaluations of the "information" they gain from others may be modified by what they gather about the characteristics or concerns of the "informant". Our evaluation of any evidence is, after all, affected by the source of that information. The concern here is to pay some direct attention to this feature of interaction which is sometimes overlooked.

WHY INFORM THE OTHER PARTICIPANT(S) OF YOUR ASSESSMENTS OF THEM?

Ever since psychologists began assessing others they have been, by one means or another, reaching conclusions about their subjects and quietly carrying these assessments away to reveal, not to the person assessed, but to colleagues or others. Thus, the one person who is probably the greatest expert on the sense or nonsense of the psychologist's assessment has virtually always been excluded from the validational issue: after all, he would be subjective and involved and anyway, he is not really competent to judge the worth of technical assessments by expensively trained professionals! My concern here is to reverse this trend. This immediately raises the question of "contaminating" the subject of our assessment because he might now change in some ways. Exactly, that's what might well happen and it would be of considerable interest to see it happen. Surely an essential feature of life is that we continually learn from experience, well or badly. This section of the procedure is seen as a kind of intensification of the normal ways of finding out more about oneself and others. Concern here is not so much with the rightness or wrongness of the participants' assessments of each other but with the ways in which each *makes use of* his own and the other assessments. People are bound to change in some ways and remain the same in others. The present model may provide a framework within which some of these options can be noted by those involved.

It may appear that the use of this model supposes that man is all cognition and nothing much else. This is definitely not so. Indeed, the approach was accepted partly because it might allow many possibilities for noting and incorporating observations of *behaviour* as well as words. It is cognitive in the sense that all science is and in the way anything which concerns making explicit what was confused, complex and implicit is bound to be. It should not be assumed that because the aim is to "spell out" psychological processes of many kinds that what is "spelled out" is limited to intellectual matters.

Fingarette (1969) notes that by observing discrepancies between what a person says and what he appears to do, clues can be obtained about the projects in which he is engaged without awareness, such discrepancies may reveal how some of his purposes may not even be open to his own inspection. Because in the conversational approach under consideration, each participant is actively encouraged to use all his ideas, feelings, intuitions and observations about himself and the other participant(s), he is bound to incorporate these in his assessments or use them as evidence in justifying the conclusions he may reach at any point. Thus, although what is written down is necessarily verbal, what contributes to these written assessments will certainly not be limited in this way.

WHY STUDY SHORT AND LONGER TERM CONSEQUENCES OF ENCOUNTERS?

Psychological experiments in general tend to be short term encounters. Even longitudinal studies are generally only cross-sections sliced out at different times. There has thus been remarkably little work on the processes whereby people go about being the same or becoming different. Partly this has been because psychologists have generally wanted to keep their subject matter "pure" and "naïve". But people are not like that and if we want to conceptualize, predict or control how we develop as people we need some ways of exploring people *in action*, not just in blurred photographic captivity. We have been very concerned to find reliability and stability, but have still not found as much as hoped for in many aspects of psychological functioning (Mischel, 1968). Might it not be that a good way to study stability is to encourage movement; especially if what we are studying is in movement anyway? If that movement is slightly accelerated, the regularities in methods and concerns of the individual may well stand out more obviously because he himself may be in more need of affirming where he stands firmly in order to deal with changing events. This present method is aimed at catching some of the patterns of movement within and between people and thus to move towards statements concerning how we both go about "standing still" and "moving along".

In some ways this model for enquiry reverses some of the normal emphases in psychological experimentation. Normally the experiment begins when the participants enter the experimental room and ends when they leave. Here, what happens in the direct encounters is of great importance, but no more so than what happens *between* encounters when each person is living his own life. In this phase, each may need to be trained in the skills of taking note of the personal "experiments" he enters into in the normal course of events as he explores personal issues raised in the encounters. Participants would here begin to specify the range and sorts of "experiments" and "experimental designs" of use in their normal living. They may also become more competent in recognizing and stating the sorts of personal and interpersonal tactics or strategies they use in order to set up situations in such a way as to make things work the way they want or to evaluate the worth of their present and proposed commitments. It is here too, that one might hope to specify regularities in the sorts of *approaches* to problems which typified oneself or others and the sorts of solutions made possible or impossible by the adoption of these approaches.

WHY ASK PEOPLE TO GIVE EVIDENCE FOR THEIR ACTIONS OR JUDGMENTS?

Surely anyone knows that people, as often as not, do not know why they do things. Surely most of our reasons for doing things are hidden in past conditioning or buried in the unconscious. This may or may not be so, but seems largely irrelevant to the present issue. Surely, as scientists, we are constantly looking for evidence; and so also are lawyers, car mechanics, politicians, dry rot experts and everyone else. What may be studied here are the *sorts* of evidence people *are able to specify* initially and at later stages when they develop greater expertise in the task. Also the kinds of beliefs, judgments or actions which they engage in *without* having any clearly or even vaguely formulated grounds may be made more manifest. Many important features of personal beliefs are *unprovable* and useful just for this reason. In this present concern with evidence it would seem useful to be able to explore further these unprovable beliefs as well as those more harshly tied to outcomes, and to begin to specify how they help maintain viable personal systems of meaning. That a person may be unable to specify some of the grounds which justify his beliefs is no reason for not exploring what sorts of beliefs or actions he can give evidence for and those for which he cannot.

In specifying the nature of evidence a person is using he will be encouraged to look at the feelings, gestures, tones of voice, discrepancies between word and action and such like, which he may not normally be aware of noting. It is this part of the exercise where each participant may develop his powers of sensitive observation and inference, prized rightly by scientists as necessary accomplishments. One further point here; in talking about evidence I refer not only to what is called formal experimental evidence. Participants will probably find it important to make use of other sorts of evidence such as varieties of *procedural* as well as *validational* evidence, discussed in detail by Rychlak (1968) and more briefly with different emphases by Bromley (1968). Awareness of the sorts of evidence which might be sought may also be heightened by a recognition that people implicitly, if not explicitly, probably work in terms of a variety of different sorts of *causal* explanations. While psychological experimenters have tended to put almost exclusive reliance on *material* and *efficient* causation, it may here be important to recognize also the uses of *formal* and *final* cause explanations (Rychlak, 1968; 1970).

WHY HAVE REPEATED ENCOUNTERS?

This model is aimed at encouraging continuing studies rather than pinpoint encounters from which few have an opportunity of learning anything or making further use of what they may have learned. In being concerned to capture not man, but some aspects of *man in motion*, these repeated engagements would seem essential means of studying the ways in which relationships develop. Psychologists have been eager to improve their capacities in predicting aspects of human behaviour. They have done little, though, to study the human use of predictions or explore or develop their capacities in making and modifying predictions in the light of what they take to be evidence. In repeated encounters, participants could focus on presenting formulations of what each *predicts* the other will have done and thought following the exchanges in the previous encounter. Each might also attempt to specify what he thinks the other will have expected him to have made of the events he faced (here something like the study of perspectives and meta-perspectives in interpersonal perception suggested by Laing *et al.* (1966) is being introduced). In Kellian terms, participants in engaging in these predictive exercises are explicitly stating their anticipations, based on their role construing of the other; explicitly attempting to validate their understanding of the other in terms of what they expect his responses to have been resulting from a "common" experience.

Now all this has been very limited and only some of the possibilities of this approach have been mentioned. Certainly more problems may have been created than solved, but some *possible* solutions have been offered for certain old problems. In these speculations *one* possible framework for exploring some aspects of psychological functioning has been outlined. It would seem to allow acknowledgment of at least the following possibilities: that individuals make personal interpretations of events; that they have personal ways of organizing their personal meanings; that people are in movement and should be studied as such; that people act in relation to their understanding of other people and events and in so doing use and change their beliefs; that much of what we do, we do not fully appreciate and that the development of greater awareness may in large part be a result of an interpersonal learning process.

By the way, I forgot to mention which of our two imaginary participants was the experimenter. Could you tell? In a real sense *both were the experimenters* and *both were the subjects*. Clearly their concerns in any investigation are not identical but their status and functions are indistinguishable; clearly their competence or skill in spelling out their engagements and strategies will differ markedly but their opportunities are similar. Thus the model seems to offer the kind of integral involvement of subject and experimenter I've been seeking and is based on the use and development of trust in a co-operative enterprise. But is it science?

Some Features of a Conversational Science

Some may feel, perhaps rightly, that what has been suggested here is quite humane in that it both elevates the subject to the status of an experimenter and brings the experimenter fully into the structure of the investigations so that he can have not merely a ring-side seat but an active part in every performance. But have we not thrown out all claims to scientific method to achieve this? Thus, in an important sense, the proposed solution to the dilemma initially posed is no solution at all.

Only a few comments on this complex topic will be made here. But before this, one thing should be made clear. I *do not* regard the conversational model and the specific methods suggested as *replacements* for existing models and methods in psychology. While this seems to be the first conclusion to which many people jump, it is not so. While it is possible that insights and information gained by the approach outlined here might encourage modifications in some existing methods for some purposes, this approach in itself cannot replace them. Rather its use may suggest some ways of broadening the scope of psychology and dealing with some problems and issues which to date have been little studied. Some people, but not all, regard "tight" experimentation as their method of choice for *really* validating their predictions and that will doubtless continue. Not everyone regards *any particular* approach as being his method of choice for *all purposes*. Acceptance of this, indeed, seems at the heart of the use of this conversational model.

Some ideas about what sort of psychology would be compatible with this conversational model have been indicated elsewhere (Mair, 1970a,b) and a few other points will be touched on here.

One thing which science is centrally concerned with is achieving *communicable results*. Is the conversational approach not an invitation to subjective exploration of the personally unique and will not everyone take something different away from any investigation? There are certainly genuine problems about the nature of communicability with this approach which have not yet been resolved, but some answers can be given now. It is true that what is found in the sort of investigation mentioned is *personal* but this does not necessarily make it uncommunicable. The results at every stage can be presented in the form of *a series of separate or interrelated statements* (*see* Bakan, 1967, Chapter 9) by each participant about psychological events or relationships between events. For the person who makes these statements, they are likely to represent *actualities* for him. For others they may also accord with their own experience of similar actualities. The more people who acknowledge the same statement, the more generality the statement may have as representing what these people think is a state of affairs. Presumably very few psychological statements have universal applicability and any science tying itself only to these would be a pretty limited venture. What we may be looking for are statements with different degrees of generality.

But suppose a statement by one person is not recognized by others (after similar investigation) as reflecting their experience; what then, is it useless? Not at all. If something is *thought true* by one person it is in that sense a fact, an actuality. For other people its revelation creates another *possibility* for explanation or behaviour which otherwise they might not have entertained within their personal systems. Thus the results of this sort of study may contribute to both a body of *actualities* and *possibilities*.

Going further, can we accept that because one or more people believe something to be true that it is so? Not necessarily. Here is where *you* bring in *your* criteria for *really accepting* that something has been proved, and here as elsewhere people differ. The tendency in psychology today is to suppose that *real proof* needs a brittle experiment set up according to the traditions of a physical-science model. This again is quite acceptable; it reflects *personal* criteria concerning proof which in turn are central concerns of the conversational approach. When some participants seek to test out the worth of some of the statements resulting from some "conversational" encounter, they will consider it right for them to do it this way. This choice would constitute part of the data for further examination concerning why and for what purposes they saw that form of validation more adequate than others. A point which often seems to be missed in talk about obtaining proof or validating a hypothesis is that evidence is sought *for a purpose*. The evidence you get for one purpose may be quite inadequate for another purpose. People differ in their purposes and in the way they gather their relevant evidence. Some methods in relation to some purposes will certainly be better (according to some criteria) than others, but which and when is here a subject for study, not for dogmatic assertion.

The problem of communicability leads directly into other important concerns of psychologists. Two of these are the questions of *representativeness of samples* and *generalizability of results*. Because the method discussed starts and returns to personal experience as a central core, will it not be difficult to generalize the results? Answers to this question presumably depend on what one wishes to generalize about. Mostly, psychologists have tried to generalize about groups of people, but if one wished to generalize about cycles of movement or of sequences of methods and aims *within individuals* and *between individuals* perhaps appropriate generalizations can only be grounded in some form of enquiry similar to the one outlined. But still, won't the usefulness of the approach be limited by the unrepresentative nature of the people who may be willing and able to co-operate? This would seem no more of a problem here than with any other approach and in some ways it may even be less of a problem. Talk of representativeness in psychology is sometimes very undiscriminating. If you want to make statements about populations, a representative sample of that population needs to be examined. But if you want to m..ke statements about ways in which people execute cycles of enquiry (raising questions, getting evidence, experimenting and revising their beliefs) it will be more informative to use people in relation to whom it is possible to get partial answers rather than get no answers at all. Some partial answers may be useful in two ways. On the one hand, in spite of uniqueness of individuals, people are in many ways very much alike. Understanding of sequential psychological processes in one person may then have considerable relevance for understanding such processes in others. On the other hand, if features of the cycle of enquiry found in one person are not found in others, these more unique relationships will contribute to our knowledge of *possibilities* and so broaden our range of options for future action or explanation. Schultz (1969) notes with some alarm that most of the experimental work in psychology has been done on white, male, American college students. Clearly he is right in noting that for many purposes this sampling is quite unsatisfactorily limited. It is possible, however, if experimenters had been concerned in many of these studies to explore the ways in which these students gained, used and revised beliefs and methods in the course of their day to day lives as well as in laboratory situations, that we might now be able to say quite a lot about how the male, American college student "ticks"; and perhaps something about some other people besides.

In adopting this conversational model, I assume a science of man in which *rules* and *laws* are created partly to sustain present patterns of behaviour and partly to be transcended. Thus, we may look for some rules concerning regularities of psychological functioning which will have a short life span (because once some people get to know of them they will want to make use of these regularities in order to become regular in some other way) and some which, hopefully, may have a longer life span. But all may have to be seen as subject to repeated revision and replacement over varying periods and in relation to different sorts of human experience. Stated more personally, rules found appropriate for describing and found useful by one person at one stage of his development may not satisfactorily reflect his actions or serve any useful purpose for him at another stage. This seems rather different from much present concern to establish *the laws of behaviour*—and that's that. Such an approach makes one nervous in case any lay person sees the books where the precious laws are recorded because he may just go out to show he can act in such a way as to prove some of them no longer applicable. The alternative approach readily accepts that people do things with the regularities they create and know; such movement is then no threat but a necessary, desirable state of affairs.

At present there seems to be the feeling among some psychologists that it's a bit of a nuisance that everyone can interpret the same data differently, that people seem wilfully persistent in preferring their own theories to those of others and that there seems to be little sign yet of final unification of viewpoint. Some seek this unification by abandoning all theories and claiming that salvation lies only in collecting *the facts*; supposing "facts" to be untouched by assumptions. Behind this there is, perhaps, the belief and the hope that when we know enough, we will have only one grand theory of man and can then go home to put our feet up—a good job well done. This is not the view underlying the conversational model. The thought of everyone thinking in terms of the same explanations and following exactly the same logic seems frighteningly totalitarian and bleak; but thankfully it also seems completely unrealistic. Surely we need to encourage diversity in viewpoint. Having people actively exploring what aspects of the world can look like and what can be done if one or another starting point is accepted. This seems vital if we are to hope for human development and if we are to prevent ourselves dying of boredom.

What may be more profitable would be to develop a number of *theories about theorizing and experimenting* and a number of *models* within which to explore the methods and theories of individual people. Perhaps the conversational model may be the beginnings of one such model (as Personal Construct Theory is one such theory). While allowing the examination of many points of view it does not leave one adrift in the choppy seas of eclecticism. Rather it provides some structure (even if a temporary and partial one) within which freely to explore, use and develop possibilities for thought and action implicit in as many theories and methods as individuals are able to create.

Perhaps some uneasiness remains in some breasts about the fact that subjects participating in investigations employing this conversational model are likely to *change* in some respects as the study progresses. Another difference between the conversational approach and the traditional kind may underlie this. I assume that one of the basic aims in psychology should be to find means whereby people can extend *their own* ways of experiencing and exploring their worlds. In other words, psychology should be contributing more directly to individual lives and the psychologist who studies people should *give* at least as much as he gets from them, not merely at some indefinite future time (beyond the grave for most subjects) but in the course of the actual investigations. Much concern is shown in psychology with effecting *control over* the behaviour of subjects in many contexts. This seems acceptable within limits, provided that primary (or at least equivalent) attention is paid both to finding ways of developing *within* people the means whereby *they* can more readily control and modulate their own ways of dealing with themselves in the world and to finding means whereby people can handle more surely the unwanted controls which others may wish to impose on them.

Psychologists as People

The dilemma facing psychologists who wish to acknowledge the specifically human features of those they study (rather than the features men share with animals) is a dilemma just because psychologists too are human. When they recognize that their subjects share many of the concerns and capacities of experimenters, they must also appreciate that they, as experimenters, share the limitations of ordinary people. Psychologists, like other people, have to work within the bounds set by their own achievements and can hope to extend their competence only through the means they are capable of employing. Each has a limited viewpoint, personal and often unacknowledged assumptions, preferred theories and explanations, favoured methods for raising and answering questions. Like others, a psychologist can only subsume the assumptions, theories, methods and actions of others in relation to his personal points of view and to the extent that his own sense-making system allows.

Personal Construct Theory seems to provide the sketched outline of a theory which recognizes and uses these personal structures and the Conversational Model may provide one framework within which these individual configurations can be employed as valued tools in the study of man rather than rejected as embarrassing shortcomings. As psychologists we seem to have an alarming tendency to transform important human characteristics into problems, weaknesses and sources of error. This largely seems due to a continuing, if often blurred, adherence to a view of science quite inappropriate to the subject matter we seek to understand.

Psychologists, in recognizing their personal limits and predilections as people, have generally sought to overcome these by *excluding* themselves as thoroughly as possible from the contexts within which they act as scientists. Thus we have often tried to use, or acknowledge, as little of ourselves as possible in our professional roles. But, as noted already, our subjects still persist in viewing psychologists, even when they act as experimenters, as human beings like themselves. If we are inevitably to be seen as this, why not make the best rather than the worst of it? Why not intentionally begin to use *all* our capacities of feeling, thought and action to aid us in creating more sensitive means to extend our understanding of ourselves and others (who are the subject matter of psychology)? It was William James who said somewhere: "It takes the whole of us to spell the meaning out completely." This being so we can convert our personal preferences in thought and action into our greatest scientific assets rather than our shameful secrets. What we discover about ourselves can contribute to our own growth and to the possible development of others, just as our discoveries about others may aid them and extend the range of possibilities we personally can employ. In all this remembering that when we study others the conclusions we reach are about *persons in relation* (Macmurray, 1961) and not specifically about us or them.

Psychology can be made different from what it has so far been and the nature of this difference depends on the imaginative possibilities which psychologists as men are able to put into effect. George Kelly explored in some detail the necessary bonds between actions and possibilities in the lives of individuals and he should perhaps have the last word here (Kelly, 1969). The actions of a psychologist, like the actions of any man, may better be understood "in an expanding context of all that is seen to be possible for him, rather than within the boundaries of his presumed nature, his reflexes, his brain, his complexes, his chronological age, his intelligence, or his culture. This, of course, means that, as unsuspected potentialities materialize, we shall probably have to keep changing the coordinates in terms of which we plot his life processes. But it does suggest, at the same time, that psychology can become a vital part of the on-going human enterprise. It is scarcely that now."

References

Bakan, D. (1967). "On Method", Jossey-Bass Inc., San Francisco.
Bannister, D. and Mair, J. M. M. (1968). "The Evaluation of Personal Constructs", Academic Press, London and New York.
Bromley, D. B. (1968). Conceptual analysis in the study of personality and adjustment. *Bull. Brit. Psychol. Soc.* **21,** 155–160.
Fingarette, H. (1969). "Self-Deception", Routledge and Kegan Paul, London and New York.
Friedman, N. (1967). "The Social Nature of Psychological Research", Basic Books, New York.

Hinkle, D. N. (1965). The change of personal constructs from the viewpoint of a theory of implications. *Unpublished Ph.D. Thesis*, Ohio State University.

Jourard, S. M. (1968). "Disclosing Man to Himself", Van Nostrand, Princeton, N.J.

Kelly, G. A. (1955). "The Psychology of Personal Constructs" Vols 1 and 2, Norton, New York.

Kelly, G. A. (1969). Humanistic methodology in psychological research *In* "Clinical Psychology and Personality" (Maher, B., ed.), John Wiley and Sons, New York.

Kelman, H. C. (1967). Human use of human subjects: the problem of deception in social psychological experiments. *Psychol. Bull.* **67**, 1–11.

Laing, R. D., Phillipson, H. and Lee, A. R. (1966). "Interpersonal Perception", Tavistock Publications, London.

Macmurray, J. (1961). "Persons in Relation", Faber and Faber Ltd., London.

Mair, J. M. M. (1969). Personal constructs and personal growth. *De Psycholoog*. **IV**, 360–377.

Mair, J. M. M. (1970a). Experimenting with individuals. *Brit. J. med. Psychol.* **43**, 245–256.

Mair, J. M. M. (1970b). The person in psychology and psychotherapy: an introduction. *Br. J. med. Psychol.* **43**, 97–205.

Milgram, S. (1965). Some conditions of obedience and disobedience to authority. *Human Relat.* **18**, 57–76.

Mischel, W. (1968). "Personality and Assessment", John Wiley and Sons, New York.

Orne, M. T. (1962). On the social psychology of the psychological experiment: with particular reference to demand characteristics and their implications. *Am. Psychol.* **17**, 776–783.

Rosenthal, R. (1966). "Experimenter Effects in Behavioral Research", Appleton-Century-Crofts, New York.

Rychlak, J. F. (1968). "A Philosophy of Science for Personality Theory", Houghton Mifflin Co., Boston.

Rychlak, J. F. (1970). The human person in modern psychological science. *Br. J. med. Psychol.* **43**, 233–240.

Schultz, D. P. (1969). The human subject in psychological research. *Psychol. Bull.*, **72**, 214–228.

Seeman, J. (1969). Deception in psychological research. *Am. Psychol.* **24**, 1025–1028.

Stricker, L. J. (1967). The true deceiver. *Psychol. Bull.*, **68**, 13–20.

Stricker, L. J., Messick, S. and Jackson, D. N. (1969). Evaluating deception in psychological research. *Psychol. Bull.* **71**, 343–351.

Wright, K. J. T. (1969). An investigation of the meaning of change in phobic patients using grid methods. *Unpublished M. Phil. Thesis*, University of London.

Wright, K. J. T. (1970). Exploring the uniqueness of common complaints, *Brit. J. med. Psychol.* **43**, 221–232.

George Kelly: An Appreciation

Don Oliver

On being asked to write a paper for this volume my first thought was that it should be something critical of George Kelly's psychological "system". There was no pressure on choice of topic or type of paper, but what else would be expected of a philosopher? Surely philosophy is nothing if not critical. Besides, what did I know of Kelly? Quite a few years ago I had been introduced to his "Psychology of Personal Constructs" (Kelly, 1955) by an admiring friend and pupil of his. It had, in large part, puzzled me, more especially in its claim to being scientific, and it had, in somewhat smaller part, caught my imagination because I sensed that I had been following paths roughly parallel to those Kelly was pioneering. The latter were vague paths as I discerned them then, perhaps because I could not disentangle them from what, by my inveterate habit as a philosopher, I could not but reject, as inept, as inconsistent, as ambiguous in his, to me, bungling attempts at what I then conceived a system to be. "He should have read Aristotle", I said, "instead of striking out blindly at what Aristotle is supposed to stand for". "He should have read Dewey, the whole of him, and studied how Dewey went about doing much the same thing that he, Kelly, was trying to do." "He should have been more careful and more subtle in drawing his characterization of the scientist and scientific method". These were by no means the only critical remarks that I voiced to myself. Still, even then, each "he should have" was accompanied by the wish that he had, for I did feel that the case he wanted to make—or that *I* thought he wanted to make—deserved to be made well.

But now that I have read, only recently, the papers included in "Clinical Psychology and Personality" (Kelly, 1969), it strikes me that I might make my best contribution not by writing as a philosopher, not primarily at least, but as a man appraising another man; or as a man appraising the humanity of another man, giving forth an answering call to a shout he has heard, even though indistinctly. For I have decided that *for me*—a phrase Kelly would surely not object to—he is not a deviser of a system, and hence not to be judged by the cold logic of consistency. Or I could turn that around and say that he *has* devised a system, but that it is a most peculiar one in that it is intended to stimulate thought, not to capture it and force it into a straight-jacket. As to the latter version, the *for me* comes in as "for me the question of whether such a strange thing can be called a system, or a theory, is irrelevant".

So to speak, it is George Kelly himself who has persuaded me to step out of my professional disguise to speak from another—that of a man (which no doubt *is* another, even a more pretentious one!). After all, I can assume no prerogatives as a psychologist, so what is left to me except myself and who would listen to me if I spoke through *that* mask? I agree that the philosopher is a man and should not forget it, just as the scientist is, and should not forget it. I think also that the philosopher should lift his eyes, from time to time, from his favourite theory or his critical ventures to take a look at men and at himself, as well as at the world he finds himself living in. I am not sure that he will always look at himself or other men as Kelly would, but almost any look that is not theory-bound would be refreshing. Useful, too, in his philosophical labours, if he has the flexibility to assimilate what he has seen.

Much of what Kelly has written has to do with creativity, more often, with what prevents it from realizing itself. This is bound to catch the interest of the lay reader. Each of us, or at least anyone who is likely to be found reading Kelly, secretly thinks that he is creative—well, not just now, maybe not in the—oh, the last ten years. If only one were not so busy, if one did not have so many cares, if one could get away from the office and the job—and the children—then. . . . We all want to be creative, but there's this business of finding something to be creative about. Something big, something important; but also something we could *do*, within our capacities, that is. And so, we will just have to bide our time, wait for the right circumstances to come along, and the right idea.

If what we expect from Kelly when we first read what he has to say about man's creative capacities is some advice about how to hurry up the circumstances and the idea, then we probably won't read him for long. He does not tell us how to outsmart Einstein, or how to invent a new airplane engine. There are no diagrams, no kits, no exercises to be done on arising in the morning and going to bed at night. And it is somewhat deflating to one's idea of creativity to read that learning *is* experience and experience learning—or that whatever living is done without learning isn't experiencing—and then to discover, by degrees, that Kelly doesn't mean very much more by "creating" than he does by "learning". Perhaps, even, not *anything* more.

In the following I wish to explore both "our" reasons for feeling dissatisfied with Kelly's account of "man, the creative animal"—the phrase is mine, not Kelly's—and the possible virtues of Kelly's description.

I suppose that most everyone links creativity with the making of discoveries. Maybe not in the "fine arts", but pretty surely in the sciences. A scientist "discovers something". Maybe it is a law, or maybe it is a new atomic particle. What is discovered is something that was there, waiting to be discovered. The creative scientist is then a man who is good at searching, uncovering. He has sharper eyes than others—if not literally eyes, then a sharper, more "penetrating" mind. This, at least, is the way that Kelly thinks people have regarded creativity in the sciences. They indeed must have if they were loyal to the conception of reality they profess: that what is real is *there*, outside of us, and that it is the business of the man of knowledge to get at what is there in some way or other and give us an account of it. As I have said, this may not be the opinion they hold of man engaged in the fine arts, but if they think that a great work of art captures or expresses a truth about something or other, then it is likely that they do.

Kelly disagrees. Of course he can not just reject this opinion outright. He has to provide a substitute for it. His rejection is of this conception of truth and reality. It is not that there is no reality, but that man has no way of making direct contact with it. He does not just open his eyes and look and there it is! Whatever man perceives or conceives he "grasps" by application of a "construct system". He can "take in" only what his construct system is capable of handling. That is to say, what it can not handle is, so far as man is concerned, mere confusion, chaos. It is not quite that he can not be aware of it in some sense of "aware", but that it can not be assimilated to his world in a reasonable, rational, or even perceptual way, so long as his construct system remains what it is. In Kelly's terminology, man *construes* that which he encounters of the real in terms of his construct system, which, in effect, sets limits on what he can comprehend.

Now for creativity: I have been speaking of *man*. Kelly writes of the individual. *Each* man has a construct system of his own, and each man does his own construing. There is no reason why the construct system of one man should be very like that of another. And construct systems are not fixed. They can and do change. Kelly has a great deal to say about how and under what conditions they change. I shall not attempt even to summarize what he does write, except to say that the conditions under which they change are all internal to the individual, and that, in a sense which I shall attempt to make clear, the latter is in control of the change. Kelly does not profess to know much of anything about reality, but of one of its characteristics he seems to be very sure. It changes, it is even in a constant flux. The individual is in flux too. Here Kelly's metaphysical position, which is never expressed very explicitly, seems to approximate that of Bergson, who regarded reality as in flux and pictured the intellect of man as an instrument for arresting the flux by imposing concepts on it. Only Kelly does not distinguish between the intellect and the rest of man, and he explicitly says that an individual's construct system, which sort of takes the place of Bergson's intellect, does change. It changes by changing itself, and that, I shall assert now and explain later, it does by being creative!

Reality as Kelly conceives it—or does not conceive it—is not much of a hindrance to him. It does not set lines within which man's experience must flow. In point of fact, if there are lines they are set by the individual's construct system, and if they are hindrances that is the fault of the individual who owns that system. What he does feel he can say about reality is that it offers man an indefinite, even an infinite, number of possibilities for construal. There is no one construal that is right or true, while all others are wrong. He does not intend this to mean that there can be no wrong construals. There can. Reality has that much structure, enough to exclude some perceptions or interpretations of it; but it is "tolerant" of a variety of construals, and an individual in construing freshly is exhibiting his creativity. One might ask whether a fresh construal is a creation in the way that a painting or a novel type of bridge is. The answer is yes, and for two reasons which may at bottom be one, but which had better be presented separately.

First, the individual is real and any change in him is a change in reality. Kelly does seem to think of a man's construct system as being the core of his personality. As such it is, or is close to being, his reality. But a construct system is changed through construals made under it. The change occurs when a fresh construal comes as a response to the failure of the conceptual system, as it then stands, to provide correct anticipation of what is to come in the experience of the individual. When the individual suffers repeated disappointments in his anticipations, that, as Kelly presents the matter, is because his construct system is inadequate. It blocks possible construals that might be more satisfactory. But it cannot be changed directly, that is to say its "owner" cannot lay hands on it and twist it into a new form. He cannot do this because it is by the construct system that he construes his world, every item in it, and he cannot "get at" it as a thing which he might change. However, a "good" construct system is one that possesses a considerable degree of flexibility. We might put it that it contains "blank spaces" to be filled in by construal; or that there are potential pathways within it that can be blazed by novel construals. It boils down to the fact that in such a construct system fresh construals can alter the structure of the system. And so, in some such way as this the individual can change by exercising his creativity, and such change is change in reality because the individual is real.

Second, the individual is active. Kelly objects violently to the "push" theories (S-R psychology) and the "pull" theories (motivation psychology) of man because neither recognizes man's self-moving, self-realizing nature. Nor does Kelly tolerate any of the usual divisions of man into faculties— the intellect, the will and the emotions, for example. He insists that the individual is a whole in the sense that no separate systems can be distinguished within him. It follows from this that no sharp line can be drawn between thinking and acting. Construing can be interpreted as either thinking or acting. We construe our worlds by actively inducing changes in them quite as much as by reconceiving them. I think that Kelly would regard a reconceptualization that was not followed by changes in active response as an *Unding*, very near to a contradiction. So we can see that a creative re-structuring of the construct-system of an individual is equivalent to the freeing of potentialities that are potentialities of reality quite as much as of the individual, and we can confidently expect that "material" consequences of that "psychological" change will, as a matter of course, put in an appearance.

I shall now begin to creep out of the present disguise and into another. Or, as I might put it, I shall drape some shreds of the philosopher's robe over my shoulders. That means abandonment of the strictly expository mood and its replacement by one of criticism. I hope it will be understanding criticism, sympathetic to the tasks he has undertaken.

Kelly has a good reason for not venturing to characterize reality. What we cannot know except through construal under a construct system cannot be known as it is in itself (this is a Kantian theme that one encounters again and again in modern philosophy). But having become convinced of this, he should have felt constrained to say nothing more about reality than that it *is*. He does recognize this constraint sometimes; but sometimes he does not. When he asserts that reality is in flux, or that it is of its nature to change, for example. Now he could reply to this sort of charge that this is but an assumption, an hypothesis, he has made to see how it aids him in making predictions. I am willing to accept this as an answer, but of course it is open to me, or to anyone, to put forward a different hypothesis respecting the nature of reality. There is no question about what Kelly's response to this sort of claim would have been. He very explicitly upholds the right of anyone to advance any hypothesis he chooses to, though it will then be his responsibility to test it by making predictions from it. In the following I propose to advance another and somewhat more complex hypothesis about reality. I shall attempt to show first that the predictions Kelly draws from his hypothesis could also be drawn from mine, and that mine would extricate him from certain logical difficulties which I believe he is caught in. Thus it is my intent not to attack his positive theory, but rather to abet it by a reconstrual of reality, and, through that, of the person. I would like to push my criticism back as far as Kelly's notion of the construct system, but I fear that cannot be done without increasing the length of this paper beyond reasonable bounds. I confine myself, therefore, to the context of the person as revealed through his treatment of creativity.

I see no good reason for ascribing but a single basic character to reality. That reality is flux is a possible hypothesis. But so is it that reality is unchanging. It might be difficult to draw predictions from that one, but so might it be from the first if we really tried to carry it through. Anyhow why should reality not be characterized by motion *and* rest? I say "characterized" because I suspect that one might get into trouble were he to say it *is* motion and it *is* rest. So in laying down this postulate I am assuming reality to be something more than just motion and rest: there is something that sometimes is in motion and sometimes is at rest. Here my difference with Kelly takes on a double aspect: I not only assert rest as well as motion of reality, but I object to his objection to the use of a subject-attribute mode of speaking. Since a good deal of what I shall have to say turns on this rejection on Kelly's part, I shall say a bit more on the subject.

I have found one mention in Kelly's writings of Korzybski. Perhaps he was influenced by him. Perhaps he had been reading Bertrand Russell, or some other proponent of symbolic logic. Korzybski, in my opinion, is a wild man, full of interesting, even exciting suggestions, but he is not a man one ought to choose for a guide. Before releasing his invective against Aristotle, he should have read Aristotle. The man he attacks, very definitely, is not Aristotle. Much the same thing can be said of Kelly. When he speaks of "traditional" or "classical" logic, he is usually talking about something that never existed on sea or land. Nor do I believe that Kelly ever realized just how much "doing" it takes to produce and to put to work a "logic of relations", i.e. a logic that does not employ the subject-predicate mode of expression. The fact is that none of the special non-predicative logics that have been invented have been put to use as languages. The philosopher, when he is interested in something more than these logics as formal systems, employs them as tools of analysis which are suggestive of possible ontologies. By employing symbolic logic in this way Bertrand Russell, among others, has been able to suggest ontologies that do not contain such elements as substances and properties of substances. It is true that the grammatical structure of English and other Indo-European languages inclines us to think of whatever we want to talk about as if it were an object bearing qualities. But, as it has turned out, philosophers who have rejected this sort of ontology have managed to express themselves quite effectively in English and other languages of similar structure. In short, a subject-predicate language can possess resources for obviating the subject-predicate "prejudice" inherent in it. Actually, the special "languages" developed by philosophers are far more prejudicial in this respect than "ordinary language". Little is gained, and much can be lost by trading off the language we are accustomed to speak for another.

It is true that if one's language offered no choice of different ways of expressing oneself, it would be truly restrictive. But when one has other languages available in which other ways of saying things are possible, one does have a choice. I make this point only to indicate that one could *choose* to speak in subject-predicate terms without being forced to by one's language. I do choose to, as many other philosophers have. It is, of course, the reasons for my choice, especially as they bear on Kelly's theory, that are important.

We commonly speak of man as a being to whom things happen, who does things to objects, who has ideas, experiences, suffers pain, enjoys successes, and so on. I think we should not be asked to give up this manner of speaking unless there are some very good arguments against it. One argument that has sometimes been thought conclusive is that no one has been able to tell us in a wholly satisfactory way what this something or other is that we call a man. We collect descriptions of him, of his exploits, of his misfortunes readily enough, to be sure, but these are all descriptions of what he looks like, feels like, does, suffers, etc. In what sense, if any, are they descriptions of *him*? If it is maintained that *he* should be that which does these things, suffers these misfortunes, thinks these thoughts, but *not* the doing, the suffering, the thinking, then of course we will never get at him, for all we encounter are these emanations from him and accidents to him. (This is only a somewhat concrete version of the argument whereby John Locke convinced himself that in man's knowledge substance can be only a "something I know not what".)

Another argument against our ordinary way of speaking is that this "empty core" of "the man himself" (more generally, of substance, which is supposed to comprise the reality of every object) invites the unscrupulous to speculate shamelessly about the nature of things. This is speculation that is especially hateful to the empirically minded critic because, protected by that insulating "shell" of substance it goes scot free of the criticism experience can afford.

But I wonder whether either of these criticisms would touch a concept of the self or of substance somewhat differently drawn. Suppose we were to say that the self is not an inscrutable substance that "lies behind" what is observed, but is revealed to us in our experience. We learn more about the self, including ourselves, as experience rolls up. Properties, characteristics, actions, reactions *are* properties of something that *has* these properties, etc. In other words, substance or the self is not unknowable. It reveals itself through its behaviour. *Only* it goes right on revealing itself. It is knowable but not completely knowable, for to be completely knowable in this sense a substance would have to have a finite repertoire of revelatory acts. We go on learning more and more about substantial things, but we never learn all that could be known about them. As we learn, we have to revise opinions already formed, for there is no reason to suppose that our learning must be passive. We do not have to wait placidly for experience to reveal what is to come next in the "performance" of an object. Indeed, what we do learn by experience about the peculiar object called "man" is that anticipation is a very prominent feature of his repertoire, and that he anticipates by forming concepts that have a variegated "filling" of what has been observed and what is speculatively suggested by the latter in man's imagination. One might say that by thus imaginatively supplying what observation has not provided, he is filling with content that "empty space" at the centre of the notion of substance. But note that this sort of content is subject to correction by further experience, just because it takes the form of anticipation.

Now there is nothing about the subject-predicate way of speaking and thinking that forbids our conceiving substance as I have just done. It is true that some philosophers and some psychologists have so defined substance that the things I have been saying could not be said. But that is an act of vandalism, a deliberate destruction of the marvellous flexibility of the language we all speak. More particularly, there is no reason why we should not think substance as active rather than passive, or as coming into existence and passing out of existence, or as particular—in the sense that the substance of this individual or object is not the substance of that. Substances can grow and change, and can collide with and alter one another, can fall into complex systems in which they mutually support one another, and so on and on.

But I must bring all this to bear upon Kelly and his theory. I shall try to show—and this will be my last point—that Kelly could not say many of the things he does, and he could not lay claim to having produced a theory of personality, if he were to adhere strictly to the restrictions he would place on the language of psychology as it is to be employed within his own system. How is one to talk about actions in the absence of an actor? If something is done, does it not have to be done to something and by something? If there is a thought, does it not have to be somebody's thought, and is it possible to reduce the "somebody" who has had a thought—or an experience, or a fear, or a fright or a heart attack—to the thought or experience, etc.? It is very easy to reply to this bank of questions, rhetorical questions, admittedly, by the accusation that I am caught in the net of a subject-predicate language. Of course one cannot avoid talking this way, so long as one has no other language in which to express oneself! This is a reply, I suppose, but surely it is not conclusive. If it were to be so, it would have to show how these things are to be done; in short, to do them. It would not help to set up equivalences, write a dictionary giving a definition of each subject term of the subject-predicate language in the new language, because the very possibility of such equivalences presupposes equivalence of the two languages. If they *are* different, then the one can say things the other cannot. If we can express the same things in both, then they are insofar equivalent. If such a word as "act" is not dissociable from "actor" in our native language, then "act" cannot be taken up by another language without dragging "actor" along with it.

Actually, Kelly has not invented any new languages, nor has he taken over and used any of the new languages that others have invented. All that he says is said in a subject-predicate language, which he occasionally does assert to be misleading. But whatever he has to say against it is said in that language, and whatever corrections he makes in it are made by utilization of the facilities it has to offer. He is still entangled in the conditions it imposes. For my part, I am content to remain entangled, but Kelly is not, and his belief that he has escaped leads him to make some questionable assertions. He talks frequently of movement or activity as being of the nature of man— and of everything else, for that matter—so that there is no need to invoke either pushes or pulls to account for man's behaviour. This I would not quarrel with. But he seems to think that in rejecting the common notion of inert matter he is doing away with the concept of substance. This is simply false. In the history of ideas, hylozoism, or the idea that matter, or nature, or whatever you wish to call it is alive and self-moving antedates by centuries the modern concept of inert substance. It was not until Galileo that the latter was given an unambiguous formulation. It is precisely the notion of a substance that is self-moving that can best account for action.

It is in his treatment of the construct system that Kelly comes closest to placing a restriction on himself that I think is suicidal. He suggests that in the theory he is formulating the person be regarded as nothing more than a construct system. It is not difficult to guess at what he hoped to gain by this move. It would undercut a vast amount of traditional opinion about the person, for instance all those distinctions between body and soul, intellect, appetite and will, emotions and concepts, perception and conception that have long been thought absolutely essential for an understanding of man. It would indeed clear out a quantity of what Kelly thought was useless baggage and leave him with a free hand to develop his own hypothesis. But if taken seriously and literally, it would plunge him into a paradox of reflexivity—a danger to which he, more than any other psychologist, was alert—and render him powerless to make assertions essential to the statement of his theory.

The paradox of reflexivity enters with the fact that here is a man, a theorist, Kelly himself, suggesting that all men be considered to be only construct systems. So he must be a construct system if his hypothesis is to be taken seriously. The other men he wishes to theorize about must be construct systems within his construct system. There is nothing especially wrong with this, provided that it is immediately pointed out that it is only by *construing* other men under his construct system that he can perceive, think about or theorize about them; *but* that there is no intention to reduce them to construals under his concept system. Of course Kelly has no intention to so reduce them. But not having an intention to do something is not always equivalent to not doing it. The question is how anyone who has this intention not to is to avoid doing it. Only, so far as I can see, by attributing a reality, independent of his concept system, to other men. To himself too, otherwise he will be nothing more than a set of construals under other concept systems. For my part, I cannot see how one is to attribute reality to oneself and other men except by granting that there is *that which* has a construct system, *that which* construes under that construct system, and a host of *thats* that are variously construed. My point is simple enough; it really was made already in my contention that if "that which acts" is to be withdrawn from our vocabulary, then "act" and "action" must be also.)

Granted, Kelly is offering us an hypothesis. He insists that it is only an hypothesis and he forecasts its eventual abandonment. It might be thought that something that is merely useful for making predictions need not encompass or mention all those factors which must be present in order that something be real. Thus man might be treated *as if* he were only a concept system. The hypothesis might work well, and no harm would be done. I think this is a mistaken argument. An hypothesis is not a machine that stamps out products—predictions. I even think it misleading to call it an intellectual tool, unless we mean by the latter that it helps us to understand. An hypothesis that lops off something that is essential to the understanding of its subject is no help to the understanding. It is especially important that it be complete in its own way if it is to be treated as, or if there is to develop out of it, a theory of personality. The latter must present the person as something that could be *real*, not as something that could never be more than a figment of the imagination. I believe that this is a point that Kelly has appreciated at one juncture at least: where he stipulates that there is a reality which, though unknowable in itself, is what is construed under each person's construct system. He need only extend this assertion about reality to the person, i.e. assert that each person is real and is potentially subject to an indefinite plurality of construals by himself and by other persons. This brings us to another subject which, in turn, will lead us back to creativity, the topic we began with.

I believe that Kelly could have ventured to say a little more about reality. Following the lines I suggested when I was speaking of substance and our knowledge of it, he might have asserted that changes are induced in reality by construal; or, what may be the same thing, construal is *one* of the ways in which reality changes. Construal need not be a screen between us and reality. (In being construed reality is revealed to the construer. Not "as it is in itself", of course, and not as everything it could be. Why not say that in a construal those of reality's potentialities that appear within this construal are realized, and that they would not have been realized if this construal had not been made, and not, therefore, if the person who made it had not existed.)

This reveals the sense in which we can assert that a person in construing himself, things, other persons is creative. He is contributing to the totality of what is. Of course this is a rather "flat" sense of creativity. What is contributed may be momentous or trivial, good or bad. A stab might be made at drawing a distinction between the momentous and good and the trivial and bad by utilizing one of Kelly's leading principles: that a person tends to modify his construct system in such a way that a maximum of freedom for its subsequent modification is achieved. (I am not sure that he *does*, but I agree that he *should*.) This would induce the desired distinction in the proposition that momentous and good construals (creations) are those that open the way to an indefinite multitude of possible construals and those that restrict or block subsequent construals are trivial or bad.

I do not think this an unlikely candidate, though it is very abstract and surely cannot serve as the sole criterion of high level creativity. The real art work and the great idea in science do seem to be those subject to—even demanding—the greatest number and variety of interpretations. They are, as we sometimes say, the works that take hold of and stimulate man's imagination. They do not stimulate it "wildly" of course. They excite and at the same time channelize, holding the activity they excite within limits, but never within such narrow limits that the induced product is trite. And it is because it is not trite that *it* does not block subsequent construal. That is to say, creativity of the momentous variety is the very opposite of the "dead end" sort of conclusiveness that some people seem to feel is the proper goal of intellectual and artistic activity.

One further comment will reveal the final twist that my suggestion would give to Kelly's psychology interpreted as a theory of personality: The person, when we insist that he be real, is not just another chunk of reality. He is an interpreter, a construer, through whom reality is enriched. To see how this could be we must manoeuvre ourselves into a mood of acceptance for the assertion that things may really be as man construes them. *Their* potentialities are released or realized in construals of them. When the construal is of a social order, this seemingly strange idea can be recognized as almost a commonplace. In the presence of chemists, engineers and social needs, iron ore becomes pig iron, pots and pans, bridges, locomotives and what not. But it is equally true that, on the individual level, in the presence of a sculptor a block of stone becomes a statue. A man is not just another thing in the universe. Would it be too much to say that reality becomes a universe only by reason of man's presence in it; man as a construing creature, of course? If all this is rather poetic and far-fetched, I do not know but that Kelly is partly responsible for it. His way of conceiving the individual, with no internal partitions, no distinctions between construing through perception, through thought or through action, makes it easy to pass right through the person to the world about him, or conversely, through his world to him. The "no internal partitions" transforms with ease to "no external skin".

References

Kelly, G. A. (1955). "The Psychology of Personal Constructs", Vols 1 and 2, Norton, New York.

Kelly, G. A. (1969). "Clinical Psychology and Personality, The Selected Papers of George Kelly" (Maher, B., ed.), Wiley, New York.

A Psychology of Personal Growth

Phillida Salmon

In trying to assess the value of psychology, it seems fair to ask how much it has contributed to the understanding, not of psychologists as such, but of people in general. Through the various media of communication in our society, most of the major claims made by psychologists do eventually get through to the man in the street. The degree to which he is able to apply these to his own experience, to achieve through them a greater understanding of himself and other people, and even to order his life more effectively, constitutes one possible criterion of the validity of the ideas themselves. Personality development is an area which is of the greatest concern to most people, particularly parents; and in considering the formal psychology which centres on it, I should like to begin by looking at the legacy which psychologists have bequeathed to ordinary people involved in bringing up children.

In this century, possibly the greatest influences on the layman's ideas about the development of children's personalities have derived from two major schools of psychology—the behaviourist school of Watson and the psychoanalytic school of Freud. From behaviourism came an emphasis on correct procedure in child rearing; the ideal child's personality was seen as the direct outcome of prolonged drilling to produce the right behaviour at the right time. The concern with rigorous feeding and sleeping schedules and with the careful timing of disciplinary measures, which can be seen in the baby-care manuals and log books of the late 1920's, suggests how strong an effect this line of thought exercised on general attitudes towards child upbringing. A little later, however, this influence was countered by that of the Freudian school. The focus was now upon the primitive, alien nature of the young child and the pathological consequences which followed any mishandling of his needs. The "right way" to develop a well-adjusted child became more obscure; both indulgence and severity towards the child's demands were equally fraught with dangers, of fixation on the one hand and repression on the other.

It can be argued that both these approaches were predominantly negative and inhibiting in their effect on parents. The correct child-rearing approach,

197

according to behaviourist thought, lay in direct opposition to parental spontaneity and casualness; while the strictures of Freud emphasized the far-reaching threats, subtle and hard to counter, implicit in everyday contacts between parents and children. To the extent that parents actually tried to follow the precepts of either school, they were likely to become anxious and confused. Indeed, by the middle of the century, some theorists were consciously aware of this situation, and were concerned to free parents from the inhibiting influence of psychology. Winnicott, for example, consistently urged that expertise in bringing up a child was the prerogative of "the ordinary devoted mother", and many other writers urged parents to "throw away the book" and follow their natural feelings in dealing with their children. A similar, even more fundamental, assumption seems built into the very empirical approach of many contemporary studies of child development. It is not merely that the child, quite rightly, has been "given back" in a moral sense to his parents; it is also that, by defining their variables in sociological, economic or demographic terms, many researchers in the field of personality development seem to suggest that psychology as such can have little to say about the processes involved.

How far is such an assumption justified? Granted that psychological theories as yet have held little that is positive or constructive to offer parents; does this mean that the scientific study of personality development must inevitably be non-psychological, or else devoid of any practical usefulness? Certainly this is not the case where cognitive development is concerned. Despite its high level of abstraction, the psychological theory of Piaget has exercised a profound and highly fertile influence on actual educational practices. Teachers, who are directly concerned with understanding and producing cognitive development, have been, as a group, greatly affected by Piaget's ideas about the qualitative changes in children's thinking, the internal logic of each developmental stage, and the function of active experimentation. The effect can be seen not merely in the theoretical formulations of teacher training courses, but also in certain fundamental changes in teaching methods. For instance, the conception of the young child as essentially intuitive, and governed by his impressions, has led, at the infant school stage, to the devising of educational situations which translate ideas into concrete, manipulable form, and which enable the child to test out his own ideas by their external expression. For teachers, Piaget's theory of cognitive development has opened new horizons, offered profound insights and given rise to fruitful extensions and changes of teaching method.

The Language of Objects

If cognitive development is accessible to psychological theorizing with such positive and fertile practical applications, the processes of personality growth seem potentially equally accessible. Yet, so far, psychological explanations of personality development appear singularly barren. This may well be because theorists in this area characteristically adopt an externalized orientation towards their subject. In Kelly's terms, they tend to use a language of objects, rather than a language of persons. Where the behaviourist school is concerned, this orientation is, of course, explicit and intentional, the "black box" approach being deliberately chosen as the only scientific and objective stance possible. More recent exponents of learning theory, such as Sears (Sears *et al.*, 1965) have considerably modified this approach. But by translating subjective concepts, such as warmth, conscience, identification or dependency, into stimulus-response sequences and patterns of reinforcement, social learning theorists strive to maintain a mechanistic view of socialization processes. The theoretical formulations of the psychoanalytic school are at first sight not derived from an externalized approach at all. In clinical rather than experimental ventures, Freud was, after all, involved in attending to the internalized, subjective view of his patients; and his writings contain numerous references to the ideas and feelings of the person he was describing. Yet his theoretical model deals in fragmented, non-personal entities, on goals which are basically biological rather than psychological in character, and on a conception of man which defines his undertakings in terms of their physical effects rather than the personal meanings which they may hold for him. In addition, the theory denies validity to the terms in which individuals themselves make sense of their lives.

The ultimate test of the usefulness of either an externalized or an internalized view of personality development can only be that of enabling prediction. On behalf of the former type of approach, it is normally argued that, being literally objective, it eliminates personal biases, ensures accuracy of observation, and does away with inference and interpretation. It may be, however, that it is the experimenter without a personal orientation, without the capacity to go beyond mere observation, to infer and to interpret, who will make the poorest job of predicting what his human subject will do next. In the laboratory situation, as many experimenters have ruefully discovered, the experiment only "works" if the experimenter rightly infers the subject's attitudes and intentions, and if the subject does not use his own inferences about the experimenter's attitudes and intentions to turn the experiment upside down. The need to be "subjective", to make inferences about the other's state of mind, is likely to be even more crucial in real-life situations, particularly where the person to be predicted is a developing child. An "object" view of the child, involving mechanistic rules and attention to the physical parameters of the situation, is likely to prove a very poor predictive model. Without an understanding of the changing psychological dimensions of the child's own developing view, it is impossible to keep pace with his changing behaviour—the outcome of his own redefinitions of the situation he is in. The disastrous consequences of an unwillingness or inability to take the child's view are evident in practical life. In her study of the mothers of delinquent boys, Cass (1952) found them to be characteristically unaware of their sons' likes and dislikes, fears, and preferences. Similarly, a study by Adams *et al.* (1965) showed that the parents of maladjusted children were frankly puzzled when asked such questions as "How does your child see that?" and "Do you occasionally try to stop and see things the way your child does?". The predictive failure of parents who are unable to conceptualize the inner world of their child seems likely to be equalled by that of psychological theorizing which sees no necessity for so doing.

Children as Persons

It is here that personal construct theory, *par excellence*, offers an alternative. The person, rather than object, orientation of this theory is spelt out by Kelly in many different ways—in the formal postulate and corollaries, in discursive argument and comment, even in the title he chose for his theoretical system. "If we are to have a psychology of man's experiences", he remarks in a discussion of hostility, "We must anchor our basic concepts in that personal experience, not in the experiences he causes others to have or which he appears to seek to cause others to have. Thus, if we wish to use a concept of hostility at all, we have to ask, what is the experiential nature of hostility from the standpoint of the person who has it. Only by answering this question in some sensible way will we arrive at a concept which makes pure psychological sense, rather than sociological or moral sense merely."

Kelly's frequent insistence upon reflexivity—the need to define the subject's behaviour in the same terms as one uses to account for one's own scientific endeavour concerning him—represents essentially the same argument. It is on the grounds that such an orientation offers the best hope of predicting human behaviour that Kelly justifies his own standpoint. In a nice description of the "strictly manipulative approach to human relations" he attacks "objective", stimulus-response psychology as doomed to fail in the understanding of people. "How often is it we hear a man who appears to be successful in handling his employees, complain that he is not really wanted at home. All his family expects of him is "financial support". His children expect candy and agree among themselves that all they need to do to satisfy the old geezer is avoid crossing him. His wife expects gifts from him rather than understanding, and she has found that all she needs to do to make him perform is prepare his favourite meal and rub the back of his neck with the tops of her fingers—while she occupies her own mind with a romantic story in the Ladies Home Journal. While all this scientifically valid psychology is being practised in the home, probably both of them have been seeing psychotherapists for some time now, and the children have likely been placed in some good school, chosen because of its staff of well-trained counsellors" (Kelly, 1969).

In its promise of an approach to developing individuals as persons rather than objects, construct theory seems worth examining. Kelly himself never explicitly applied his theoretical system to the topic of personality development, and restricted his comments on children to an occasional, thought-provoking aside. Tracing a construct theory view of personality development must therefore necessarily be an inferential and tentative exercise. But since personality change in the psychotherapeutic situation represents the original focus of the theory, some of its fundamental implications for this area have already been spelt out. As in all such explorations, Kelly's own "invitational mood" seems an appropriate one here. Adopting for the time being a construct theory viewpoint need not imply any final decision to reject all other viewpoints. However, the implications of this particular theoretical orientation seem most likely to stand out clearly if they are contrasted with those of other theoretical systems; and since contrast is an essential aspect of construct theory, an attempt will be made throughout this essay to point up differences on every level between existing influential positions and the construct theory view being elaborated.

Change—from Without or from Within?

By definition, a crucial concept in any account of personality development is the concept of change. Yet it is with precisely this concept that object-oriented theories meet the greatest difficulty. Identity, continuity, stability— these are aspects of people which can be handled quite easily by object language accounts; but the notion of change presents them with fundamental problems. Since objects are naturally static, any change which they undergo has to be explained in extrinsic terms. Hence the classical learning theorists' account of personality growth in terms of the physical reinforcements produced by the environment; and hence, in a more elaborate description, that of the social learning theorists who cite variations in parental attitudes and practices—themselves redefined in reinforcement terms—as the agents of personal changes in the child. In order to account for different effects on children of apparently the same environmental events, trait differences, inherent in the children, may be postulated; these, however, are essentially static, representing permanent predispositions to respond in particular ways, and are not themselves the active principle of change.

Quite apart from the question of the degree of success which such explanatory attempts have achieved, this kind of approach can be criticized on grounds of lack of theoretical parsimony. The use of two qualitatively different languages is inevitable in these accounts, since they rest upon an intrinsically static model of the child and must, therefore, explain change in terms of extrinsic forces. One language covers stable, constitutional traits, with concepts such as drive level, sex-determined tendencies, or introversion; another covers change, using concepts like conditioning and reinforcement. In practice such an explanatory system seems likely to fail in accounting for two opposite kinds of situation—on the one hand, change which occurs in the absence of new external events, and on the other, lack of change under conditions of maximal environmental variation.

A rather different explanatory approach to change is taken by the proponents of the maturation school. Such theorists as Gesell account for change in personality, as in all areas, by reference to inbuilt principles and structures. The process whereby a child acquires a moral outlook is governed by a predetermined sequence, just as are the stages through which he passes in his locomotor or manual grasping skills. In this account, it is the environment which plays the passive part, merely presenting enabling or inhibiting conditions for such sequences to manifest themselves. Different though such an explanation is from a learning theorist account, the same fundamental criticism applies. A maturationist theory also rests upon two clearly different sets of concepts, although in this case it is those relating to the individual which involve the principle of change, and those relating to the environment which are essentially static.

In placing the agency of change within the child himself, this type of theory seems to represent a more person-oriented approach than does a learning theory account. Yet, on examination, the maturation principle reduces to an ultimately non-psychological level of explanation. By deriving its laws normatively from behavioural aggregates, this account abandons a concern with process. In turn, by rejecting process, it can offer only a mechanistic and fundamentally tautological explanation of change which is not linked in any essential way with the psychological content of the changes to which it refers.

Construct theory seems to offer a way out of the dilemmas of both these theoretical approaches. Of all concepts, that of change is the most integral to Kelly's formulations. "Man", he claims, "is a form of motion [who] exists primarily in the dimensions of time, and only secondarily in the dimensions of space." It is the time-line, in terms of which a person's experience and behaviour must be understood, which represents the fundamental difference between a person and an object. "A rock that has rested firm for ages may well exist in the future also, but it does not link the past with the future. In its mute way it only links past with past. It does not anticipate, it does not reach out both ways to snatch handfuls from each of the two worlds in order to bring them together and subject them to the same stern laws. Only man does that" (Kelly, 1969).

This view of change as the essential feature of human psychology is in obvious contrast with that of the behaviourist school, which meets problems in accounting for changes at all. Construct theory, by placing the principle of change firmly within the person and by referring to the environment only in terms of the person's changing constructions of it, also avoids the dual language system of learning theory formulations. By the same token, this view can cover changes occurring in the absence of environmental events, since "whatever exists can be reconstrued", and changes in behaviour are a function of changes in one's construction of the situation. The other side of the coin is that, by construing major recurring themes in one's own life, it is possible to view two physically very different environmental situations as essentially the same, and, therefore, to behave in the same way towards them.

Construct theory also avoids the mechanistic and circular nature of maturationist explanations by defining psychological change in essentially psychological terms. Where the Gesell school substitutes normative sequence for process explanation, Kelly underpins his notion of changing man with a clearly psychological principle—the motive of anticipation. The Gesellian child changes despite himself, by the operation of a universal mechanism— that of maturation. Kelly's child changes as a function of his own endeavours to grasp the nature of his world, to understand himself and those about him, and to find out what new possibilities life may hold for him.

The Language of Change

If externalized theoretical approaches meet major problems in accounting for the fact of psychological change, the question of what terms should be used to trace it seems no easier for them. The logically appropriate dimensions for some such approaches are physicalistic, and to some extent, the theorists concerned have succeeded in building these into their account of personality development. The use of chronological age as a major dimension represents one such attempt, as does reference to biological events, such as weaning, excretory control, or puberty. Frequently, indeed, these two kinds of para- meters are combined to produce a stratification of development by age-cum- biological stage. Most current textbooks on child development are based on this approach, as a glance at their chapter headings shows: this child is segmented into Pre-natal, Neonatal, Infant, Pre-school, Middle childhood and Adolescent. Despite its common-sense appeal, this approach to per- sonality development seems basically unsatisfactory. One reason is that, unless, as in the psychoanalytic school, a common underlying theme linking all stages is postulated, there is little to identify the same child throughout all his different stages. The content of the account differs according to the particular stage involved, referring, for example, to differential tissue growth in prenatal life, locomotor skills in infancy, peer group identification in middle childhood and sexual problems and aspirations in adolescence. It is because the causative agents of change are viewed in physicalistic terms that the psychological content chosen to describe each stage is inevitably somewhat arbitrary.

Another kind of dimension, used by social learning theorists like Sears, Bandura and Dollard, is that of molar behavioural tendencies—aggression, dependency, morality and so on. For these theorists, the task is to define such tendencies in physicalistic terms, and then to trace their antecedents, also defined physicalistically, in terms of environmental—particularly parental—variables. Although the focus of this kind of approach seems more genuinely psychological, at least in its origin, than that of the previous approach, certain fundamental objections seem to apply here also. In the first place, there is again an absence of any unifying principle to sew together the segmented child, who in this case is cut up horizontally rather than vertically, that is according to separate content areas, rather than by segments of time. Secondly, any attempt to pin down a concept like aggression in a final, once-and-for-all physicalistic definition seems bound to fail. As Escalona's detailed study (Escalona and Heider, 1959) showed, the prediction of young children in such specific terms, over only a few years, proved unsuccessful.

A very different use of molar dimensions of change is made by Erikson in his theory of psychosocial development. Combining psychoanalytic notions of ego growth and sex-differentiated tendencies with those of social and cultural pressures, Erikson's system is an account, in stage-linked terms, of successive dominant themes. On certain counts, his theory seems an attractive one; it is based on genuinely psychological content, it contains an organizing principle in the form of ego growth and, unlike almost all current theories, it extends the notion of personality development over the whole life span. Yet, again, even this theoretical system rests on an arbitrary approach to the child insofar as it defines the content of development in advance, and reduces it to certain universal, generalized themes. It seems ironic that Erikson, so aware of cultural differences, should nevertheless claim universality for a particular set of values and goals. His theory is also open to objection in that, despite their descriptive vividness, his themes are loosely derived in their bipolar contrasts, in their sequential order, and in their relation to social and cultural contexts. One might ask, for example, why guilt should represent the opposite pole to initiative, or inferiority, to industry. The priority in sequence of autonomy, followed by initiative, seems similarly unjustified; and indeed the distinction between these two dimensions is not clear. Where Erikson argues a relation between each stage and a particular type of social institution, his argument seems still more arbitrary, as in the link postulated between initiative and economic institutions.

The basic assumptions of construct theory clearly rule out both physicalistic terms of change and universality of psychological content. On the one hand, Kelly's notion of man "as a creature who himself devises constructions", represents an explicit rejection of the physicalistic approach. On the other hand, the emphasis placed on individuality is incompatible with the definition of change in terms of any universal psychological content. The uniqueness of each person, differing from all other persons in his constructions of reality, demands a psychology which describes change within the context of particular construing systems. Since it is essentially the recurring themes, by means of which a person defines his undertakings and anticipates his future, which give him his continuity and identity, it is these, rather than any *a priori* content, which must form the anchors of a construct theory account of personal change.

A construct theory approach to personality development has so far been defined negatively. The terms in which it would discuss change would be non-physicalistic, since a child's activities can be understood only in terms of the constructions he places on them. They would also be non-preemptive, because the child is himself an individual, for whom every situation has a unique, personal meaning. Having thus said what this approach would *not* be, I should like now to attempt a more positive account of what it might offer.

The Construing Group

At first sight, an explanation of personal development in terms of the individual's own constructions seems an impossible undertaking. If every child has a unique construing system, and if, even within that system, the dimensions of content are continually changing, no generally applicable terms of reference appear feasible. Indeed, Kelly admits that to account for the behaviours of any individual it is necessary to "keep changing the co-ordinates in terms of which we plot his life processes". It seems therefore, that in our anxiety to match psychology to the protean forms of the child, we may have introduced insuperable problems to the task of explanation. Yet construct theory offers a way out of this predicament, through its assumptions about commonality and sociality.

Despite its emphasis on individuality, Kelly's theory is not solipsistic. The idea of shared areas of personal meaning is made explicit in the commonality corollary. "To the extent that one person employs a construction of experience which is similar to that employed by another, his processes are psychologically similar to those of the other person". The importance of agreed interpretations and of social validation is also implied throughout

Kelly's references to interpersonal relationships. From the point of view of personality development, these assumptions suggest that it would be appropriate to focus upon the increasingly wide areas in which children share the constructions of others. During early stages of development, it seems likely that the mother helps to define the relevancies of situational contexts for the child, thereby offering him a construction in terms of which he can act towards the situation, and at the same time relate to her own construction of it; this argument underlies a current investigation by Newson, Shotter and Treble (Newson, 1969). As Shotter argues, "After setting him a task, keeping his attention on it, and then selecting relevant from irrelevant activities, the mother shapes up the child's spontaneous actions in a way that he would not do himself if left on his own" (Shotter, 1969). Later, through verbal communication, dimensions of appraising himself and others are explicitly taught to the child, who is likely to incorporate them, for a time at least, within his own construction system. As his social experience widens, he will meet other dimensions from the peer group, older children, and adults; and the degree to which he adopts these dimensions, as a basis for his behaviour, as well as the particular poles which he applies to himself and to other important people, will represent one kind of definition of his personality.

Commonality with others in a developing construing system thus offers a way in which the changing content of personality may be described. Another approach to content, which seems potentially still more fruitful, is in terms of sociality. Kelly lays considerable stress on this aspect of interpersonal relationships, and his definition of role rests upon it, since, according to his corollary, a social role can be played towards another person only insofar as one is able to construe his constructions. Since relationships with others are central to the concept of personality, and since expanding role playing abilities define the ever-widening limits of the child's interpersonal relationships, the concept of sociality seems a key one in the psychology of personality development. Several lines of approach are possible here. One might focus upon core role construing, which defines the central parameters involved in all social roles and sets the limits on the roles that may be played by the person. The, by now, numerous experiments, such as that of Campbell and Yarrow (1961), which show that reputation acts to influence the child's behaviour, or which, like that of Rosenthal (Rosenthal and Jacobson, 1968), reveal the effect, on his achievement, of the expectations of key people, all serve to indicate that core role constructions are intimately linked to the constructions which others have of the individual child. My own study of primary school boys (Salmon, 1969) suggested that the values the child adopts, and which underlie his behavioural response to conformity pressures, are to a significant extent a function of the particular group with which he identifies himself, this in turn being mediated by the degree of acceptance which he has held in the group—that is, the constructions which the other group members have of him. Thus, self-concept is critically bound up with the social roles the individual plays.

A rather different line of approach to personality growth, in terms of sociality, would be to examine the changing constructions which the child holds of others. The studies of Little (1968) suggest a general trend in developing constructions of other people, from highly concrete, physicalistic constructs, to abstract, truly psychological ones. The intermediate stage appears to involve reference to specific figures or functions, such as "like my mother", or "like a teacher". The very interesting approach outlined by Flavell and others (Flavell *et al.*, 1968), and underlying their experimentation with children, seems based on the same assumptions of progressively growing subtlety and abstraction in the child's construing of other people. Morse's (1966) study of the ways in which students construe others represents a different extension of the same line. His results showed three main categories of construing among his subjects. The first group tended to view significant others along largely the same dimensions with which they defined themselves, and to construe them mainly at the same poles of these dimensions as themselves. The second group, though using the same dimensions to construe themselves and important other people, tended to view the latter as being at the opposite poles to themselves. The final group consisted of subjects who tended to use different dimensions altogether for defining themselves and other significant people. Although Morse's was not a developmental study, it seems likely that individuals may pass through more than one of these categories in the course of development, and that they may, therefore, represent stages, rather than final modes of construction. All these studies suggest the fruitfulness of exploring an individual's changing construing of others, particularly since such construing represents his own "personality theory", which, as Kelly maintained, may be the best definition so far of his own personality.

Analysis of Systems

Whereas both commonality and sociality refer essentially to content, construct theory also suggests the usefulness of a structural approach to personality. Kelly's concern with organization and patterning, with mathematical analysis of conceptualization, and with the development of techniques of measurement lending themselves to quantification, shows the considerable stress which he lays upon structure. Many of the formal corollaries relate to structural rather than content features. On one occasion, Kelly even remarked that if the element and construct labels were eliminated from a repertory grid, the data would still convey a good deal about the subject. It is appropriate, therefore, to try to trace the implications of this structural emphasis for an analysis of personality development.

The most obviously relevant aspect of structure for any examination of a developing system is that of its degree of organization. It seems probable that very young children differ from older ones not only in the smaller number of constructions in their repertoire, but also in the lesser degree to which these are organized. One of the advantages of such lack of systematic organization may be the relative ease with which constructions can be changed; and it may be that the child's first temper tantrum is a signal that his constructions of himself and others are now sufficiently tightly organized to produce hostility when change is imminent. As Kelly defines it, hostility represents "the attempt to extort validational evidence from a social situation in which the prediction has already been recognized as a failure". This, after all, is not likely to happen unless constructs are systematically inter-related: to be wrong in one's predictions only matters if more than the predictions themselves are at stake. At the other extreme from the non-organization of early life, stands the child whose construing is very tightly organized indeed. The rigid children studied by Leach (1964) with constructions of interpersonal behaviour which were entirely rule-bounded, and could admit of no exception to these rules, would probably represent an example of such over-organization.

A quite different aspect of structure concerns the degree of consistency within any system. As Kelly states in his fragmentation corollary, individuals may have separate subsystems whose lines of inference are mutually inconsistent. While this situation may be normal, and even useful, in some areas of construing, it is likely to lead to difficulties in constructions of oneself. Here, fragmentation may well produce the development of two different personalities—one the "home" child, and one the "school" child—which can be successfully maintained only until the child meets some situation in which pressures from both contexts operate simultaneously.

Perhaps the most crucial structural feature, from the point of view of personality development, is the permeability of the system, since it is this, as Kelly argues, which ultimately allows for creative growth. According to his definition, "a construct is permeable if it will admit to its range of convenience new elements which are not yet construed within its framework". Thus, the child who develops, from his early construct "like my mother", the more widely usable construct of "motherly", is achieving greater permeability in this aspect of his system. Since permeability, according to Kelly's argument, is what enables the individual to think both "tightly" and "loosely", this feature of a system seems a critical one from the developmental point of view. Failure to achieve it is likely to be reflected in two opposite modes of adjustment, seen on the one hand in the many individuals who lose their spontaneity of thought and feeling all too early in life, and on the other in those who, equally tragically, fail ever to come to grips with reality, and wander through their adult years with childish non-comprehension.

Having sketched briefly some of the major dimensions of personality growth which might characteristically arise out of a construct theory orientation, I would now like to consider how this theoretical position compares with others in the model of development which it implies. All theoretical accounts are based, either explicitly or implicitly, on some model of how the relevant processes operate and how the antecedents in the causal relationships affect the consequents. Omitting those theoretical systems in which the causative factors are entirely physicalistic or sociological, and which make no reference to purely psychological processes, three major types of model invite consideration as comparable in some respects with a construct theory model. These are, first, systems in which maternal attitude is the major causative factor, secondly, the role theory model and thirdly, the Piagetian model.

The Causative Mother

Theoretical systems based on maternal attitude take as their focus the young child's first relationship with another person—a focus which is also consistent with construct theory's stress on commonality and sociality, as well as with Kelly's frequent stress on the fundamental importance of human dependencies, on the centrality of interpersonal relationships for psychology, and on a "deep concern with social relations" as one of the key features of human beings. It is when such models set out the process whereby the effect of maternal attitude operates, however, that many points of divergence from construct theory emerge.

Systems in which maternal attitude represents the major causative factor typically take as their starting point the measurement of maternal attitude differences. Using questionnaires, rating scales, interviews or observation methods, data are obtained as to differences in maternal views, feelings or practices, and these are then subjected to statistical analysis to yield major factors or components. The resulting dimensions form the antecedents in the model and consequents are then looked for in child behavioural differences. Any associations found are built into the model and hypotheses are advanced to account for the processes linking the two dimensions, these normally being expressed in some kind of reinforcement terms.

Standard though this procedure may be for the analysis of maternal attitude, it stands in direct opposition to the approach demanded by construct theory. Since the focus of such a procedure is on "individual differences", measured first in the maternal and then in the child sphere, the process whereby these two are argued to be linked, inevitably comes *post hoc*. A primary concern with process, crucial to construct theory, implies an experimental design in which "individual differences" do not merely come second, but are unlikely to feature at all. "The variables . . . that explain the differences between persons are not to be confounded with the ones that explain what happens to people or what can happen to them. So when we look for variables by which persons can be distinguished from each other, we should not expect to find the variables of psychology by which personal lives have variety and accomplish change" (Kelly, 1969).

The effect of this very fundamental difference in approach can perhaps be seen in the unsatisfactoriness, from a construct theory point of view, of the dimensions which typical maternal attitude models employ. Acceptance-*vs*-rejection, and control-*vs*-neglect, despite their common sense appeal, are labels having to do with generalized adults' constructions of the mother, rather than with those she or her child may be using. Similarly, child behaviour dimensions such as aggression or dependency are essentially reflections of generalized adults' reactions to the child's undertakings, and make no reference to the personal meanings they hold for him or for his mother. As such, both types of dimension are value-laden, often being couched in the "language of complaint", and are meaningful as aggregate descriptions rather than applying to individuals. Another aspect of the deficiency of such dimensions is the large area of mother-child interaction which they omit. The few studies which have concerned themselves with mothers' own constructions of their relationship with their child have suggested that ideas broadly termed philosophical may be extremely important in influencing the child's developing personality. The concern with objective reality and with "truthful" verbal expression, which emerged in the Newsons' interviews with some mothers (Newson and Newson, 1968) represents one aspect of this neglected area; while Bing's (1963) maternal variables of encouraging the child's interest in the physical world, and inviting active experimentation in it, as a source of validation, seem to be relevant also.

In so far as it is possible to state the content of a construct theory account of "maternal attitude", this would perhaps be likely to centre around the capacity of the mother to "provide an enabling structure" for the child's "progressively shifting referents of behaviour". Such a capacity implies the mother's readiness to adopt a non-manipulative, empathic approach to her child, to respond to what the child means by his ventures rather than to a literal definition of his behaviour, and to be concerned with what he is undertaking rather than with the state he is in. However, the relationship would certainly not be viewed as one-way, and, in this, the mother's position is much like that of the psychotherapist, who "does not know the final answer either—so they face the problem together. Under the circumstances there is nothing for them to do except for both to enquire and both to risk occasional mistakes. So that it can be a genuinely co-operative effort, each must do what he can to help the other understand what he himself is ready to try next" (Kelly, 1969). It is because the process is essentially interpersonal that ultimately such an account must rest on an analysis of individual mother-child pairs, rather than one of mothers-in-general considered independently from children-in-general.

The process typically postulated to account for observed associations between maternal and child variables is in terms of reinforcement. Acceptance, or love, is seen as operating because it is essentially a reward, for the sake of which the child will conform to socially prescribed behaviour. Similarly, discipline, whether of the power-assertive or love-related type, works because it imposes a punishment which the child wishes to avoid. From a construct theory point of view, this account of motivation is quite unacceptable. The client who "feels guilty because he doesn't feel guilty", the delinquent who feels guilt for being "a good boy", the person who persistently seeks out and produces the rejection and hostility which confirm his cynical view of others—all these are Kelly's illustrations of the active pursuit of "punishment" and avoidance of "rewards" which people are frequently apt to show. In a theoretical account where anticipation is the driving motive, reward and punishment have no ultimate meaning. A man's behaviour "is governed, not simply by *what* he anticipates—whether good or bad, pleasant or unpleasant, self-vindicating or self-confounding—but by *where* he believes his choices will place him in respect to the remaining turns in the road. If he chooses this fork in the road, will it lead to a better vantage point from which to see the road beyond or will it be the one that abruptly brings him face to face with a blank wall?" (Kelly, 1969).

Serious Role Playing

Role theory, as originally put forward by Norman Cameron, offers a general model of personality development which has been used by a number of psychologists both in the field of psychopathology and in accounting for normal development. In many ways this theory seems to parallel construct theory in the model which it sets up. Its focus on social interaction, rather than on individual attributes, as the source of fruitful analysis of personality, is very much in harmony with Kelly's emphasis. The definition of role on which it rests also has much in common with Kelly's concept of sociality. Cameron, for example, argues that roles involve knowing the contexts in which certain behaviours are demanded, others permitted, and still others, excluded. This fits in well with Kelly's idea of roles as involving an awareness of other person's constructions and expectations, as does Cameron's argument that successful role playing consists in shifting one's perspective and in reacting to oneself as a social object, to be appraised, criticized and controlled. Finally, Cameron's concern with development, whereby the child gradually acquires, through participating and reciprocal relationships, a variety of differentiated roles, matches Kelly's focus on growth, through time, by active, committed undertakings.

Despite the close similarities in focus between role theory and construct theory, the models which the two views employ have some important differences. The first concerns the relative lack, in role theory, of attention to system. Role playing seems to be viewed rather as though it represented a series of skills. By contrast, construct theory stresses organization and hierarchy; its model is of central, core-role constructions governing less major, more differentiated roles and by the same token precluding certain roles, regardless of environmental opportunity. In this view, role-playing is not so much a skill, as a direct expression and elaboration of an individual's personal construct system, with the unique set of priorities, choices and implications which it holds. The same structural emphasis of construct theory also implies a rather different picture of process from that of role theory. Where role theory stresses the function of accepting attitudes towards the child, of opportunities for him to identify and engage in reciprocal relationships, construct theory additionally suggests the importance of such aspects as the developing degree of structure, the permeability or the fragmentation of the child's construing system. Since acquiring new roles constitutes one way of elaborating one's personal construct system, the structure of this system is likely to be crucial in determining whether, for instance, the new role demands are seen as highly congenial or highly threatening, as holding major or merely superficial implications, as endorsing or out of keeping with core roles, and so on. This difference may derive from contrasting emphases, rather than from any underlying difference in assumptions; yet it seems likely that the concern of role theory with social rather than psychological parameters entails some inevitable disregard of the individual's particular system of organization.

A further, more subtle point of divergence, concerns the view implied by the two theories of the fixed or fluid nature of social roles. Role theory suggests, though without explicitly stating this, that social roles represent definite, well-established patterns of expectation and behaviour, governed largely by the social context, whether this is one of family, work, counselling, club, or any other setting. The creative nature of interpersonal interactions, so much stressed by Kelly, seems to play no part in this conception. From a construct theory viewpoint, however, the capacity of individuals to transcend the accepted parameters of the situation by inventing new ones, is what is essentially human about behaviour and what gives interpersonal relationships their most exciting quality. A role, like any other human endeavour, can best be understood by considering the ingenuity of individuals, who launch "unprecedented behavioural undertakings", and who "though continually challenged by circumstances, are never dictated to by them". Rather than picturing a social role as a channel of communication already established and implicit in the context, construct theory suggests that interpersonal relationships of all kinds are forever being created anew by the individuals involved in them.

This difference is of course related to the relatively passive part allocated to the individual in a role theory account. Where construct theory focuses upon the person and upon what he is currently undertaking, role theory stresses social context and the expectations of others, implying that these constitute the essential source of the role that is to be played. Kelly himself underlines this contrast between his own view of role and that of most other theorists in some remarks about the notion of role (1966). The traditional concept of role, he argues, is as a course of activity articulated with that of others. More recently, roles have come to be regarded as the set of expectations held by others, with which a man finds himself encompassed. Unlike both these views, the idea of role in construct theory implies the active, experimenting nature of the person. "Role can be understood in terms of what the person *himself* is doing, rather than in terms of his circumstances. . . . Anyone who attempts to understand others in terms of the outlooks they may have, rather than their behaviours only, may indeed play a role" (Kelly, 1969, his italics).

Piaget's View

In several important ways, Piaget's model of cognitive development has much in common with a construct theory model. Like Kelly, Piaget lays great stress on the idea of system and organization. For both theorists, a behavioural event can be understood not as a single act but insofar as it reveals a systematic orientation, governing a whole network of inter-related implications. In both theoretical accounts, change is seen rather in structural than in content terms. The concepts of space and time, though as familiar to the six-year-old as to the sixteen-year-old, are far more densely and complexly interrelated for the latter in Piaget's account; just as, for Kelly, the matrix of relationships between constructs about people is likely to become increasingly less simple in its factorial structure as the individual gains in personal maturity.

Another point of similarity between the two models is that in both an overall, governing theme, an overriding principle, forms the basis for their systems. Where Kelly's governing theme is that of anticipation as the driving force in human behaviour, Piaget builds his system of cognitive development around the principle of adaptation. In both cases, the whole theoretical system is derived from the central governing theme, so that not only does this apply to the individual's behaviour in any particular situation, it also accounts for the direction of his overall development. Thus, while Kelly uses the anticipatory motive to explain the choices a person makes in psychotherapy, Piaget explains a baby's reaching out and grasping the rattle he sees, in adaptational terms; and while Kelly accounts for progressive elaboration of construing systems as increasingly refining and extending the channels for anticipating reality, Piaget defines the substages of intelligence in terms of ever-growing adaptational efficiency.

Not only do the two theoretical systems seem comparable in terms of structural features; there are also points of similarity in the content of their accounts. Piaget, like Kelly, adopts an essentially internalized point of view. Using methods designed to elicit the meaning to the child of the situation he is in, Piaget sets up a model in which each stage of development, however different from an adult's outlook, has its own coherence and its own logic. By presenting a sequence of development which "makes sense" all the way along, Piaget seems as person-centred as Kelly, who argues that, however meaningless a person's behaviour may look from the outside, to him it is the logical and sensible thing to do. A further common theme in the two theoretical models has to do with the active nature which they both assign to human beings. Just as Kelly's model man lives by reaching out to reality in his behavioural ventures, so Piaget's child grows through his active experimentation with ever wider and deeper aspects of his environment.

Yet despite these major features in common, Piaget's theoretical model differs in one crucial way from that of construct theory. It is on this account that construct theory cannot be viewed as an extension of a Piagetian model to the field of personality development. In their philosophical assumptions, Piaget and Kelly stand far apart. Piaget's theoretical account rests on an absolutist view of truth. Assimilation, one half of the adaptation process, is defined as shaping outer reality to the inner conceptual world, while accommodation, the other half, represents a modification of the inner world to fit the demands of outer reality. Underlying such an account is the assumption that a person can directly experience pure reality and can distinguish between this and his inner conceptual world. This view runs counter to the philosophical basis of construct theory, whereby reality can never be known in any final, absolute way, but only through our constructions which, as a result of the varying validational outcomes of the behavioural experiments we make, are subject to continual revision.

The absolutist view of reality seems closely bound up with Piaget's choice of the cognitive area of human experience as the focus of his theory. In dealing with our knowledge of movement, density or arithmetical operations, Piaget has recourse to laws which have extremely wide consensual agreement.

From a construct theory point of view, these laws are none-the-less constructions, and are not the direct expression of the real world, however useful they may be at present as guidelines for certain behavioural undertakings. However, the degree of consensus about the physical world enables Piaget to present cognitive growth in this sphere as progress towards an understanding of certain universal, absolute principles. It is a different matter when it comes to the world of interpersonal relationships. Here, there are clearly no absolute laws or entities, since values, goals and psychological attributes inevitably entail judgement and interpretation—with rather poor inter-judge agreement, at that. Indeed, Piaget himself recognizes the relativism implicit in morality and his account of moral development attributes the notion of moral absolutes in an immature developmental level. But having traced moral development from absolutism to relativism, Piaget has little further to contribute to the understanding of morality. His theoretical model, deriving from the principle of adaptation to reality, cannot in fact account for the conceptions and procedures governing people's relationships with each other, where probably every social convention that has ever existed has been turned upside down by some social group, and where there can be no rules beyond what works for the particular unique human venture in which the individuals concerned are engaged. It seems no accident, therefore, that Piaget devised his theoretical model to cover the development of thinking primarily about the physical world. In accounting for personality development, such a model seems bound to fail, and it is by the same token that construct theory appears promising.

The Emphases of Construct Theory

Kelly claimed that the crucial test of the validity of any theoretical framework was that of fertility. In the field of personality development, how far can his own theory be said to contribute a new and fruitful view?

In the first place, it must be said that construct theory represents a metatheory, rather than an explanatory system designed to account for any one of the traditional "fields" of psychology. Although psychotherapeutic change was the starting point for Kelly's theorizing, the formal theory—standing as it does at a high level of abstraction and claiming to embrace virtually the whole range of human psychology—has little specific content to offer those concerned with "child psychology" or with "personality". Indeed, since Kelly was hostile to such text-book categories, it would be surprising if he had devoted much thought to *ad hoc* explanations covering particular fields. In the long run, such freedom from conventional delimitation of the area of personality development may well prove fruitful. But its immediate consequences seem to entail a great deal of work on the part of the psychologist in this field, who is obliged to establish for himself the relevance and the application of Kelly's theoretical position to the area. Kelly himself said so little about children, and so far no one has attempted to trace the implications of his theory for an area in which children are so essentially concerned. Any attempt to do so at this stage can only represent an act of faith.

Nevertheless construct theory does seem to offer a distinctive approach to the processes of personality development—an approach which, by presenting a novel definition of personality and its growth, suggests many areas of investigation so far untouched. In terms of this theory, personality consists, not in the static attributes of conventional psychological terminology, but in the behavioural ventures arising out of continual revisions of anticipatory systems. Its sphere of action is interpersonal rather than intra-individual, since it is essentially defined by socially agreed roles; and this means that the only "real" personality an individual can ever have consists in the shared interpretations which he and others make of his own behaviour. Personality development, in this theoretical system, represents neither the function of time nor that of inbuilt maturational processes, but the outcome of continuous anticipatory effort on the part of the individual. Again, the concern of such anticipatory effort is the behaviour of other people, just as the source of its validation is a social one.

The interpersonal nature of personality and the dynamic of anticipation which construct theory attributes to it, suggest a research focus which is rather different from the conventional ones in this sphere. In the first place, any investigation of personality development needs, according to this definition, to concern itself with more than one individual. If the content of personality is interpersonal, the construing of other people must be taken into account in tracing the personality development of any particular person. The dimensions in terms of which any individual defines his behaviour towards others have not been selected out of thin air; they are derived from the roles which he has played with other individuals, the frame of reference which he has elaborated in common with them and the agreed network of implications which he has shared with others in crucial interpersonal relationships.

Any attempt at a comprehensive account of personality development in these terms must clearly begin with the first significant person in the child's life—normally, his mother. Her construing gives him the basis of his own, however much he may later elaborate his own view. It is she who provides him with the first dimensions for appraising his own behaviour, just as the first role relationship he plays is played with her. Without falling into the trap of assuming her own construing system to be static, and to be unaffected by the validational evidence which the child himself provides for her, it is relevant to examine as thoroughly as possible the mother's construing of herself and of others. In particular, the ways in which she sees herself to be like her child, and to be different from him, seem to be crucial. The absence of any shared content in her view of herself and of her young child is likely to prove disastrous, in that without this, there can be no basis for a true role relationship, nor for any creative building together, through such a role, of progressively enriched shared experience. Further even than this, the lack of any dimensions which she attributes to both of them, offers the child no material out of which to elaborate his own view of himself, and in so far as he is defined in this purely negative way, his own construing of himself and others is likely to remain very impoverished and empty of implications. On the other hand, a mother who "identifies" with her child to the extent of using precisely the same network of constructions, modified only by her concessions to the concept of age, is likely to produce equally fatal results for her child's personality growth. The severe restrictions which this places on the behaviour he can display, on the roles he can engage in, and on the constructions he can build for himself, must act to inhibit grossly the essentially creative endeavours whereby a child normally establishes his own developing self. Some differentiations, on certain levels, between a mother's system of construing herself and the one she uses to construe her child, seem essential. Equally her constructions of both of them must be permeable and open-ended if they are to enable the child to work out his anticipatory system by his behavioural ventures. This is also necessary to enable the mother to elaborate, through her relationship with the child, her own construing system.

Though the first basis for the child's construing of himself in relation to others normally derives from his mother's construction system, he is likely before long to meet a challenge for further development in the construing of other individuals. The constructions he has acquired as a function of his relationship with his mother will prove inadequate to enable him to comprehend the behaviour and the demands of other young children, of his older brothers and sisters, of his father, or of the nursery school teacher. The construing systems of those with whom he now comes into contact are likely neither simply to endorse, nor simply to contradict the constructions he has hitherto held; by offering quite new constructions and by defining his role in quite new ways, they demand an extension and redefinition of himself which is much more than a simple confirmation or reversal of his previous construction system. The construing systems of such figures, together with those of school mates, family members and adult friends need also to be explored, since in becoming involved with the child they provide the content of further development in his own construing. Insofar as, potentially at least, personality growth is endless, the construction systems of a whole succession of people with whom the individual relates in his life span, merit the same exploration.

In examining and comparing the construing systems of any two individuals who are involved together in a relationship, similarities and differences of structure are as important as those of content. A school age boy and his father may use much the same labels to describe their own and each other's behaviour; but the organization system of the child is likely to be far simpler than that of the adult. This means that the validational evidence which both meet within the context of their relationship is likely to be very different. For the boy, whose constructs relate to a relatively simple organization, certain events bearing on his construing system will carry much more validational weight than they will for the man, who sees them as relatively peripheral, with few implications. One has only to listen to the comments made by father and son on a film they have just seen together to realize how much greater is the impact of such experiences on a child than on an adult. Conversely, other events, meaningful to both of them, will convey a great deal more to the adult than they could to the child, if they relate to super-ordinate constructions within the former's relatively complex system. Slight changes of emotional tone in his mother's voice, treated quite casually by the child, may well be of major significance for his father.

The differences between individuals in terms of what constitutes evidence, for them, bearing on their relationship are important as defining one reason for the varying interpretations which those involved so often make of the same "event" in their interactions. Since the parameters of personality and social role are seldom made explicit, and since arriving at a common under-standing is usually a highly intuitive procedure, such differences between people are unlikely to emerge at a conscious level in interpersonal interac-tions. Thus among friends, mutual sympathy and enjoyment is less often disrupted by explicit disagreement than by the perception, by one, that the other has abandoned the unspoken stance upon which his part of the re-lationship rested. To the latter, the occasion had no bearing on such a stance.

In content terms, one major theme which seems to affect personality development at certain stages has to do with the competitiveness of some roles. This theme is particularly associated with the family context. When a child has been allocated an agreed identity by the various members of his family, he may feel threatened if a brother or sister seems to be "trespassing" on it. The boy who is regarded by all the family as 'no good at lessons, but a real sportsman', may be furiously aggrieved if his younger brother, "the clever one, but hopeless on the games field", begins to take an interest in sport and to compete for athletic honours. The little girl who is recognized by the family circle as musical will feel it a personal injury if her sister takes up the piano too—and will be speechless with indignation if she adds insult to injury by learning "her" piece of music. This possessiveness about role definition, whereby a particular role is jealously guarded, and viewed as private property, seems to be the outcome of rather simple systems for construing personal identity. It is therefore not surprising to find such views among children, who are striving to establish separate, differential personalities in their relationship with each other and with adults. If such narrow and restricting definitions of identity are not endorsed by the adults in the family—who alas, sometimes have equally simple views of personality— these conflicts of role do not seem permanently to block further personality development. Indeed by subsuming these roles within a broader, more superordinate construction, so that they no longer seem mutually exclusive, children are able to progress to a higher level of personality functioning.

Personality as a Contract

The idea of exclusive roles is relevant also to a question which arises directly out of a construct theory view—why personality so often seems to stop developing. Though the concept of psychological maturity, after which growth will cease or become retrogressive, is in keeping with many theories of personality, it clearly does not accord with a view of human beings as endlessly seeking further understanding, and as never achieving a final comprehension which need be revised no more. Undoubtedly, nearly all individuals improve their ability to anticipate themselves and others, and to play social roles effectively, as they move from childhood to adulthood. Yet, even for the most perceptive of adults, it certainly cannot be said that there is no further room for improvement. Insofar as every new individual one meets demands a special, tailor-made psychology to do justice to his uniqueness, and insofar as even the most familiar of one's intimate friends are themselves liable to change, the scope of further elaboration in one's construing system is plainly limitless. The reason why all too often personality seems to crystallize in middle age, if not still earlier, has to be sought, again, in the constructions of the individual himself and of others with whom he is involved.

It has been argued that personality is the accord which others have, together with the individual himself, of the mode of interpersonal activity in which he engages. In many social groups there is something of a conspiracy, albeit not a conscious one, to nail down the characteristic role which a person is expected to play. Any attempt on his part to break out of this role is likely to meet with hostility, in the form of accusations of inconsistency, or acting out of character. Since his new interpersonal ventures, by definition, demand from others, who relate to him, new orientations towards him, this may easily threaten their own sense of stability and hence arouse strong resistance which, if it is maintained, can effectively prevent him from living out his new role constructions.

If other people often impose an unduly limited conception of personality upon an individual, this is no less liable to be true of the individual himself.

Having forged out of his experience, in the long journey through childhood and adolescence, a construing system which seems to cover most of the interpersonal situations he has met so far, he may then settle for this as the best model he can hope to achieve, and may as a result cease, in Kelly's terms, to "experiment with his life". The backing of others, with the consensual definition of maturity in relatively fixed terms, may endorse this lack of growth, until, as a result of some personal crisis, he is likely to "have to go through a lot of chaos before he can make anything more of himself"; and it is here, of course, that Kelly's own account of psychotherapeutic change is relevant. Just as with children's competing and mutually exclusive roles, it seems likely that a subsuming of the individual's current role under a superordinate construction, whereby he is able to see it as one of several possible roles he could play, rather than as an ultimate definition of himself, offers the way out of this block to further development.

It is essentially this view of the creative nature of man's endeavours and of the infinite possibilities of change and growth, that gives construct theory its distinctive contribution to the psychology of personality development. Seen within this framework, personality development is not simply one aspect of child development; it is the whole social core of an individual's progression through life. If so far psychologists working in this area have been able to offer only static, barren and unexciting conceptions of personality growth, this is because they have, in their thinking, fallen far short of the ordinary person engaged in living. As Kelly, with slight paraphrasing, has put it: "The psychologist has only to participate in the human enterprise to find that man does what 'personality' tests have said he cant."

References

Adams, P. L., Schwab, J. J. and Aponte, J. F. (1965). Authoritarian parents and disturbed children. *Am. J. Psychiat.* **121,** 1162–1167.

Bing, Elizabeth (1963). The effect of child-rearing practices on the development of differential cognitive abilities. *Child Dev.* **34,** 631–648.

Campbell, J. D. and Yarrow, Marion R. (1961). Perceptual and behavioural correlates of social effectiveness. *Sociometry* **24,** 1–20.

Cass, Loretta K. (1952). Parent-child relationships and delinquency. *J. abnorm. soc. Psychol.* **47,** 101–104.

Escalona, Sybille and Heider, Grace M. (1959). "Prediction and Outcome", Basic Books, New York.

Flavell, J. H., Botkin, Patricia T., Fry, C. L., Wright, J. W. and Jarvis, P. E. (1968). "The Development of Role Taking and Communication Skills in Childhood", Wiley, New York.

Kelly, G. A. (1966). Transcript of tape-recorded conversation with Fay Fransella.

Kelly, G. A. (1969). "Clinical Psychology and Personality: Selected Papers of George Kelly" (Maher, B., ed.), Wiley, New York.

Leach, Penelope, J. (1964). Social and perceptual inflexibility in school-children in relation to maternal child rearing attitudes. *Unpublished Ph.D. Dissertation*, University of London.

Little, B. R. (1968). Factors affecting the use of psychological versus non-psychological constructs on the Rep Test, *Bull. Brit. psychol. Soc.* **21**, (70), 34.

Morse, E. L. (1966). An exploratory study of personal identity based on the psychology of personal constructs, *Unpublished Ph.D. Dissertation*, Ohio State University.

Newson, J. (1969). Comments on the nature of non-verbal communication between mothers and their children in the age range 10–20 months. *Unpublished notes.*

Newson, J. and Newson, Elizabeth (1968). "Four Years Old in an Urban Community", George Allen and Unwin.

Rosenthal, R. and Jacobson, Lenore (1966). Teachers' expectancies: determinants of pupils' I.Q. gains. *Psychol. Rep.* **19**, 115–118.

Salmon, Phillida (1969). Differential conforming as a developmental process. *Brit. J. soc. clin. Psychol.* **8**, 22–31.

Sears, R. R., Rau, Lucy and Alpert, R. (1965). "Identification and Child Rearing", Stanford University Press.

Shotter, J. (1969). Personal communication.

Men, the Man-Makers: George Kelly and the Psychology of Personal Constructs

John Shotter

". . . historically the questions that men have asked turned out to be more important than the conclusions they reached."

George Kelly

Introduction

The aim of this essay is a very broad one and to do with the foundations of Psychology: It is to work through a number of the implications in George Kelly's (1955) "The Psychology of Personal Constructs" and to discuss what might be the source of such constructs.

Kelly's model of man was, so one might say, of man with a model, an essentially *reflexive* idea which at first sight might seem to be an unproductive tautology. Tautology it may be, however it is certainly not unproductive; it is just those sort of logical structures, which in a sense *contain themselves*, that Chomsky (1957, 1965, 1968) is using to such powerful effect in his description of language. They allow, in the v. Humboldtian phrase, for "infinite use of finite means". It is because of the "reflexive creativity" immanent in Kelly's model of man that this essay refers to "Men, the man-makers." This is one theme we wish to explore.

Another related and no less important one we wish to explore is to do with the question "What must be the essential character of our knowledge, both of ourselves and nature, *that is expressible in language* (in symbols)? This is a question which, in one sense, Chomsky (1965) has been raising when he wonders whether ". . . the general *form* of a system of knowledge is fixed in advance as a disposition of the mind. . . ." (It is tantamount to the question "Are there any clear limits to scientific knowledge—especially to such knowledge of ourselves?").

Our discussion falls into two main parts: In the first, we discuss the power of man's self-images, and ponder upon the history of those currently represented in Psychology (and some which are not). We then take Kelly's notions of *construct* and *construct-system* and see "what we can do with

223

them" (Kelly's criterion of acceptability for ideas). We find that they have consequences in the planning and regulation of an individual's actions, and also in the co-ordination of our social interactions.

In the second part, I suggest an extension of Kelly's scheme to account for the process by which man acquires his 'models', taking up Kelly's (1969) points on the priority of behavioural *encounters*. The 'knowledge' that we gain by such bodily activity (for that is what *encounters* are) is ordered only in bodily terms and cannot be reordered; it is in the sphere of social interaction that schemes of ordering—*constructs* and *construct-systems*—are invented, and these may then be *imposed* upon such knowledge so that it can be reordered (or re-*construed*, in Kelly's terms) in different ways. And thus, to our question on the limits of our explicitly expressible knowledge, we reply, "Yes there is a limit, it must be expressed in terms of differences, in terms of *constructs*, with all the inherent limitations that that entails." All the other limitations on our knowledge are due to our bodily nature. Further, if 'knowledge' gained in our bodily encounters with the world and others cannot be expressed through a construct-system, because none exist, then that 'knowledge' remains inexpressible in anything other than *spontaneous** bodily activity—it can only become *both* anticipatory and voluntary as a result of (in Kelly's terms) a construal. So, while for us as individuals our 'feelings' are *absolutes*, 'known' in terms of the encounters that produce them, their systematic expression must be in *relative* terms, in terms of the differences that we can make.

The essay is brought to a close by pointing out that, until now, a thoroughgoing behaviourism (like Kelly's) has not been possible as previous approaches (e.g. Miller *et al.*, 1960) have been confounded by mechanistic diversions. For the understanding of *order*, the focus of attention should not have been upon the orderly actions of the individual, but upon the sphere of social interaction from whence that order arises. Thus if Kelly has any occidental (there seem to be many oriental) spiritual brothers, they are Mead (1934), Vygotsky (1962), and Wittgenstein (1953).

Constructs Have Consequences—In the Actions of Men

THE CRISIS IN MAN'S KNOWLEDGE OF HIMSELF

By now it is almost a platitude to say that there is some sort of crisis in western thought (and life). It is perhaps not quite such a platitude to say that it seems to stem from what is perceived as a discrepancy between what men know and feel about themselves, personally, and what their accepted public image (or plethora of images) allows as their nature. In short it is a division between hearts and minds. While, so it is said, there has been an

---

* Spontaneous as contrasted with *deliberate* I take the term from Vygotsky (1962, p. 92).

explosion in knowledge, there seems to have been a contraction in our understanding of ourselves—it is our self-image that has shattered.

This is disastrous, for these are the images which we use to plan, regulate and co-ordinate what we think of as our *rational* activities in the public sphere. If these images are inadequate or conflicting, we run the grave risk of all our actions in that sphere being irrelevant to our needs or of being in conflict. Cassirer (1944), from whose *Essay on Man* I have taken this section heading, ended his statement of the problem thus:

". . . our wealth of facts is not necessarily a wealth of thoughts. Unless we succeed in finding a clue of Ariadne to lead us out of this labyrinth, we can have no real insight into the general character of human culture; we shall remain lost in a mess of disintegrated data which seems to lack all conceptual unity."

Is it possible, then, to construct for ourselves a self-image which does not, in his words "cripple our own form-shaping powers", which will make us *whole* once again? Cassirer saw the key in the understanding of *symbolism;* we shall find the key to the understanding of symbolism (at least that aspect relevant to the sphere of Science, not that relevant in myth and magic) in the understanding of George Kelly's notions of *construct* and *construct-systems*.

MAN AND HIS IMAGES

Kelly was one of the few psychologists to systematically point out the discrepancy between the "personal" and the "public" knowledge of men, between the way someone talked about himself and the way an external observer talked about him. He (Kelly, 1955) observed that while *man-the-scientist* could entertain "theories", "ideas", "thoughts", "images", "mental-pictures", etc., of what man might be *like** (notions which serve to define *what* is being sought and to guide *how* to look for it), *man-the-scientist's-subject* can only be, scientifically speaking, as the psychologist's theories allow him to be. However, because so-called "mentalistic" terms are allowed no place in an *objective* science, the psychologist's subject cannot be influenced by his "theories", "ideas", etc., they must be determined in some quite other way—by, say "stimuli". Thus the split between the two ways of understanding man is set and cemented in right at the foundations of modern Psychology.† How has this come about and how was it justified?

In the past, and currently too, psychologists thought that if they were

---

* I italicize "like" only to draw attention to the process involved—*comparison* in terms of similarities and differences. Currently we are asking ourselves whether we are like our own creations, i.e., computers. But more of this later.

† Not that this totally negates it as a possible endeavour of man, to divide himself in this way (Kelly, 1969, p. 133 *et seq.*). He can use such *construct-systems* to achieve this aim, up to a point, i.e., within their *range of convenience*.

going to be "scientific" (i.e., act as if they were going about their business as accredited scientists do), it was necessary to model their activities upon the ways of going on, invented myth has it, by Galileo and Newton for the study of the, then *given,** material world. These were the ways, the "paradigms" (to use Kuhn's (1962) term), that Hobbes and Locke (which some look upon as the fathers of our modern approach) used for their study of man. In applying the "new method" of Galileo, and starting from the premise that we too were *material* beings (what else could we be?), Hobbes (1651) has this to say:

> ". . . what is the heart, but a spring; and the nerves but so many strings; and the joints so many wheels, giving motion to the whole body."

Thus inaugurating our present phase in Psychology—the phase of "man is a machine actuated by its circumstances"—as the last transformation in a fantastic sequence of such conceptual transformations which we can trace back at least to Plato.

This sequence seems to have gone something like this: to begin with there seemed to be *chaos* and *reality;* only the *real* was *intelligible* (via ideal forms); only that which can be *said explicitly* may be *true* or *false;* only that which is arrived at by *rational* thought and is thus *beyond dispute* can be *true; truth* and *falsity* are matters of logic; the *logic* that deals with the *real world* is *mechanics;* thus *mechanics* must be applied to man for a true understanding of man, who is part of the real world. Each new phase was an abstraction from its predecessor, and its significance could only be fully understood within the terms of the whole tradition: it was this whole tradition which Kelly repudiated.

If we had gone back to deeper roots, to the pre-Platonic philosophers for instance, we might have found there seeds which, due to lack of nurture, have not yet grown and blossomed so; seeds which might have brought forth Kelly-flowers.

What of Protagoras, who thought each man to be "the measure of all things, of all things that are that they are, and of things that are not that they are not," thus for him there was no objective truth in virtue of which one man is necessarily right and the other wrong? But his writings are lost and only known through Plato.

Kelly's true Hellenic ancestor seems to be Heraclitus. That the world is full of "things", he thought, was an idea arrived at as the result of "analysis" —a human activity practised, he alleged, by such men as Protagoras, consisting of classifying the constituents of an aggregate according to a "table

* That we cannot take *the form* of the material world as *given* follows from Kelly's idea that we *impose* construct systems upon it.

of opposites"*—this does not give us an account of how the world actually *is: only how we think it to be.* To attribute any absolute or fundamental significance to such an analysis would be a mistake (alternative analyses are to be had); it would be an inexcusable failure to understand what Heraclitus called, the *logos*—the way that words work to give only a one-sided determination of the ever changing flux, a determination arrived at as the result of one analysis among many.

It must have been the dawning realization of the power of logic which made Heraclitus unintelligible to his successors, for a sequential expression of the results of different analyses yields what in logic are thought of as paradoxes. Heraclitus summarized his position, in what to us, but not necessarily to him, was an extended paradox:

"Things taken together are wholes and not wholes; being brought together is being parted; concord is dissonance; and out of all things, one; and out of one, all things."†

THE USE OF "CERTAIN KINDS OF LANGUAGE FORM" IN SCIENCE

At various points in this essay words will appear in single quote marks, this will be to indicate that "*as if*" is intended. Thus men may have models (no single quotes) which they hold in their hands and the word "model" could only have been devised and learnt by reference to such situations. To say that "Man has a 'model'" is to say that he is behaving just *as if* he had a model in his hands to which to refer in pre-enacting his possible courses of action prior to actually encountering the situation so modelled. It is *as if* he possessed such a model but in any obvious material sense does not; it is somewhere "inside" him. Clearly, in deciding upon such a usage for the word "model" behavioural criteria must be involved.

The "*as if*" language-game [to use Wittgenstein's (1953) term] was well-known to Kelly (1964), for him it was a sub-game in the great "Language of Hypothesis" game. Illustrated below, in an extract from one of his writings on this topic, are many of the focal issues which he expressed in one form or another throughout all his writings. He is discussing whether a floor is *really* hard or whether it is *really* soft—is it a matter of *proof?* Or:

"Suppose instead we employ the language of hypothesis. We say, in effect, 'To be sure the floor may be regarded as hard, and we know something of what ensues when we cope with it in the light of such an assumption. Not bad! but now let us see what happens when we regard it as soft.' Out of this further exploration may come, not so much confirmation that it really is hard, or soft— as Descartes would have reasoned—but a sequence of fresh experiences that invite

---

* A very important idea which we shall meet again and again.

† Kelly (1962): "To sum it up, then, we may say that each of us finds meaning in his life not only by identifying things for what they are, but also by noting what they are not."

the formulation of new hypotheses . . . the object of the discourse (above) is only to suggest how a certain kind of form of language can enable us to extricate ourselves from the kind of realism to which our so-called objective language has bound us . . . one can see most clearly how man can be trapped by his indicative verbs and how, in turn, he has been led to believe that he must choose between mutually exclusive versions of reality . . . but the language of hypothesis enables his therapist (or the scientist, or the person himself) to say 'But only suppose the floor is to be regarded as hard.' "*

For Kelly then, there is no division in Science into pure and applied, the one concerned with the *proof* of an idea and the other with its exploitation; Science's primary concern is with *possibility*. In summary its characteristics are: Science functions in the sphere of instrumental activity; it does not provide a description of "reality", but schemes for the ordering of experience; scientific observation is not a passive process, but an active one, and what one observes is relative to what one does; there are no questions about which view is "true" in some ultimate sense, only the question of whether we can (and should!) use it to guide our actions in some way or other—questions of logical justification can arise only within schemes not between them; the achievements of one science thus do not negate those of another (Kelly, 1969, p. 135); only in logic is choice mutually exclusive, of the A *vs* not-A kind; elsewhere, even in the conduct of science (Kuhn, 1962), it is what Kelly calls a "double-entity" choice—choosing between one way of going on or another, choosing not to go on at all is only available to us in extreme circumstances.

All these characteristics of science†—at least these—follow as a consequence of accepting Kelly's model of man; we shall find more during the course of this essay.

"Ways of going on", then, can depend upon the invention of, for example, "a certain kind of language form," which once in man's possession can be put to special kinds of uses. Yet it is a construction of man, no less real because of its intangible nature than any of his more material constructions. To understand its nature (*one way* of understanding, Kelly would point out), is to discover both how he made it and how he uses it, and this, as we shall find later (p. 241), seems to be related to the problem of how we can come to do *deliberately* what we can already *spontaneously* (Vygotsky, 1962), and

---

* Again the shades of Heraclitus arise. He was perhaps trying to make some of the same sorts of points with such aphorisms as:

> "Sea is the cleanest and the dirtiest water:
> for fish it is drinkable and salubrious but for
> men it is undrinkable and poisonous."

† One can find all but identical views to Kelly's in Kuhn (1962), where he has documented the changing paradigms in the natural sciences, arguing that they were all "scientific" in their own terms.

how what we learn is first reflected on our spontaneous activity and only after *instruction* by another person can be expressed in language. But to understand the details of this process a close observation of it is necessary. To think that there are no empirical issues at stake here just because the material world is not under study would be a great mistake.

To turn now to Kelly's model of man.

KELLY'S MODEL OF MAN: MAN WITH A 'MODEL'

In the face of a Behaviourism which incorporated all the features of the Platonic-Hobbesian tradition outlined above, Kelly's heresy was to allow the psychologist's subject all the capacities of his investigators. Thus all men could be regarded as "scientists" to the extent that they used "theories", "ideas", "thoughts", etc., in the planning and regulating of their individual actions, and in the co-ordinating of their activities with others: Kelly's model of man was one of a man who is as if he owned a model of his world as a personal possession, to use just as he saw fit—to use in rehearsing a situation prior to its actual occurrence. Such a model that contains itself, so to speak, is *reflexive.*

The key to this idea is to realize that man is not meant to contain a model of himself as a *material* thing, but as a *form-producing process.* Just as a seed does not materially contain the plant, but produces it from the chaos of materials in the soil around it, organizing them into a plant which goes on to produce seeds for further plants, and so on, Kelly's model must be understood in the same sense; but it is to do with man's ability to *impose* upon the chaos around him *forms* which he finds *intelligible.* Thus when we use the term "invent" and say "Man *invents* the things in his environment", we shall not mean that he conjures them up out of nothing, we shall mean that he *imposes* upon what was once for him chaos, *constructs* and *construct-systems* which enable him to decide *what to do* in the face of such chaos.

The idea of "reflexivity" as a form-producing process is of relatively recent origin. As "self-replication" it occupies a central position in genetics (Beadle and Beadle, 1969) and as "recursive function theory" in the foundations of computing (Davis, 1958). It has turned up in Psychology in the computer simulation of problem solving (Newell *et al.*, 1958) and is the essential property that makes Chomsky's grammatical schemas *generative.*

One way of viewing this essay is as a working through of similar such implications in Kelly's position.

A MODEL FOR 'MODELS'

Kelly's "Theory of Personal Constructs" (1955) is to do with man's *psychological* constructions—in that way it is aptly named, but we shall find that, in one sense, *constructs* are not *personal* at all.

(A *construct* is invented when a man notices a difference, draws the attention of a fellow to it, and they agree upon a way of *representing* it. A *construct* is *used* when a man makes (expresses) a distinction using the agreed ways of representing it, such as: strong/weak, high/low, voiced/unvoiced (phonetic distinction), etc. . . . To establish (or erect) a *construct* is more than simply making a discrimination; we shall find that a social psychological process is involved.)

A *construct-system* is invented when a whole set of related distinctions is involved. The best example of an explicit system that I know is the distinctive feature analysis imposed upon the sound system of a language (Jakobson *et al.*, 1952). We shall discuss it on p. 244 of this essay.

However, to repeat, *constructs* are *imposed* upon "something", they are involved in a *form-producing process* not a *knowledge acquisition one*. Can this "something" have a nature quite apart from any analysis which we might impose upon it? (We are back, here, with the problem of "the-thing-in-itself"; there is no avoiding it.) When we give an analysis of some object, *what* might be the nature of our 'knowledge' of that object upon which our construct-systems are imposed, and *how* might that 'knowledge' be acquired? We shall deal with the first part of this problem here, the second part is left for a later section (p. 235).

A working solution to the first part of the problem is deceptively simple*: The "something" upon which constructs are imposed, the 'model', *is like* an actual material possession of the individual—as we have said before.

If we are going to give an analysis of an object, we take it in our hands and begin to describe it—this way and that, from one point of view then another, turning it over, looking inside it, feeling it, and so on. Our description of it depends upon how we examine it. Can we do the same for objects which we know well, in our imagination? Well, yes we can . . . to some extent (it is because of such differences which cannot be gone into here that I call this only a "working solution"). And we can see that *constructs* enter only into the *process of description*, and not into the memories of our once palpable contact with the object. For our memories are open to *construal* in a number of different ways, by the imposition of a number of different construct-systems upon them. We do not just remember our construals of a situation, we remember what for us was the situation.

If this seems to upset received ideas about the nature of knowledge— that true "knowledge" is what is put into books and stored upon library shelves—well . . . that is our heritage from Plato. In this issue there is a sharp distinction to be made between *our* 'knowledge' of a situation which we,

---

* And highlights, incidentally, the fact that construct theory, difficult though it may be at first to appreciate, does not actually deal with any *inner* entities directly whatsoever. It is based in observables, in behaviour.

as individuals, *derive from our actions in it,* and the knowledge of it transmitted to us by others, *which they express within a certain scheme of established conventions,* within a scheme invented by men. Thus there is a very clear distinction to be made between *constructs* and that upon which they are imposed. The latter *is* personal, absolutely so. We shall have to wait until later (p. 240) to see that there is a sense in which a *construct-system,* but not a *construct,* is personal also.

THE RELATION OF FACT TO THEORY

Psychologists seem to be in some confusion about the nature of *facts;* they do not seem to realize that their appreciation depends upon a psychological process which cannot itself be taken for granted. Not only do they seem to require Science to give us the facts and nothing but the facts, but they do not draw a clear distinction between facts of an everyday nature and "scientific facts". Furthermore, they often fail to notice that the word "theory" refers indistinguishably to both a *conceptual system* (an organized body of knowledge somewhere inside us) and its *formal expression* (in ink-marks on paper), a requirement for scientific theories.

Individuals who share in a culture seem to take "the world" (their world)— in which they think, love, hate, play, do things and find one another's actions intelligible—as "given". While everyone who possesses what some might call a culture's *Weltanschauung* can agree about everyday facts, how can they agree about the possibilities which might be made to follow from them?— there are no existent circumstances to which to refer. However, if we could decide upon objects by which to represent them, we could refer to arrangements and rearrangements of these. It is in mediating judgements of this sort that scientific theories (their formal expression) seem to have their function.

One of the important distinctions between a *Weltanschauung* and a scientific theory is that, while both reflect a conceptual system, the former is intuitively held, there being no way to reveal and characterize its nature, as alternative views with which to contrast it are (usually) unavailable, the latter, however, *must be publicly expressible,* and furthermore, if it is to be properly tested, of a form amenable to comparison with alternatives.

Thus it is that no matter how substantial the circumstances might seem that an allegedly factual statement describes, there is in the appreciation of that statement a theoretical component, a psychological process is involved in its understanding. It is, to my mind, this process which Kelly's theory illuminates.

For Kelly, a person's actions, and this includes what he says as well as what he does, can only be understood by another person to the extent that he possesses a construct-system similar to that upon which the person's actions are predicated.* Someone "can express† himself only within the framework of his construct-system, words alone do not convey meaning" (Kelly, 1969, p. 83). And it is the job of whoever it is who must understand him to construct for himself a similar system of constructs. (Perhaps in Experimental Psychology the opposite often happens: during an "experiment" the subject comes to construct a system similar to the experimenter's, operating only within his predetermined options—this is perhaps what "warm-up" or "practice" periods are for.) If the formulation of the construct-system is being undertaken within the sphere of science, then it must be made explicit and expressed by being represented materially to yield an account available for public examination and manipulation.

In Physics the lack of a clear understanding of the relation between fact and theory is tolerable—*any* way of doing something against our environment may be useful to us. But in Psychology it is quite intolerable, it might lead us to accept, as a scientifically proven fact, that our nature is determined in quite unalterable ways, and we might easily forget that the ways in which we construe our own nature have been invented by us, and are relevant only to how we achieve our purposes and not to how we formulate those purposes in the first place. Science has nothing to do with the formulation of *ends*.

To return to the relation between fact and theory, we can note that others have made the point, similar to Kelly's, that "a fact" only has significance if an individual possesses a way of interpreting it, otherwise, it is literally nonsense. A "scientific fact" is not, Cassirer (1944) says:

> ". . . given in any haphazard observation or in a mere accumulation of sense data. The facts of science always imply a theoretical, which means symbolic, element."

For example, Galileo's law of motion referred, not to actual bodies, but to idealized ones. And what Galileo did was not just to find his law by painstaking observation and measurement, but to *invent* the mode of idealization which determined the nature of the measurements he made.

There is no way in which it makes sense to talk of a "pure fact", *in toto* undistorted, with no construct-system imposed upon it. Kuhn (1962) puts it another way:

> "Scientific fact and theory are not categorically separable, except perhaps within a single tradition of normal-scientific‡ practice.

---

* Laing (1959, 1969) has, of course, been expressing similar views for similar reasons.
† Later we shall have reason to modify this and distinguish between *spontaneous* and *deliberate* expression. We shall find that Kelly is only really dealing with our intellectual activity, activity with a purpose as contrasted with purposeless play.
‡ "Normal-science" is for Kuhn a technical term. It is science in tranquil, problem-solving times, when scientist's activities are all coordinated via a shared paradigm which provides the currently "true" view of things, only in these times are "facts" nothing but facts. But normal-science ceases during paradigm change, during times of revolution, and previously established "facts" again become problematic.

. . . Men whose research is based upon shared paradigms are committed to the same rules and standards for scientific practice. That commitment and the apparent consensus it produces are prerequisites for normal science."

So, however one looks at it, what can be expressed in scientific terms, that is, explicitly written down or unambiguously encoded into some permanent physical system of expression, depends for its interpretation upon those encountering it possessing the appropriate 'model' and constructs: otherwise, it is just part of the unknown flux.

Goethe expressed it all in a sentence: All that is fact is already theory.

DIFFICULTIES WITH OUR PRESENT IDEA OF WHAT SCIENTIFIC PSYCHOLOGY SHOULD BE LIKE

A number of important implications for scientific Psychology follow from the discussion above: First it is not possible to base Psychology upon "facts". It is not good enough to assert that Psychology is a science because psychologists approach their subject matter with a scientific attitude—"a disposition to deal with facts rather than with what someone said about them" (Skinner, 1953). It is one of Psychology's tasks, one which in my estimation Kelly has done much to elucidate, to account for how we come to agree upon what constitutes a fact, and how what is construed as a fact from one standpoint is not so from another.*

Next: If a science cannot exist apart from its means of expression yet within its existent means, there are serious limitations when it comes to giving expression to many well-attested modes of human feeling and conduct —as indeed there seems to be with the language of science, see what Wittgenstein (1953) said about Wittgenstein (1922)—then psychologists should not feel inhibited as instituting new forms of reliable communication (if any can be invented).

(Perhaps they already exist and it is a matter of empirical investigation to discover them. This must have been the case with *logic*, for as Ryle (1949) says:

"Rules of correct reasoning were first extracted by Aristotle, yet men knew how to avoid and detect fallacies before they learned his lessons, just as men since Aristotle, and including Aristotle, ordinarily conduct their arguments without making any reference to his formulae. They do not plan their arguments before conducting

---

* Not that this means that one standpoint is as good as another, and that there is nothing to choose between them. Some have much more extensive *ranges of convenience* than others; some are couched in terms of *constructs* unavailable to people without special instruments; and so on. And, of course, the final arbiter is, as always, a conformity between one's expectations and what actually happens—construct-systems can be *falsified*. However, it is clear that the process via which one is abandoned and another taken up is more complex than has previously been imagined (Kuhn, 1962).

them. Indeed if they had to plan what to think before thinking it they would never think at all; for all this planning would itself be unplanned.

Efficient practices precedes the theory of it . . .''

In Science, we have bound ourselves, as an article of faith, to aim (we always fall short, necessarily) at a particular language form *made for reasoning* —a form which limits itself to *names* and patterns of *relations* between them. Surely, now, it is possible to allow other forms?)

Finally: It seems that once and for all Psychology must relinquish its Newtonian dreams (hasn't Physics) of the one single unified edifice of knowledge available to morons in cookbook form. It is to commit our students to yet two hundred years more of a Psychology without people for Broadbent (1961) to say:

> "Against the perspective of two thousand years the speed of our advance in studying behaviour seems more cheerful. At a rough guess, two hundred more years may bring the study of behaviour up to the level which physics reached in Newton's time. The problem to be faced is less tractable than that of the organisation of the Solar System . . .!*

For it ought not to be forgotten that Newton's laws do not deal with particular bodies or masses, but with any point-masses whatsoever. Laws which are about *any people whatsoever*—hypothetical proto-human forms with features common to cave men, wild boys, aboriginals, modern western europeans, etc.,—will exclude at the onset any account of what we think of as our humanity. For, as we know, babies born to us need not grow up to be what we understand as human; their humanity is transmitted to them after birth. It is inherited, but like houses and cities not like blue eyes, and it is of course the responsibility of a culture to make sure its young get their birthright: the inventions of their ancestors. The laws of proto-human forms phrased, if that is imaginable, in psychologically equivalent terms to point-masses, would ignore such inventions, thus denying us just those abilities by which we identify ourselves as human.

These are just some of the implications that we can draw out of Kelly's understanding of the relation between fact and theory. Later we shall take up a related issue: the way that "laws of nature" depend for their means of expression, their mode of existence, upon "rules of social conformity" —that is, "rules" are epistemologically prior to such "laws", which cannot, thus, be turned round to provide an explanation of our behaviour. *For explicit explanations we are locked within our own constructs.*

However, we must turn now from the discussion of what we can do with constructs once we possess them, to a consideration of how we might acquire

---

* Pascal remarks somewhere that the whole of infinite space is in one's mind.

them—construct them—and how we acquire the 'knowledge' upon which they can be imposed. We shall then be in a better position to understand their nature further.

Actions Have Consequences—on the 'Knowledge' and Constructs of Men

THE PRIORITY OF ENCOUNTERS

For Kelly, man was not something which in its natural state was static and upon which, action, motion and life had to be superimposed. It was taken as given that he was a self-active being in the world; also, *he was a creature who made his own circumstances*. What, then, might be the capacities of such a being? Why, he defines them for himself: "It is by his actions that man learns what his capabilities are . . ." (Kelly, 1969, p. 33). He utterly repudiated the "Darwinian assumption" that most psychologists seem to impose on men—although he was not sure that Darwin himself would have made it—that mankind had finally stopped evolving, and thus all that psychologists had to do was itemize his nature. It is a question of invention, not discovery.

> "Out of . . . further exploration may come not so much confirmation . . . but a sequence of fresh experiences that invite the formulation of new hypotheses . . ."

That quotation appeared earlier, within the body of a more extended quotation from Kelly's comments on the "Language of Hypothesis". Here, as in many other places, he emphasized the role of action, behaviour, as the primary source of man's new 'knowledge' both about the world and himself. But here again, I feel that Kelly did not sufficiently work through the powerful implications in his own position, even though the comments littered about his writings were obviously informed by an intuitive appreciation of them. We will explore the consequences of taking bodily activity as a logically prior datum. One might be forgiven, at this stage, for saying "So man does what he does because he does what he does, does he? Tell me something new." Admittedly it is an avenue of exploration which, *prima facie*, does not seem especially fruitful. However, it is not quite as circular as it may seem, it does have a basis, a starting point: *We must accept that we are responsive to a situation in a way quite apart from any construction which we might put upon it*—we can in a rough and ready way respond to the actions of other beings even when they do not or cannot talk to us. And thus, prior to the possession of any construct-systems, we must assume that, innately, we respond in a differential manner to our circumstances (as must all living things), albeit in a *counteractive* rather than *anticipatory* manner.

In this section of the essay, then, I would like to outline a mythology (Shotter, 1969) and a set of suggestive questions which will carry us from the datum of bodily activity to the theory of constructs, both *personal* and *public*.

Showing the behavioural origins of constructs will amount to outlining a behaviourist theory both of behaviour and the genesis of what we think of as *mental activity*. Thus it will be substantially different from any of those within the Platonist/empiricist/rationalist/associationist/mechanistic traditions.

I will first present a mythology—a new one to replace the old—and then the suggestions.

A NEW MYTHOLOGY OF MAN: MAN AS THE CREATORS AND POSSESSORS AND USERS OF CONSTRUCT SYSTEMS

We begin with proto-beings who are not self-aware individuals at all (Mead, 1934). They live together, initially like animals: reacting to one another directly and spontaneously, but in ways modified by 'knowledge' initially derived from their *encounters* with the world and each other. Before they created language, they were aware of nothing of their own nature and planned nothing consciously or deliberately.

But then they *created amongst themselves* a means for co-ordinating their communal activities: language. In doing so, not only did they make themselves aware of aspects of their otherwise spontaneous activities, they also provided themselves with a means for modifying these activities in a deliberate fashion. Once it was possible to request an act of another, and he of you, it was possible to request it of oneself (Luria, 1961). As ways of life ("forms of life", Wittgenstein, 1953) became stabilized and it was possible to request *organized sequences of actions* of another, and he of you, it became possible to *plan* and to *regulate* one's own activity (Vygotsky, 1962).

While it was the *internalized actions of the individual* that made the material for thought (Piaget, 1952), it was the *internalization of dialogue* (Vygotsky, 1962) that provided schemes for the ordering and re-ordering of such material.

Whereas the original creations of men were blind—there was no pre-established plan or guide—children now *re-invent* (Chomsky, 1968) them again, but with their mothers and friends as guides. Men can learn such things as language because men created such things—learning them is *guided invention*. But learning the things of men is different from learning the things of the world, the first are governed by *rules of social conformity*, the latter by *laws of nature*. Our means of expressing the latter depends upon the prior possession of the former (Wittgenstein, 1953).

THREE SUGGESTIONS TO DO WITH THE GENESIS OF "MIND"

The above is a story, pure fiction. Can we get away with saying "But then they created . . . language", as if it raised no problems? When Locke (1690) was discussing language, thinking that men were *endowed* with it, he said ". . . nature, even in the naming of things, unawares suggested to men the originals and principles of all their knowledge . . . (Bk. 3. Ch. 1. sec. 5)" and that was the story *he* had to tell to get on with the analysis he wanted to make. It was a useful myth, as so too, I hope, is the one above in its own way.*

One consequence of it is that everything which we think of as "mental" activity, or a product of "mind", is an invention of man—even "mind" itself is a cultural product. "Nothing which happens in the brain can be described except in terms supplied by the mind" (Mumford, 1967). And, Kelly would say, to find the seat of the mind do not look into the brain, look at those responsible for it, look at men, whole men with their fellows in the world.

Now to frame some questions (we will take spontaneous activity as given):

1. "What if 'knowledge' could only be derived from the self-instigated actions of the body?"
2. "What if the unknown is 'felt' first via bodily encounters; and only later when it is so known can it be construed into parts, one way by one construct system, another way by another, where the invention of construct-systems arises out of co-ordinated activity within the sphere of social interaction?"
3. "What if, *within the sphere of social interaction*, a construal (one among many) of spontaneous, context-bound, non-conscious, "need-depen-dent," activity can be imposed so that *an act* (a unit) can come to be done deliberately, out-of-context, to alleviate no present need? It could then be interpolated into spontaneous activities thus modifying them, and action could then be emitted in anticipation, *voluntarily*."

These are not to be taken as formal propositions to be proved, but only as suggestions to be discussed. Let us take each one in turn and see what we can get out of it.

"Thought derives from the abstraction of one's own action upon things" (Elkind, 1969)—Does it?

Only the behaviour of organisms that in some sense can acquire 'knowledge' could possibly become *anticipatory*—initially the aspect of its activity influenced by its environment must be *counteractive* in character, and without being modified by 'knowledge', remain so. But even for such activity of this primitive kind to be possible what goes on *outside* the organism must affect its behaviour in *a differential manner* (we might want to say that its movements were mediated by its "feelings", but that is not necessary at this stage).

---

* For a full scale attempt to speculate upon the origin of language see Mumford (1967). The account here is fundamentally influenced by it.

This necessitates a fundamental assumption that must be made about all organisms:* they must contain "internal regulators" which function to 'guide' (in the absence of all other guides) their activity—regulators which determine, regarding its current circumstances, whether at least the organism is *to go on* or *to withdraw*. It is to these very primitive regulators that we will appeal to guide the protohuman's actions until he has acquired some 'knowledge' and some constructs for construing it, and thus become human.

We have not yet, though, made contact with *construct theory*; simply *acting* and *acquiring 'knowledge'*—if one is going to be able to put *alternative* constructions upon it—is not enough. To show this I am going to use in a modified form an analysis of concrete bodily needs to be found in Dreyfus (1967).

Imagine a wild-boy divorced from any human community. He might develop his own abilities and knowledge of the world in the following way: At first he would not know what was the nature of his world *nor what his needs were*; he would simply begin by being in some state of restlessness or discomfort. And this is not a determinate state that can always be alleviated in the same way. He would have to actively cast around for a way of easing it, inevitably, in the process encountering his environment. Once a way was discovered he would come to know his need in terms of what he had done to alleviate it, and to 'know' the structure of his world in terms of the actions within which he had encountered it. And next time he recognized himself to be in the *same* state of restlessness he could do *what he did before*, but this time *in order to* relieve it. Presumably, he could discover many needs to himself in this sort of way, and he would 'know' his world in terms of his needs and the actions that he must initiate to satisfy them. Furthermore, we might presume that his 'inventions' would become 'polished' with repetition, as he discovered that not all aspects of them were relevant to his "needs".

Both animals and wild-boys may 'teach' themselves in this way, and I feel that it does reflect Kelly's intuition that "It is by his actions that man learns what his capabilities are. . . ." However, it does cause some difficulty. It provides only *one* construction, one which is tied to the organism's needs —alternative construals are impossible. So although we now have behaviour that is anticipatory, it is still not so in the sense Kelly meant. We can only solve this problem when we turn to suggestion number two.

Before we do that, however, it is necessary to comment upon our title for this section [taken from Elkind (Piaget, 1968), who uses it to express Piaget's key notion of "reflecting abstraction".]: The "things" of the child's world are not the "things" of Elkind's or Piaget's world. His is still the statement of an external observer. Does thought derive from the child's actions upon Piaget's "things" or from those upon his own "things"?

* At least about those which interest psychologists.

While 'thought' may be derived from our actions, we seem to derive from them both our own nature and "things." Elkind's statement, elegantly phrased as it is, ultimately is unhelpful.

". . . *the development of thinking is . . . from the social to the individual (Vygotsky, 1962)*"

As the title for this section, a discussion of suggestion number two, I have taken a statement from Vygotsky (p. 20) in which he was totally disagreeing with Piaget's (1923) then interpretation of language development: That it was a transition from an egocentric to a socialized use of speech. While the child's view of the world may be egocentric, and this expressed in his speech, his *use of* speech could be, Vygotsky showed, initially for nothing but social purposes; this, after all, was the situation in which it was learned.

"Egocentric" speech emerges, Vygotsky thought, when the child starts to use his language to plan and guide his own actions. It is only incomprehensible to others because it omits to "mention" what is obvious to the speaker. Such a language form seems to disappear when the child's speech becomes sharply differentiated between the two functions: overt communication and covert self-regulation and planning.

Thus it was that Vygotsky invented a thesis, the full implications of which are still to be worked out: An organized pattern of social interaction (and there are many other examples other than language) initially *between* two people (a child and others), creates a means for that child, at a later date, to organize *his own* behaviour.

The reason why this is so important is because it shows that there is so much more to learning to talk than just making acceptable patterns of noises with one's mouth. It is not that first there is language,* and once learned it can then be used by the child in co-ordinating his social relationships. For, as Wittgenstein (1953) put it:

> "If language is to be a means of communication, there must be agreement not only in definitions but also (queer as this may sound) in judgements . . ." (S 242).

Associated with the process of getting a child to re-invent a language, as those around him and their ancestors originally invented it, are many other processes not obviously linguistic. To put it shortly here, although I will

---

* Here, by the way, we are not just talking about *communicating*. We must assume that we can, and always could, all communicate without any special training—that the activities of living things have some sort of significance for use, and we can use this fact amongst ourselves to co-ordinate our activities in a rough and ready way without the use of language. By "language" is meant *skilful* communication, where speaking as an activity, is a structured skill at social interaction *invented by men*.

expand on this a little in the final phase of this essay, they are to do with getting him to structure, to partition and attribute significance to the world in the same way as his mother. And this process, if words are later going to serve any communicative function, *begins before the child learns, as we think of it, to talk* (Newson, 1969). In Wittgenstein's terms, it seems as if "agreement in (at least some) judgements" between mother and child is a prerequisite for the development of language.

Thus a child inherits (like a house, not like eye colour) at least two possessions when he is inducted into a culture, separable only as an analytic convenience: A special way of 'seeing' the world, of attributing significance to it, and interwoven with it, a skilful way of co-ordinating his social interaction in its terms.

It is not as if the wild-boy in the previous section would not develop his own special way of 'seeing' the world; he did. But what language enables our children to do, which the wild-boy could not, is *to re-arrange the component parts of his 'view' into new patterns*. And it is a 'view' that represents and incorporates knowledge gained from *the many different stand-points of his fellows*. Thus our child may now construct for himself many different construct-systems for alternative construals of a situation—something inaccessible to the wild-boy. Furthermore, our child may make a *personal selection* of constructs and construct-systems. And it is thus that we can once again give a sense to the word "personal" in personal constructs.

But we are departing from some of Kelly's (1969) very fundamental points here. He looked upon it as "*the creative capacity of the living thing to represent the environment, not merely respond to it . . .* to represent other forms of reality, while still retaining its own form" (p. 8). Thus the ability to "construe" situations characterized *all* living things. If the views above are correct, it is an ability only of man, because only men can 'see' the world *as others see it*. This, however, is a departure that makes no practical difference to Kelly, concerned as he was, only with men; but within the broad panoply of Psychology it is a point worth making.

"*Our new activities are our old spontaneous ones deliberately reconstituted into new ones*"

For the discussion of our final suggestion I have modified some comments of George Miller's (Miller and Chomsky, 1963) in which he ponders the source of our new plans: "Presumably, our richest source of new plans are our old plans, transformed to meet new situations" (p. 486). While that may be our richest source, it cannot possibly be our only source. The trouble with Miller and Chomsky's scheme is that it will not get us beyond the possibilities implied *within* our current symbolic schemes, and then only with our *logical* schemes at that.* For in their scheme plans must be treated as "objects that can be formed and transformed according to definite rules." Yet as Kelly (1969, p. 31) says:

> "There are first-time occurrences in the history of mankind . . . a psychology that pins its anticipations on the repetition of events it calls 'stimuli' . . . will find its accurate predictions confined to the trivialities of man's least imaginative moments and to the automatisms of persons given in despair."

So how are we to get beyond these limitations in our symbolic systems and yet come to give an account of the human innovative process within them?

Let us return for a moment to the idea of *reflexivity:* Chomsky (1965) has shown how a "finite means" can give rise to "infinite (in the sense of 'uncountable') creativity", as long as the rules in the system have a "recursive" property. The point which Chomsky misses is that men not only "create" *systematically* according to their own rules—they "create" the rule systems too! This type of invention (I would like to call it *transcendental* to contrast with systematic) proceeds not in terms of symbol manipulation, but by the invention of new activities, new "forms of life" within which others can share (and which later come to support a "language-game"). It is how man can modify his own actions without plans that is the problem; and this is the problem of free-will, volition and consciousness too.

For the key to the puzzle, we can again turn to Vygotsky (1962, p. 90): "In order to subject a function to intellectual and volitional control, we must first possess it." And it is *instruction* (of the child by the adult) that effects the transfer of *spontaneous* actions to the realm of the *deliberate*. Its effect is not to make the child do what he cannot, but to *restructure* what he can do already into new forms—and this first proceeds without language, and provides a frame of reference within which the particular language of the child's culture can develop (Newson, 1969). However, once *linguistic* communication is underway it can function first, as the *instrument* (Vygotsky, 1962, p. 56ff) for the mother to cumulatively restructure the child's actions, and later, for the person (that the child becomes) *to restructure* his own. As Goethe said: "Language makes people more than people make language."

This is obviously an area of investigation with undreamt of riches; the discussion above is little more than an assay which, in my estimation, indicates that full-scale mining operations are worthwhile. Its implication here is that there is a close involvement of construct theory with language and language development; that essentially what we think of as "free will" or "deliberate" action is to do, not with acting in accord with a construct-system, but with *selecting* or *constructing* that particular construct-system

* Appeals to Turing's Hypothesis (1936–7) that such schemes are equivalent to the ultimate in *logical* expression, notwithstanding. The limits of mechanism are not our limitations; we *invent* our own forms of life, mechanical ones included.

in the first place. Thus, although we disagree with Miller's idea about the source of plans, the disagreement is only partial; we think that the 'knowledge' for plans comes *from bodily activity* and the structuring of it into component parts and the schemes for their organization and reorganization, *from instruction*.

CONCLUSIONS

Constructs, as we have already said, are binary distinctions. What I have attempted to do in the preceding sections is to construct at least two sets of generically (i.e., each new distinction arising out of the last) related construct systems for the analysis of *behaviour* and *knowledge*.

Clearly, there is no monopoly on construct-systems, we must remember that constructs are just as much as all our other artifacts, constructs. And if we think that *all* human actions are guided by a definite and limited set of fundamental constructs which can be described, once and for all, we shall run again into all the difficulties from which Kelly tried to save us. Yet the choice of constructs is not at all an arbitrary one, and much of Kelly's (1955) book is to do with such problems of choice at the personal level [as Kuhn's (1962) is at the scientific level].

Current Issues

THE EXPRESSIBLE AND THE INEFFABLE: THE NATURE AND
DEVELOPMENT OF CONSTRUCT-SYSTEMS

"What must be the essential character of our knowledge both of ourselves and nature that it is expressible in language (in symbols)?" For Plato, the world of sense experience was a flux, but "true" knowledge was of "real" and unchanging things; it was infallible, it allowed one to do with an expectation of success what one could not do before. (It ought not to be forgotten that the Greeks were concerned, for the conduct of their practical affairs, to instruct their slaves appropriately—much as we are now concerned to programme our computers to relieve us, adequately, of some of our chores.) Plato thought that true knowledge could be arrived at by viewing the flux against an unchanging set of limits or ideal forms. And this set the philosophic task for centuries after: To discover the nature of such forms. Thus it is that we still ask such questions as "What is perception?", "What is motivation?", etc., expecting to be answered with a set of templates which will cover all possibilities.

In Fig. 1, I have depicted the results of a Kelly-Heraclitian process of construct-system development. As we have already discussed people encountering the flux about them may sense it in a differential manner, and furthermore agree amongst themselves upon ways of indicating this. Taking system A, on the left, essentially what it depicts is that a group of people encountering the flux, f, have found in it a difference and have invented a distinctive indication, A_1, which allows them to show how to mark off f into two distinct regions f' and f''. Noticing that there is a difference must come first, agreeing on its nature and representing it next, and realizing that the two distinct parts are still related last. After having made A_1 they next, say, notice a difference within f'' and mark it with the term A_2. But again this

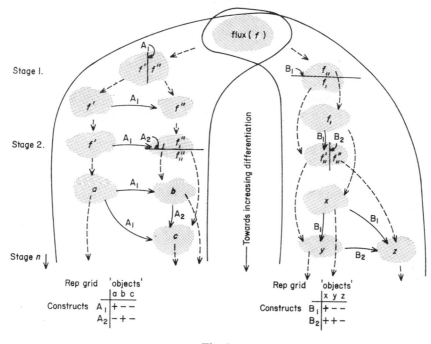

Fig. 1.

involves the process of first simply sensing differences, then agreeing upon which are of significance and representing them symbolically, and only finally realizing that what has been made separate is still related, now much more complexly, to its opposites. The process of noticing differences and so on, in other words, the process of developing construct-systems may, presumably, be continued indefinitely. But note this, once a distinction has been made, we may quite reasonably choose to ignore it, thus, although the diagram depicts, from top to bottom, systems of increasing differentiation, the lower are *generically* related to the higher and are logically included in them.

The system so produced is best described as a system of *compartments*,*

* A system of structured vacancies.

where the compartments are distinguished from one another in terms of binary distinctions, i.e., *constructs*, and where each compartment may be identified by the relation that it bears to all the others in the system. This is where the repertory grid comes in: We might like to name the compartments, in the case of system A, I have named them, arbitrarily, a, b and c. Aspects of the flux in which we can sense A_1 but not A_2 qualify to be called a's, those without A_1 but with A_2 qualify as b's, while those with neither as c's. (Not a very rich system as depicted here perhaps, but with eight binary distinctions (256 possible compartments) we can encompass the sound system of a language (about 40 distinct phonemes) with about 50% redundancy.)

To hark back to Heraclitus on Protagoras: a set of constructs is obviously like a "table of opposites"; however, a construct-system demands not just a list but properly inter-related constructs.

While each compartment is, in isolation, uncharacterized, its nature is known in terms of its relations to all the other compartments in the system. [And we might, as Kelly (1961) did, imagine an algebra of such systems.] However, what it is important to realize is that constructs are not passively acquired, but result from action of some kind, and that gaining conscious possession of a construct involves the social psychological process discussed on p. 239. When it comes to construct-systems in science, this process is not just involved in the making of a construct, but is involved in the making of *a whole system*. The task of science (as distinct from technology) does not lie in just discovering new facts, but in discovering an orderly arrangement for many, many facts, one which depicts the nature of all their interconnections.

Now, as has been mentioned before, what is observed depends upon what is done. In the diagram I have shown two construct systems A and B which have been imposed upon the same flux, *f*. To take a particular example, imagine the "flux" to be the unanalysed "proto-noise" of speech. The construct system A might be the distinctive feature analysis* of Jakobson *et al.* (1952), where speech sounds are distinguished in articulatory terms: vocalic/non-vocalic, consonantal/non-consonantal, compact/diffuse, etc. While the construct-system B might be a physicist's analysis of the proto-noise in terms of: high/low frequency, high/low intensity, short/long duration, etc. The two sets of objects (a, b, c) and (x, y, z) so produced bear no relation to one another having been obtained by *different means* of analysis serving *different purposes*; there being no general or "neutral" analysis to be had as there is no general or superordinate communal activity

* Those readers familiar with this will recognize repertory grids as similar to "distinctive feature classification", which clearly expresses de Saussure's dictum (1960, p. 120): "in language there are only differences." Kelly (1962) expressed the same intuition thus: "Probably the most important deviation of psychological logic from classical logic is in its use of contrasts."

from which it could arise. So while both phoneticians and physicists are talking about what we obviously feel are *the same* noises, they are both viewing them through their own "paradigms" (to use Kuhn's term), their own research training and practice, or their own scientific "form of life" with its associated "language-game(s)" to use Wittgenstein's (1953) terms. Kelly talked of a construct-system as having a *range of convenience*; I hope the discussion above goes some way towards explicating that idea.

Now, as what scientists observe depends upon what they do, the intelligibility of the account they give depends upon whether one is a participant in the appropriate scientific community, for their accounts are only of relevance (i.e., of use in exploiting the possibilities inherent in them) to those who possess the same means for affecting the world as those who originally produced them.

This seems to suggest that explicit construct-systems follow from a particular orderly activity (see suggestion 2, p. 237), and need not be at all implicated in that activity. This raises a most important issue. A child does not first learn the distinctive features (constructs) of his language in order to decide what is the right way to talk: he must first 'talk', try to talk, in order to find out what the distinctive features of his language are. [And he seems to go through the sort of development depicted in the diagram, i.e., his early constructs are different from his final ones, but *generically* related to them. The process of differentiation seems to stop when he has made enough distinctions for all practical purposes (Brown, 1965, Ch. 6).] Thus an analysis, in terms of some final set of constructs, such as Jakobson *et al.*'s, *cannot be involved in the process of learning to talk*, it can only be constructed and imposed *as a consequence* of knowing how to talk. Talking is learned *by trying to talk* to an adult, by bodily activity being shaped under instruction. [Here we are very close to Skinner (1957) as I shall acknowledge in a moment, p. 249.]

It is because of this that we cannot make machines, which lack bodies and thus non-linguistic means of communication and so on, learn to talk as we do, no matter what this author (Shotter, 1968) once thought.

Unfortunately, we cannot spend time working out the implications of this diagram here, though it obviously has many to do with systems of knowledge, concepts, universals, etc. But it is clear, I hope, that the answer to our initial question is: "The essential character of the knowledge we encode in symbols is that it is expressed in terms of differences, i.e., it is *relative*, and based in 'knowledge' derived from our direct encounters with the "world".

OBJECTIONS TO THE IDEA THAT EVERYTHING ESSENTIAL TO HUMAN INTELLIGENCE CAN BE FORMALIZED

It might seem that Chomsky's (1957, 1965, 1968) brilliant analyses of linguistic

9

rule-systems has, along with our *linguistic competence,* brought the whole nature of our competencies as such within the realm of logic and computation. At the moment Chomsky (1968) is "assigning to the mind, as an innate property, the general theory of language that we have called 'universal grammar'."

> ". . . very deep inborn principles, probably of a highly restrictive nature, that determine how knowledge of language emerges in the individual, given the scattered and degenerate* data available to him (Chomsky and Hampshire, 1968) . . . the general features of language structure reflect, not so much the course of one's experience, but rather the general character of one's innate capacity to acquire knowledge—in the traditional sense, one's innate ideas and innate principles" (Chomsky, 1965).

And Chomsky seems to think that in some way these very deep inborn principles can be characterized. As indeed he must if his ideas about a "universal grammar", and language acquisition, and so on, are not to be vacuous. This is a powerful claim and if correct would have startling consequences, if not in all of Psychology, at least for construct theory: If Chomsky is right, and our linguistic (and possibly other) competencies are so structured because of "innate mental dispositions," then the consequences are exciting. For it would suggest that the *form* of our knowledge is limited in discoverable and well-defined ways (Chomsky, 1965, Chomsky and Hampshire, 1968), i.e., *that a basic set of constructs could be found from which all others could be derived.*

However, if such people as Kelly and Wittgenstein are right, languages are not built upon such constructs, constructs are a consequence of the process. Languages appear to share deep common characteristics simply because all peoples of the world share the same basic bodily form, live in the same world, discover their capacities to themselves in the same way, and so on. In other words, the fact that our linguistic structures seem to be limited in well-defined ways is no more remarkable than that we locomote on our feet rather than on our knees and elbows.

The activities that we carry out in the social sphere do not just depend upon the "dispositions" of the "mind", but upon the whole person. Chomsky's constructs are constructs; they can only be *imposed* upon a language by someone who already knows that language. Grammatical transformations are, in his own words "*structure dependent,* in the sense that they only apply to a string of words by virtue of the organization of those words into phases"

---

* Chomsky does not take into account the use of intelligible actions as meaningful accompaniments of "grammatically degenerate" sentences. Work involving the videotaping of mothers 'teaching' their pre-verbal infants a task, currently conducted at Nottingham, indicates the importance of these (Newson, 1969).

(Chomsky, 1968). That is, they can only be applied if it is already known how to construe sentences into phases.

Obviously language *is* innate in the sense that it has come out of man's own resources, but we inherit its structures not like blue eyes but like all the other constructs of man.

MENTALISM, MECHANISM, BEHAVIOURISM, SOCIAL INTERACTION

". . . words are connected with the primitive, the natural, expressions of the sensation and used in their place. A child has hurt himself and he cries; and then the adults talk to him and teach him exclamations and, later, sentences. They teach the child new pain behaviour.

"So you are saying that the word 'pain' really means crying?"—On the contrary: the verbal expression of pain replaces crying and does not describe it" (Wittgenstein, 1953, S 244).

For Behaviourists to attempt to banish mentalistic terms from their vocabulary—terms that they called "mentalistic" because they were supposed to refer to private inner states—was quite unnecessary.

When as an adult we refer *to ourselves* by use of such terms, we do it against a personal background of thought and feeling which we must recognize as familiar in some way. Thus there is for us, we feel certain, a particular private inner state associated with the use of such words, and it is to that which we think they refer. But that is not how we were taught them; that is not how the words were used by those who taught them to us. They observed *our behaviour* and used such terms *to refer to us, not to themselves*. It was a case of "adultmorphism" for Behaviourists to think that the epistemologically prior use of mental terms was for self-reference. Furthermore, it was yet another example of the "double-viewed"* approach, to use such terms in setting the goals of a Behaviourist psychology—an account of "mental" activity in terms of S-R laws. They did not realize that even in their very contention that such laws were "objective" or "public" they were appealing to implicit "rules of social conformity" involving just the process such "laws" were meant to illuminate: perceptual judgements, agreements, their symbolic representation and so on.

Kelly's Psychology is not mentalistic, quite the opposite. For him we do 'talk' to one another with our behaviour.

"Two people, say a mother and a newborn child, may not have a full intellectual meeting of minds the first time they try to enter into a discourse with each other in the maternity ward. But by sharing their encounter with events—including the events produced by their own behaviour—some mothers and daughters do develop a fair understanding, each of what the other is talking about" (Kelly, 1969, p. 28).

* The other example is the one Kelly pointed out: "man-the-scientist" and "man-the-scientist's-subject."

And it is no exaggeration to say that in fact Kelly's is a thoroughgoing behaviourism [like George Mead's (1934)], so thoroughgoing that one cannot use it to find out within it anything about man's very fundamental natures any scientific accounts that we might achieve we will still have *invented!* But yet it deals with just those activities of man which are thought of as intellectual, conscious and deliberate.

In relation to this, turning now to the problem of mechanism, it is noteworthy that it is just the "higher" mental functions of man that have proved easiest to simulate upon a computer. Something, such as the extensive recognition of friends faces, which even what we think of as the most moronic among us can do, is very difficult to simulate—if not impossible for it to be done in the same sense as we do. In Wittgenstein's terms, the language-games of our "higher" mental functions, e.g., mathematics and logic, arise out of extremely circumscribed and orderly forms of life: those that revolve around the arrangement and re-arrangement of patterns of marks on paper. That such orderly patterns of social interaction should give rise to activities which can be mechanized is not, then, surprising. A machine to do these tasks could be an expression of those very same inventive impulses that originated the social interaction in the first place. Thus it is not at all remarkable and we should expect to be able to invent a rational description (a mathematical model) for all our rational activities, as Chomsky has done for those aspects of our language usage that Bernstein (1964) would call "elaborated".

Thus we may only be able to simulate on a computer, in any genuine sense, those of our activities which we ourselves have both *invented* and, most importantly, *closed to any further inventive development.*

Comments such as these, I think, should make us suspect that there is more to being intelligent than having a "mind" (and that computers are more like electronic "minds" than "brains").

The simulator's dreams of designing "a species of superior intelligence to replace ourselves as lords of the Earth" (Sutherland, 1968), seem to be nothing more than thinly disguised "death-wishes" to be able to escape from the responsibilities of being able to act consciously and deliberately by choice.

> "No wonder so many of us would like to become scientists and be content to win prizes without having to take the awful responsibility for people (Kelly, 1955)."

The Frankensteinian-myth, of making creatures more powerful than our selves but which still remain within our control, is obviously very powerful. And scientists' activity no matter what public relations story they put out, is still clearly tinged, unavoidably, by mythico-magical thinking.

For example, computer programmes must be written in 'words', in symbols

—whether these are patterns of punch holes on paper tape, patterns of magnetization in core-stores, or whatever. Is it not "word-magic" to hope that one day, if the pattern is long enough, or complex enough, we shall hit upon the right combination to make the machine "intelligent"? Also, if "principles of reinforcement" (Skinner, 1957) were *all that there was* to learning language, we would have to accept, as Locke said, that the origin of language really was a shaping process by Nature: ". . . nature, even in the naming of things, unawares. . . ." If we call that a myth, a story we tell ourselves to make the world and ourselves intelligible, then the notion of "innate ideas" is no less a myth. And in the absence of any alternatives, such myths guide us in our corporate affairs until we can invent more empirically well-founded alternatives. There are, I think, reasonable grounds for preferring Kelly's myth.

Finally, in this section, I would like to give some indication of how one can proceed in a behaviouristic fashion while investigating the most complicated of topics: the instruction of a young child by its mother.

I am fortunate enough to be involved in a project* at Nottingham investigating pre-verbal communication between mothers and their 10–20 months old infants. I feel that we are beginning to uncover the processes at work by which they create a mutual construct-system between them *before* language proper develops. We are simply watching (and video-taping) how mothers go about trying to get their young children to do form-board tasks, i.e., putting different shaped pieces in their appropriate place, otherwise the situation is entirely unstructured by us.

> "Mothers shape the child's whole activity by selecting and emphasizing happenings which are task-relevant (as the mother sees it) at the expense of those which are not. In this sense the mother structures the child's spontaneous activities in a way which he himself would not do if left to his own devices.
>
> Out of all this mutual activity, mother and child develop a shared frame of reference. Each knows the happenings to which the other is responsive, and they are thus in a position to communicate their intentions to one another. It may well turn out that this form of rapport is essential to the development of linguistic communication as a later stage" (Newson, 1969).

In other words, the mother is responsible for some of the very fundamental constructs available to the child. She, obviously, is not responsible for his activity and what he discovers to himself as result, but she is responsible for getting him to *select* among his actions.

Clearly here, some version of a reinforcement theory is needed (and here we acknowledge Skinner's ideas of "shaping" and "reinforcing"), but quite why a child is responsive to some of his mother's actions and not

---

* With Susan Treble and John Newson.

others, why her "Ohoo . . . o there's a good boy" seems to relax him and terminate his ongoing activity, we only just now are working out ways to investigate.

All we can say at this stage is that patterns of interaction are, in some degree, idiosyncratic. The mother must watch the child, and the child the mother, there are no pre-established rules, only continual improvisation. It is the creative exchange, *par excellence*, of people making people.

Conclusions

The essence of a recursive scheme is that it can give rise to an indefinite number of different forms. This is the nature of Kelly's model of man; he may take on many forms. In no sense can Kelly's Psychology boil down to a Galilean or Newtonian formula, quite the opposite: it gives us the beginnings of an account of how the scientific process functions, how rational thought can grow out of thoughtless and irrational activities; it suggests that rather than seeking after the one single "true" system we should proceed with a proliferation of construct systems, each, if they are of any relevance to man's needs at all, with their own special range of convenience. As we discovered on p. 244 a particular *analysis* is achieved by a particular *means* for a particular *purpose*, and the analysis is only intelligible and of use to those who understand and possess the means via which it was originally achieved. Thus if a construct-system is to be of any use at all *it must bear a relation to the methods that people have available for taking some sort of action in the world.* But even if it can meet these conditions, whether it should then be used ("should" always implies agreements amongst people) is another matter. Once we possess an accredited construct-system we can use it like we use a map, letting it dictate most of our actions, proceeding not in terms of a differential sensing of our environment, but by letting it determine a sequence of ready-made units of activity relevant to the achievement of certain purposes. Thus it is in the sphere of instrumental activity that construct-systems have their importance; however, it is in the sphere of non-instrumental activity (I shall for convenience call it "play"), that construct-systems are invented. Play is the sphere of activity where we are not under compelling external circumstances, they are such that we can "selectively non-attend".

To some the mere mention of the irrational, or non-rational, is to court disaster; here I have spent much time discussing its value. This is not because I wish to advocate the abandonment of rationality, far from it. I hope that if we can understand its roots more clearly we can transform it from a fragile plant, always fading away, to a robust one, a hardy perennial.

What Kelly shows us is the nature of our actions when they are regulated by rational schemes, what he cannot show us is how to choose between alternative schemes; this sort of intelligent and responsible choice cannot itself be encompassed within any rational scheme, our individual choice is still important.

The consequences of Kelly's Psychology in the long run are quite unforeseeable, and not without its dangers because of that. We should not, I think, as psychologists, as a specialist group with specialist methods, make any sort of prescriptions about the possibilities we might invent. We must appreciate that for a person to 'see' a possibility as relevant to himself, it must have a basis in his own preferred construct-system. Presenting people with new options between which to choose but with no basis upon which to choose, can only lead to what might be called "the existential horrors".

In summary then, for the three areas of concern, Psychology, Science and People, we can say: In Psychology we have distinguished between the 'knowledge' which we derive from our actions and the schemes of organization, derived from social interaction, which we can impose on it. Thus that which the child learns about his physical world is different from that which he learns of human inventions; he has to *re-invent* (Chomsky, 1968) the latter but *discover* (Skinner, 1953, 1957) the former. (Thus it is not so much that Chomsky's and Skinner's views are mutually exclusive; they have not admitted that their construct-sytems have a limited range of convenience.) Psychology must find a way of illuminating both these areas; it cannot, just because it arbitrarily chooses to ape the natural sciences, ignore our inventive activities.

For Science, the implications are that it cannot provide a one single "true" account of "reality" with pure science to *prove* the view, and applied science to *exploit* it. The essence of Science is that it should invent construct-systems which, ultimately, make empiricism unnecessary (whereas Technology exploits the empirical method). Science is to do with the creation of networks of relations which can be arranged and rearranged according to determinate rules thus allowing us to derive possibilities from actualities. The different descriptions of phenomena, the possible derived from the actual, are 'maps' to use in our investigations; they tell how, even though we may do different things, "how to go on in the same way". Thus the question is not of which view must be logically true, but of whether we can use it, not just in the material sphere but in the *personal* sphere also. But a description is only of such use if it relates in some way to the methods that people have available for taking some sort of action in the world, that is, relates to their 'knowledge' derived from bodily activity.

And finally for People, as we have already said on p. 225 their most important possessions are their construct-systems of themselves; of themselves in their culture; and of their culture in the world at large. Such construct-systems tend to be self-fulfilling as they determine peoples' rational and deliberate ways of going on. To meet new circumstances (which we as a consequence of our one actions create!) we must continually transform and *re-create* ourselves. By not realizing the nature of this process and thus not having proper provision for it in our accepted public images, we seem to have allowed our self-image to fragment, and in the process, ourselves.

My purpose in this essay has been to try to show that it might be possible to combine Kelly's Psychology with insights from the writings of Wittgenstein, Mead, Vygotsky and Cassirer to produce a new self image of man, for man, which will integrate his scattered fragments.

References

Bernstein, B. (1964). Elaborated and Restricted Codes, (Gumpers, J. J. and Nymes, D., eds.). *Am. Anthro. Sp. Pub.* **66**, 2, 55–69.

Beadle, G. and Beadle, M. (1969). "The Language of Life", Panther Books, London.

Broadbent, D. E. (1961). "Behaviour", Eyre and Spottiswoode, London.

Brown, R. (1965). "Social Psychology", The Free Press, New York.

Cassirer, E. ʻ1944). "Essay on Man", Yale University Press, New Haven and London.

Chomsky, N. (1957). "Syntactic Structures", Mouton, The Hague.

Chomsky, N. (1965). "Aspects of the Theory of Syntax", M.I.T. Press, Cambridge.

Chomsky, N. (1966). "Cartesian Linguistics", Harper and Row, New York.

Chomsky, N. (1968). "Language and Mind", Harcourt, Brace and World Inc., New York.

Chomsky, N. and Hampshire, S. (1968). A Universal Grammar, *The Listener* **79**, 687–691.

Davis, M. (1958). "Computability and Unsolvability", McGraw-Hill, New York.

Dreyfus, H. L. (1967). Why computers must have bodies in order to be intelligent, *Rev. Metaphysics* **21**, 13–32.

Hobbes, T. (1651). "Leviathan".

Jakobson, R., Fant, G. and Halle, M. (1952). Preliminaries to Speech Analysis, *M.I.T. Ascoust. Lab. Rept.*, **13**, (2nd Ed. 1963, M.I.T. Press, Cambridge).

Kelly, G. A. (1955). "The Psychology of Personal Constructs", Vols. 1 and 2, Norton, New York.

Kelly, G. A. (1962). The abstraction of human processes, *Proc. XIV International Congress of Applied Psychol.* **2,** Gerhard, Neilson, Copenhagen.

Kelly, G. A. (1964). The Language of Hypothesis: Man's Psychological Instrument. *J. indiv. Psychol.* **20**, 137–152.

Kelly, G. A. (1969). A Mathematical Approach to Psychology, 1961, read to Moscow Psychological Society, April 10, 1961 and Ontological Acceleration, *In* "Clinical Psychology and Personality: The Selected Papers of George Kelly (Maher, B., ed.), Wiley, New York.

Kuhn, T. S. (1962). "The Structure of Scientific Revolutions", University of Chicago Press, Chicago.

Locke, J. (1690). An Essay Concerning Human Understanding.

Luria, A. R. (1961). "The Role of Speech in the Regulation of Normal and Abnormal Behaviour, Pergamon Press, London.

Mead, G. (1934). "Mind, Self and Society", University of Chicago Press, Chicago.

Miller, G. A. and Chomsky, N. (1963). Finitary Models of Language Users, *In* "Handbook of Mathematical Psychology", Vol. 2 (Luce, Bush and Galanter, eds.), Wiley, New York.

Miller, G. A., Galanter, E. and Pritram, K. H. (1960). "Plans and the Structure of Behaviour", Holt, Rinehart and Winston, Inc. New York.

Mumford, L. (1967). "The Myth of the Machine", Secker and Warburg, London.

Newell, A., Shaw, J. C. and Simon, H. A. (1958). Elements of a theory of human problem solving, *Psychol. Rev.* **65**, 151–166.

Newson, J. (1969). Comments on the nature of pre-verbal communication between mothers and their children in the age range 10–20 months, Mimeo, Department of Psychology, Univ. of Nottingham.

Piaget, J. (1923). "The Language and Thought of the Child", Routledge and Kegan Paul, London.

Piaget, J. (1952). "The Origins of Intelligence in the Child", Routledge and Kegan Paul, London.

Piaget, J. (1968). "Six Psychological Studies", University of London Press, London.

Ryle, G. (1949). "The Concept of Mind", Hutchinson, London.

Saussure, F. de (1960). "Course in General Linguistics", Peter Owen, London.

Shotter, J. (1968). A note on a machine that 'learns' rules, *Brit. J. Psychol.* **59**, 173–177.

Shotter, J. (1969). What can programmed minds do? *In* "Aspects of Educational Technology III", (Mann, A. P. and Brunstrom, C. K., eds) Pitman, London.

Skinner, B. F. (1953). "Science and Human Behavior", Macmillan, New York.

Skinner, B. F. (1957). "Verbal Behavior", Appleton-Century-Crofts, New York.

Sutherland, N. S. (1968). Machines like men, *Science J.* **4**, 10, 44–48.

Turing, A. M. (1936). On computable numbers with an application to the Entscheidungs problem, *Hroc. Lond. Math. Soc. ser.* 2, **42**, 230–265.

Vygotsky, L. S. (1962). "Thought and Language", M.I.T. Press, Cambridge.

Wittgenstein, L. (1922). "Tractatus Logico-Philosophicus", Routledge and Kegan Paul, London.

Wittgenstein, L. (1953). "Philosophical Investigations," Basil Blackwell, Oxford.

Behaviour is an Experiment*

George A. Kelly

This afternoon I am in the embarrassing position of being reminded of a funny story, and, at the same time, realizing that I was not invited to come here to tell jokes. To make matters worse, I have already let slip the fact that I think the story is funny. If you are like most audiences I am sure you would have preferred to let the story speak for itself.

Humour, on most occasions, is intended to illustrate some minor point the speaker hopes to make. You can therefore take it or leave it. Now and then a thoughtful speaker will invite laughter out of consideration for the digestive processes that must accompany every address scheduled so soon after lunch as this one was. He may have a weak stomach himself. More often it occurs, however, and in spite of anything the speaker may intend, the story succeeds only in diverting attention from what, if anything, he means to say. Thus it can serve admirably the intentions of the audience—making the whole performance palatable for those who came mainly because they thought they ought to, as well as bearable for those conventioneers who came because their feet hurt and they wanted to sit down.

But the humour I have in mind has a certain lethal quality to it. If you should get the point of the joke there would be no way you could escape the point of the speech. Moreover, I am caught in this predicament myself; there is no way for me to make the speech and avoid the joke. The best I can do under the circumstances is to string out the story long enough to make it sound like the speech. Perhaps it won't seem so devastatingly funny that way.

Psychology Tries to Join the Science Club

There is something pathetically incongruous about a textbook in psychology —every one I can remember reading, at least. It took me nearly fifteen years to notice what it was. When I did I think I became a more empathic psychologist. I have been chuckling and wondering to myself ever since. Even the sometimes dreary rituals of our profession have become more endurable. Perhaps it is

---

* This is a write-up of an address to the A.P.A. Division of School Psychologists in 1966 and it has been left in its informal 'spoken' form.

appropriate, therefore, to pass along my private formula for happy psychologizing to my colleagues, some of whom must lead incredibly dull lives, if one may judge from what they publish.

Probably what took me so long to catch on was that whenever I read a book I read it as a loyal member of the Straight Faced Society of Publishing Psychologists, rather than as a man freely observant of the human scene. I believed that psychology textbooks expounded what psychology was, rather than exhibited what psychologists were. It was a long time before it ever occurred to me that I was witnessing the curious things a person, once he had started thinking of himself as a psychologist, could be led to say.

Now there is a rather touching story behind the spectacular rise of modern psychology. Charles Darwin figures in it somewhere, though I doubt that he ever intended it to turn out the way it did. It seems that, once upon a time, psychologists became enamoured of science. It was quite a passionate affair, but very one-sided. Psychologists were deeply hurt by the harsh turn of events. But instead of abandoning their suit, as any objectively minded psychologist would advise others to do, they loudly protested their continuing infatuation, taking advantage of everyone who could be made to stand still and listen. This usually turned out to be students, who, though they would rather talk to psychologists about matters of greater concern to themselves and their friends, were mostly willing to lend a sympathetic ear. Young people are notoriously tolerant in affairs of the heart.

I used to think this public display of blighted affection bordered on the ridiculous. Why didn't psychologists get on with the job of understanding man? If they did their job well the Scientific Establishment would soon enough lay claim to all they had achieved—perhaps too soon for them ever to find out what was wrong with it. Such things have happened before in the demure flirtations of scholars. There are too many characters abroad who know a going thing when they see it, and they will seize upon the slightest shred of knowledge as justification for arrogant practices, rather than reading it as a passing notation in the draft of a scholarly composition. Not all such fellows, may I say, smoke pipes, wear white coats, or drive Cadillacs.

So I was amused. The over-serious involvement with science had culminated in rejection. Yet the psychology I found so amusing is the harlequin among the sciences. In that classic theme man is reminded that the clown he observes is himself. The audience may become contemptuous of the harlequin's pomposity, be annoyed by the effrontery into which it degenerates, and linger to laugh all the louder at his subsequent frustration. But this is never the end of the encounter, for the laughter is followed by the sense that the fool has portrayed with a depth he cannot understand, and that, in turn, by the sharp realization that the harlequin is one's own pathetic self. So it is with psychology, a discipline so entangled in its own consistencies that it moves from pomposity to pathos, and, in doing so, portrays man better than it knows.

Some Curious Things Scientists Believe

By hanging onto the notion that they were scientists, psychologists have confronted themselves with the task of spelling out just what it is the scientist does that makes it possible for them to say they are like him. The ensuing descriptions of the processes of science may prove to be the only thing of great human significance psychologists have so far attempted. Yet this may be just what we are looking for. Perhaps to the extent and depth we can understand science we can begin to understand human behaviour, for science is one of man's most revealing activities.

Surely we cannot hope to grasp the potentialities of man without paying some attention to the most adventuresome things he does. Specifically, this suggests to me that unless mankind is seen in the terms we psychologists— who are no more than men ourselves—use to understand our own initiative, what we shall do will remain forever alien to the human enterprise.

But not many psychologists, I am afraid, are prepared to agree with me just yet. Most of us may be like the lonely lover who tosses about in his sleep dreaming of a lady-love far away who will have nothing to do with him. At dawn he rolls over and finds she is . . . finds she is just *leaving*. But now I am ahead of myself. Psychologists haven't rolled over yet.

If this concern with the process of science is as important as I think it is, it will be worth our while to have a look into how psychologists deal with it.

Textbook authors usually make their pitch for science in the introductory chapter. They start the discourse with a gratuitous concession to logic, which, like most scientific concessions to logic, turns out to be premature. Science, they say, knows from the outset that nature is organized, except, possibly, human nature; *that* sometimes is easier seen as disorganized, as in schizophrenia. (But this is an exception not likely to be mentioned in the first chapter, where everything is made to appear as rational as possible.)

Knowing all this, though I am not quite clear as to how they know it or why it should be necessary to make a point of it, psychologists go on to argue that the job of science is to test the truth of everything man believes. The idea seems to be that in a deterministic world everything has to be nailed down. The possibility that there may be more appropriate grounds for exercising scientific curiosity is not likely to be mentioned.

Nevertheless, as in the case of "organized nature", there is one convenient exception to this consuming eagerness to test everything. That is in the case of determinism itself. There is no testing that, unless you take as a test of it the fact that scientists disregard it outright when making up their minds about what they themselves want to do. But then I suppose if initiative should

ever cease to be a special prerogative reserved for scientists, and should be
rashly conceded to human nature in general, the whole present structure of
psychology would collapse. As long as there is no test of determinism it
should be possible to stave off such a proletarian disaster.

Exceptions, exceptions! But perhaps it is just as well. Otherwise, the
ultimate truth of the universe might snap shut on us and there would be no
place to go—except, possibly, to heaven, where I understand one might be
indulged with some latitude in amusing himself, in a more or less predetermined sort of way, and as long as he was careful not to turn up anything
unscheduled or unexpected. That is probably the reason the place is reserved
exclusively for dead people. Live ones might not fit into such an orderly
scheme of things, no matter how scientifically enlightened the management
might be.

The Psychology of Man-the-Scientist

But when the psychologist stops making dogmatic claims in the name of
science, and starts describing how scientists behave, the reading perks up.
The scientist, he says, plays guessing games. These little affairs start with
hypotheses and one plays by wagering as little as possible of his own time,
and as much as possible of the Government's money, on what will happen
when they are put into operation. Some hypotheses are supposed to be worth
more than others. There are those who think that when they bet on them they
should use only the special blue chips provided by the National Science
Foundation.

The hypotheses, the writer continues, are sometimes deduced from theory,
which is supposed to be the most elegant way to come by them, or they are
induced from years of observation—all right for Darwin, but too tedious if
you want to get ahead in these more competitive times—or, in some cases,
one goes after them with a dragnet, commonly known as "collecting items".
There is some difference of opinion as to whether the object of the game is
to confirm hypotheses or disconfirm them. Most graduate students I have
talked to seem to be of the opinion that it is better to confirm them. For my
own part I am inclined to think it depends mostly on what people may run
out into the street and start doing when they read about it in the paper, or
what kind of research the scientist will try next.

The nice thing about hypotheses is that you don't have to believe them.
This, I think, is a key to the genius of the scientific method. It permits you
to be inconsistent with what you know long enough to see what will happen.
Children do that. What is so wonderful about the language of hypothesis is
its refreshing ability to free the scientist from the entangling consistencies of
adulthood. For a few precious moments he can think again like a child, and,

like a child, learn from his experience rather than adhere stubbornly to his professional identity. But now I'm getting ahead of myself again.

The chapter goes on to tell about how experiments are designed, controls are instituted, comparable observations are made, and anticipations are pitted against the outcomes. Hypotheses stand or fall—though I have noted privately over the years that mostly they sort of lean, at about the ·08 level of confidence. When the experiment is over the scientist picks up the pieces and reflects on the whole undertaking, wondering if his sample was un-representative, his hypotheses improperly drawn, his controls ineffectual, or if there might be something at fault with the theoretical foundation on which the enterprise was based. You want to know about the scientist? This is the inconclusive story of his life. It is also the continuing story of man.

Psychology's Hidden Personality Theory

Now, as I have suggested before, the trouble with most of this is that we take it, as I once did, as no more than a faithful description of something quite external to man—called science—rather than as a perceptive account of a man who thinks he is a scientist. But is it not a most illuminating way to see the striving of all mankind in the perspective of human accomplish-ments and disillusionments?

In this over-view man can be seen moving through the centuries, as well as through the seasons of his own life. He does not endlessly repeat himself, waiting for some unusual concatenation of stimuli to point his nose in a new direction. He is not driven by the forces he inherits, nor is he helplessly buffeted by his circumstances. Instead, he repeats what seems promising, he mobilizes the forces at his command, and he recognizes his circumstances as his best resources. Like a growing child, he finds the meaning of his behaviour, not in the inculcated habits that restrain its impulses, but in what his imagina-tion can do with it.

What a personality theory! It is such a marvellously enlightening way of looking at man that I suppose one should not be surprised that psychologists should try to reserve it exclusively for explaining themselves. And that is precisely what they do.

When the writers get around to explaining the behaviour of ordinary men—usually in the last chapters of the book—you should see what they say. What man does is a response to stimuli to which he was plugged in when he wasn't looking. He is lashed into slavish endeavours by his motives, sucked into vacuums created by his needs, betrayed by his upbringing, addicted to his reinforcements, and, when he gives up looking for any sense in all this, he yields to self-destruction. And no wonder!

When one stumbles into this kind of reading he can be sure he has reached the section on "personality theories". The creatures described are not philosophers. They are not physicists. They are not even psychologists. Yet the persons you and I know—children and adults—are all of these. The would-be scientist who wrote the book is having his nightmares, unaware of what has been lying softly beside him from the moment he finished the first chapter.

The Function of a Theory

If one is to use the paradigm of the scientist as the basis of a personality theory, it is important to be clear about what a theory is. To begin with, we shall have to rule out two common notions. It is not a collection of information, regardless of how carefully catalogued it may be. Nor is it an account of a sequence of events, no matter how well authenticated.

In essence a theory is simply a way of highlighting events so they may be viewed in some kind of perspective. And yet, regardless of how well events are illuminated, it is quite unreasonable to hope they ever can be so completely revealed there will be nothing left to look for. The best one can ever expect of a theory is that it will enable him to see what he has never seen before, and that it will be succeeded in time by another theory which will disclose some of what still remains hidden.

Starting, then, with the psychology textbook writer's account of the behaviour of the scientist and regarding it in a more general way as a theory of the behaviour of all men, we can proceed to the next step. If we do, it will be interesting to note that we shall not retreat into the mentalism which some of our humanistic colleagues see as the only alternative to behaviourism. Behaviour will remain one of the most important concerns of psychology. But its role in the life of man will be seen as vastly different from that envisioned by either psychoanalysis or classic behaviourism.

Behaviour Is Always a Means; It Rarely Remains an End

Instead of being a problem of threatening proportions, requiring the utmost explanation and control to keep man out of trouble, behaviour presents itself as man's principal instrument of inquiry. Without it his questions are academic and he gets nowhere. When it is prescribed for him he runs around in dogmatic circles. But when he uses it boldly to ask questions, a flood of unexpected answers rises to tax his utmost capacity to understand.

It is true that in most of psychology's inquiries some patently desirable behaviour is sought as an answer to the question posed. But the quest always proves to be elusive. In the restless and wonderful world of humanistic endeavour, behaviour, however it may once have been intended as the embodiment of a conclusive answer, inevitably transforms itself into a further question—a question so compellingly posed by its enactment that, willy nilly, the actor finds that he has launched another experiment. Behaviour is indeed a question posed in such a way as to commit man to the role and obligations of an experimenter.

In pursuing the theoretical venture I have proposed we shall not so much be asking *what makes* people behave the way they do, nor *how to get* them all to behave in the way that threatens no one, but we shall ask, instead, how can *behaviour be employed* to seek the answers that stir human curiosity. And when we see behaviour that distresses us we will spend less time wondering what conditioned it and ask, instead, what is the experiment that is being performed, what hypotheses are being tested, how the outcomes are to be assessed, and whether it opens or closes the door to any man's further adventure.

From the vantage point offered by this kind of theorizing behaviour is not to be regarded as the terminal goal of the psychologist's effort. His objective is not to get man to display himself in all the enlightened ways of which he is capable, or even to exhibit the healthiest living habits prescribed by licensed psychiatry. How man is to act will rather be determined by the nature of his vital inquiries. What may represent actions of great self-fulfilment today will properly be considered senseless repetitions when it comes time to ask tomorrow's questions. No scientist performs the same experiment over and over just because it gives him a warm feeling inside. If he does perform the same experiment over and over, as I have noted some of them do, I shall suspect he is still looking for the answer to a question he knows no better way of asking.

A School for Experimental Behaviour

Let us now try looking at some behaviour in this theoretical perspective and see what comes to light. For the past two years Mrs. Penelope Upton, a trained teacher and herself the mother of five, has been operating the Banbury Cross Nursery School along lines suggested by personal construct theory— a theory which embodies the point of view I have been outlining. The effort is frankly experimental, which will come as no surprise after what I have just said. It would have to be, if it were human, though one would not need to be as frank in admitting it as Mrs. Upton is. Being honest with herself about what she is doing she makes a running analysis of what goes on, and this, in turn, has produced a continuing series of methodological transitions. In other words, she uses her own behaviour to ask questions, just as the theory would suggest, and she examines her children's behaviour to see what questions they may be asking and how their questions may be better posed.

The primary object of a good school is not to control behaviour, or even to "give" the child experience—two goals frequently cited by educators. In a society convinced that freedom is more than a happy personal convenience, that it also enables men to make the most of their capacity to help each other, a school cannot allow itself to become an instrument for keeping the underprivileged in line by squelching their impulses. Moreover, the school cannot permit itself to take the position that experience, instead of being a prerogative of all human life, is to be doled out in calculated amounts by the educational establishment. Yet none of this is to say that limits on behaviour are to be abandoned or that experience cannot proceed in an orderly fashion.

In Mrs. Upton's words, "The *primary* object of the school is to give each child the opportunity to discover through his own ventures who he is—and what he might become." In such a setting one becomes aware that the limits are as often imposed by the child as by the teacher. It is her observation that "the most stringent boundaries seem to be self-imposed". But regardless of who imposes them, they serve as guard rails permitting freer experimentation within presumed limits of safety. Occasionally one finds the limits have been set altogether too far out and a child shrinks back from exploration. Sometimes they are set too close in and he explores coherently only within infantile orbits. When he must function outside the limits his behaviourally posed questions are observed to be frantic and his experiments inconclusive.

As for *experience* in such a school, it is recognized, first of all, that it must be the outcome of the child's own experimental efforts carried through to some point of conclusion; it is not the direct consequence of his being bombarded at an early age with pedagogical demands, as seems to be envisioned by Project Head Start. The teacher's role is to help, as best she can, to design and implement each child's own undertakings, as well as to assist in interpreting the outcomes and in devising more cogent behavioural inquiries. But usually she has to begin, as any apprentice begins, by implementing what others have designed; in this case, what her children have initiated.

To be a fully accredited participant in the experimental enterprise she must gain some sense of what is being seen through the child's eyes. That is to say, she must do what personal construct theory technically terms, "enact a role". Otherwise the experiment performed will be hers and not the child's, and the hypotheses apparently confirmed or disconfirmed will bear solely on her own venture, while those versions enacted by the child, and confirmed or disconfirmed by his experience, will be secret ones to which she remains oblivious. Children do not learn from events just because they happen, but from contrived adventures in coping with them.

What Happened at Banbury Cross

Instead of teaching the children "how to play games", Mrs. Upton seeks to play a contributory part in the games children play. The following excerpts are taken from her notes. They describe three incidents in the life of Larry, a boy who has difficulty modulating his behaviour outside the safety of the boundaries he has imposed on himself. She starts by making observations of how two other children have transcended boundaries. She writes,

"Debby, in the mother role, tells me *not* to go up Centre Street. When I ask her what her own mother might do if she—Debby—were *a little girl* and ran up the street, she replied, 'She would turn *the girl* into soup.' Ann's father also reported to me that Ann, after having been spanked by him for taking Polly's toys, started waving her hands over the baby and said, 'I'm Polly's fairy godmother. I'm turning she into a cow'."

To be sure, the boundaries explored by these two children were not altogether self-imposed. The one Debby transcended was defined by taking her mother's role while Ann used her ingenuity to examine the far side of one her father had tried to impose by spanking her. Nevertheless, from these child-inventions Mrs. Upton develops a notion of how Larry may experiment more conclusively outside his present enclosure. Her notes go on to say,

"These two exchanges suggested to me that some children transcend a boundary, or contemplate the results of such a transcendence, by employing fantasy to explore what lies beyond. It occurred to me, therefore, that this device might provide me with an approach to Larry, whose locus of control seems to be largely internal and whose boundaries stand in the way of reciprocal relations with other children. So I arbitrarily cast him into a fantasy role through which I hoped he might be able to make some kind of effective contact with his peers.

"The first day I attempted this approach, I tried to contact him the same way I thought he might initially choose to contact another person—either child or adult. This is to say, I entered what I thought might be *his* game, rather than suggesting that he enter *mine*. I did this by 'driving a truck up behind his and crashing into it.'

" 'Hi, Joe', I said.

"Larry looked startled, then laughed and said, 'Didn't you see the red light?'

"It was interesting to note that thereupon, in the role of 'Joe', he did have some success interacting with his peers. Debby spontaneously joined the game and entered into the spirit by helping 'Joe' load lumber onto his truck. When the lumber had been hauled to its destination, Ben joined in and helped Larry unload the lumber and construct a house. The participation of both children was accepted collaboratively by the fictional 'Joe' without the friction characteristic of Larry when he is forced to contact children outside the perimeter of his own entrenchments.

"Later, at clean-up time, 'Joe', at my request, put the lumber back on the truck and put it away. This is not what Larry would ordinarily have done."

Mrs. Upton's notes then tell us more about Larry. "Larry", she says, "has a particularly difficult time entering into activities in the circle." By "the circle", she means a group activity in which children sit in a ring facing each other and take part in some kind of community activity, such as singing or story-telling. She comments, "He is wild, imaginative, and appears to be totally absorbed in a private game." She goes on to say,

"In a father role the following day, Larry again had difficulty making contact with his peers. He insisted upon throwing every single tiny piece of equipment into the toy sink. Sally, who was playing a mother role, was furious and kept putting things away. Finally, after Larry had thrown everything into the sink for the third time, Sally left the game.

"Larry then climbed up on a tall divider, transgressing a teacher-imposed boundary. There, at my suggestion, he 'repaired the roof' and then climbed down. I had hoped to give him a reason for being up there and a way of getting down without losing face. He seemed quite willing to go along with my suggestion, but the game he and Sally had been playing had ended abruptly and apparently inconclusively."

Two months later Mrs. Upton comments,

"Larry and I had a conversation about hunting during which I mentioned that pygmies used darts dipped in poison for hunting and for defence. This intrigued Larry. Half an hour later he approached me with a stick and jabbed it into my leg.

" 'There, Don, she's dead.'

"I slumped over, playing my part in the game.

"Larry became very excited and shouted, 'Let's bury her, Don!' As he tried to pick me up I collapsed on the floor and Larry started shoveling imaginary sand on top of me. Sally came into the room and, finding me 'dead' threw her arms around my neck and started to cry. I reassured her, and then noticed Larry curled up on the floor behind me.

" 'I wonder what you are doing?'

" 'I'm just lying here feeling sorry for you, Mrs. Upton'."

Mrs. Upton concludes,

"In this experiment, Larry, having had the opportunity to act the whole scene out, was able to experience feelings bound naturally to the consequences of his actions, as well as those immediately identified with the actions themselves. Had he not *carried it through* we may have seen the same experimental fragment—jabbing with a dart—repeated over and over."

Analysis of a Four-year-old's Experiment

In these briefly recounted anecdotes we see first the teacher's sensitivity to the nature of human inquiry. She notes the limits Larry maintains, outside of which he finds himself confused by unspecified variables and his behaviour unmodulated. So also the accredited scientist sets limits, which he calls "experimental controls", in order to avoid becoming lost in a multivariant universe. She sees, furthermore, that Larry, as many another scientist, is both hemmed in by the boundaries he has defined and is rendered ineffectual outside them. This is science in the flesh—the personal methodology of man. If this truly natural science is to be understood in depth it must be examined psychologically, not merely formalistically.

So the teacher goes on to help design an experiment—a human one. In this case the methodology she employed for transcending Larry's constrictive controls was ingeniously derived from the observation of two children, Debby and Ann, who, being incipent scientists too, had something to offer a puzzled teacher. She calls the methodology simply "fantasy", and she hopes it will help Larry get on with his experimental project. Via the imaginary "Joe" she reaches behind what the logic of science formally calls "hypothesis" and picks up the basic human process by which all hypotheses are derived.

Larry then, in posing his question behaviourally and in the terms of this basic form of hypothesis, finds out what other scientists who employ the language of hypothesis also learn. He finds that as "Joe" he can produce outcomes not attainable by the "Larry" in terms of whom he ordinarily approaches his world.

In the next episode we find Larry posing a question in a familiar way, again behaviourally, and having to face up to what appears to be an inconclusive outcome, or at least one that must be contemplated from the height of the room divider. We do not know what hypothesis is being tested— probably not another "Joe", but possibly an aspect of what he assumes to be "Larry". The experiment takes an abrupt turn when Sally, presumably his principal subject, walks out on him. The teacher then attempts to salvage something from the project by having him "repair the roof" up there. Then, like the reluctant gods, who, as their human experiments go awry, must eventually descend from their lofty contemplations atop Mount Olympus, he comes down.

In the last episode, two months later, Larry is engaged in a much more penetrating inquiry, and we are given a glimpse of the resolving effect of a completed experiment. Designed by himself, and carried, with the teacher's co-operation, through its full natural cycle, the experiment reaches the point of being a significant experience when Larry, finally prostrate on the floor beside his "victim", says, "I'm just lying here feeling sorry for you, Mrs. Upton." How much more psychologically significant this was than to have offered a guilty apology for what he had done. I cannot refrain from mentioning a parenthetical comment I found in Mrs. Upton's notes for this day. She says, "There is so much that goes on in the course of the morning that never is noted it distresses me".

Pete Smith: Panacea or Experiment?

Let me turn quickly now to two more illustrations of the way in which human behaviour can be regarded as experimental—"fixed role therapy" and "behaviour therapy". The first suggests how a person may use is behaviour to pose hypotheses about a different kind of self, and, by being alert to the outcomes, attain a better vantage point from which to launch the sequence of further experimental ventures we call "life". The second suggests how much more lucidly a procedure, in which *a subject* is usually envisioned as being "treated", may be understood if the person is regarded instead as *an experimenter*, and his behaviour changes as an orderly progression of hypotheses.

About twenty-five years ago A. J. Robinson (1941) and Ethel Harkness Edwards (1943) collaborated with me in developing a form of psychotherapy that has come to be called "fixed role therapy". It makes no use of psychodynamic or motivational concepts, or of "insight" into one's customary behaviour, or of past influences in a person's life, or of learning by reward or contiguity, or of calculated verbal reinforcements, or of affective support, or of environmental control. In fact it discards about everything either the hard scientists or the soft scientists claim is essential—everything, that is, except that outcropping of intrinsically human methodology we call "science". The particular method consists in the design and execution of an experiment. And it is carried by the client through a full experimental cycle to a point of conclusion, one where it may become a significant personal experience in his life.

The client—call him John Jones—is shown a tailor-made self-characterization sketch "written" by a fictional person called, say, Pete Smith. If, on reading the sketch with the therapist, Pete seems like a genuine person and one whom he would like to know, John is asked to imagine that he himself is going to the mountains for a two-week holiday, and in his place there materializes Pete, whose part the client is to enact as faithfully as he can, twenty-four hours a day. He is to think of himself as Pete, talk like Pete, treat others as Pete would, execute Pete's daily habit pattern, entertain himself as Pete might, and, if he can, even dream as Pete would dream.

In frequent sessions during the enactment the therapist rehearses the part with the client, paying particular attention to situations involving the client's peers, his supervisors, his spouse or girl friends, his parents, and his religious outlook. At the end of the period the therapist insists that John Jones come back and take over. After John has returned, and done what he can to pick up the pieces, the client is free to make what he wants out of his experience, and to go ahead and start making something out of his life.

Of course there is much more to it than this. Before the enactment is proposed John has written his own self-characterization, and there are serious pitfalls that experience has shown can be avoided when this step is taken. The Pete Smith characterization, that binds together the clustered hypotheses of the experiment, must not omit certain features, notably a clear axis of contrast between Pete and John, and *role constructs*—as that notion is precisely defined in personal construct theory. It is important that the enactment not break down into a conglomeration of impulsive bits of self-expression whose outcomes can have no apparent bearing on any clearly perceived component of the undertaking. Without the theme of Pete Smith the experiment becomes incoherent.

Finally, it needs to be clear that the part of Pete Smith is not a doctor's prescription for the improvement of John's mental health. Pete may turn out to have more faults than John. Nor can any evaluation of John be inferred from the proposal itself. Besides, the therapist, his fee structure notwithstanding, is only an inquiring scientist himself, and not a prophet. He is in no position to know precisely what is best for his erstwhile research colleague, and he had better be frank about it. Both of them must wait for the data to come in.

The central purpose of the enactment—which both therapist and client must keep in constant focus—is to see what ensues when the hypothesis of Pete Smith is put to the world—and to one's self—in the terms of a behavioural commitment. No matter that Pete Smith is not the client's presumed self; a hypothesis is always a venturesome departure from the dogmatic world of certainty. And that indeed is its genius, a genius practiced spontaneously by children and self-consciously by scientists.

Since what is proposed is never intended to be a panacea for the vacationing John Jones, who was too grown up to imagine being anything but himself, outcomes can scarcely be judged as patent successes or failures. But how much more exciting it is anyway to be confronted with some of the amazing things that may happen in a world that is differently approached. When it is all over, the returning John Jones, who just once in his life was a Pete Smith, can decide, from among the countless variations his own ingenuity might contrive, what kind of a person he wants to be, and get on with the undertaking.

Perhaps I should add parenthetically that fixed role therapy is not a method I choose to employ in all cases—perhaps only one in fifteen. There are too many other novel and exciting approaches to the world of psychotherapy. As a therapist, I, too, can be a Pete Smith instead of a John Jones. Besides, fixed role therapy is hard work. There ought to be still more facile ways to help man participate in the human enterprise.

In Behaviour Therapy, Who is the Experimenter?

Now what about "behaviour therapy", which is supposed to be at odds with humanistic psychology, and precisely so because it is "rigorously scientific"? To my mind the only thing wrong with the accounts of behaviour therapy I have read is that they fail to mention who the principal investigator was. They call him a "subject", while the fellow with the doctoral degree, who turns out to be only the technician in the project, is given credit for doing the experiment. Sounds familiar, doesn't it? Nevertheless, the psychologists who write about this sort of thing may be about to turn over and find what is in bed with them. But they haven't done so yet.

Take, for example, the reverse snake charming experiment, which has become the popular prototype for behaviour therapy. The task is for a person who shudders at the sight of snakes to come to appreciate how very charming a snake can be. The first step is to entertain the hypothesis; although, like any proper hypothesis, it may not appear to be very realistic— at least not for the person engaged in the undertaking. The next step is to make a behavioural investment, that is to say, to pose the question behaviourally. That may not be what a philosopher would do, but it is what a scientist, who always doubts uncommitted rationality, must do. So the part to be played is the part of a scientist.

But a man making up to snakes may find himself floundering about in a multivariant predicament. Like Larry, when he had to approach other children outside the safety of his guard rails, one may find, in the presence of too many snakes, that his behaviour has lost its composed directionality. If the old boundaries of safety are to be transcended in his approach to snakes, and there is to be a conclusion to the experiment, new boundaries must be established *ad hoc*. In research language this means that each successive experiment must be "controlled" if the researcher is not to become lost in a sea of "variables". Moreover, the specific hypotheses in each sequential inquiry must be clearly defined, else the principal researcher will not be able to determine what is confirmed by what.

And there is one final ingredient in the science of being charmed by snakes. The scientist—I'm still talking about the fellow who is trying out a new slant on snakes—must be left free at the conclusion of each step to decide just what experiment is to come next. Here, as elsewhere, the outcomes of scientific endeavours are often best judged by what the scientist, after searching his own reactions to his completed undertakings, decides to do next. It is preposterous to assume that the mere overt outcomes of one experiment make the scientist's next venture a cut-and-dried affair.

Now let us notice how the Wolpe type of behaviour therapy artfully contrives a procedure to enable the patient to become his own experimenter. Preliminary interviewing focuses attention on the general hypothesis that he can learn to live with snakes. It is, of course, only a hypothesis and therefore a ventured departure from the reality of the patient's world. The criteria against which accurate predictions will be assessed are defined in terms of the state of relaxation the patient may experience. He then practices relaxation so he will recognize it when he sees it.

Next the patient's fear is calibrated and a useful scale of aversion is constructed out of a graduated series of pictures of snakes, or actual distances measured from the snake itself. Experimental controls are established as *ad hoc* boundaries which can be successively moved out as the patient becomes bolder. Fantasy, or make-believe, is employed as the patient imagines his approach to the snake before he actually attempts it. This, as in the case of

Larry, constitutes the formulation of intermediate hypotheses in terms of which his experimental behaviour is to be attempted, step by step.

The patient is not pushed beyond the limits established for the current phase of his inquiry. Before each successive venture he must decide where the guard rails are to be placed, and he is free to return to their protective enclosure whenever he is threatened with incoherence. He does not surrender his initiative to another investigator. He observes carefully what happens— how frightened he is, or, rather, how relaxed he is, relaxation being operationally a better defined criterion for him than fright—and he notes how differently the snake appears as he approaches it. Finally, it is the patient, now a scientist planning his own actions, who decides what the next step in the experimental series will be. In this kind of therapy, behaviour is so clearly an experiment.

Behaviour is the Method of Man-the-Scientist

In conclusion let me suggest only that when psychology, that harlequin who turns out to be ourselves, rolls over it may realize that, while intellectualization is the method of man the incipient philosopher, behaviour is the method of man the scientist. The philosopher asks questions by disengaging from facts; the scientist inquires by confronting himself with events of his own creation. This is true, whether the scientist is a psychologist, a Larry, a John Jones, or Adam's impressionable girl friend who thinks "snakes really have *a lot* to offer".

References

Edwards, Ethel D. (1943). Observation of use and efficiency of changing a patient's concept of his role: A psychotherapeutic device. *Unpublished MA thesis*, Fort Hays Kansas State College.

Kelly, G. A. (1955). "The Psychology of Personal Constructs", Vols 1 and 2, Norton, New York.

Kelly, G. A. (1964). The language of hypothesis. *J. indiv. Psychol.* **20**, 137–152.

Kelly, G. A. (1965). The strategy of psychological research. *Bull. Brit. psychol. Soc.* 1–15.

Kelly, G. A. (1966a). Sin and psychotherapy. *In* "Religion and Mental Health" (Mowrer, O. H., ed.), Rand McNally, Chicago.

Kelly, G. A. (1966b). A psychology of the optimal man. *In* "Goals of Psychotherapy" (Mahrer, A. W., ed.), Appleton-Century-Crofts, New York.

Krasner, L. and Ullmann, L. P. (1965). "Research in Behavior Modification: New Developments and Implications", Holt, Rinehart and Winston, New York.

Lazarus, A. A. (1964). Crucial procedural factors in desensitization therapy. *Behav. Res. Ther.* **2**, 65–70.

Robinson, A. J. (1941). A further validation of role therapy. *Unpublished MA thesis*, Fort Hays Kansas State College.

Wolpe, J. (1958). "Psychotherapy by Reciprocal Inhibition", Stanford University Press, Stanford, California.

Author Index

271